The Hidden Form of Capital

The Hidden Form of Capital

Spiritual Influences in Societal Progress

Edited by
Peter L. Berger and Gordon Redding

ANTHEM PRESS
LONDON · NEW YORK · DELHI

Anthem Press
An imprint of Wimbledon Publishing Company
www.anthempress.com

This edition first published in UK and USA 2011
by ANTHEM PRESS
75-76 Blackfriars Road, London SE1 8HA, UK
or PO Box 9779, London SW19 7ZG, UK
and
244 Madison Ave. #116, New York, NY 10016, USA

British Library Cataloguing-in-Publication Data
A catalogue record for this book is available from the British Library.

Library of Congress Cataloging-in-Publication Data
The Library of Congress has cataloged the hardcover edition as follows:
The hidden form of capital : spiritual influences in societal progress
/ edited by Peter L. Berger and Gordon Redding.
p. cm.
ISBN 978-1-84331-832-3 (hardcover : alk. paper) – ISBN
978-0-85728-952-0 (ebook : alk. paper)
1. Economics–Religious aspects. I. Berger, Peter L., 1929- II.
Redding, S. G.
HB72.H53 2010
261.8'5–dc22
2010003314

ISBN-13: 978 0 85728 413 6 (Pbk)
ISBN-10: 0 85728 413 4 (Pbk)

This title is also available as an eBook.

TABLE OF CONTENTS

CONTRIBUTORS

Peter L. Berger is Professor Emeritus of Sociology and Theology at Boston University's College of Arts and Sciences and School of Theology. From 1985 to 2009, he was also Director of BU's Institute on Culture, Religion and World Affairs (CURA), a research centre committed to the study of beliefs, values and lifestyles, especially religious ones, as they affect economic and social change in different parts of the world. He has written numerous books on sociological theory, the sociology of religion and Third World development, which have been translated into dozens of foreign languages. His most recent book is *Questions of Faith: A Sceptical Affirmation of Christianity*.

Gordon Redding has for the last seven years served as head of the Euro-Asia and Comparative Research Centre at the European Institute of Business Administration (INSEAD). He is also Professor Emeritus at the University of Hong Kong, where he founded and directed the business school. He is the author of several books and research papers on the relationships among culture, religion, modernization and development. Among his publications are a series of theoretical papers on the correlations between economic progress and religion, including: 'The thick description and comparison of societal systems of capitalism' (*Journal of International Business Studies*, 36, 2005), and 'Rationality as a variable in comparative management theory and the possibility of a Chinese version' in B Krug (ed.) *China's Rational Entrepreneurs*, London, Routledge Curzon, 2004.

Ann Bernstein is Director of the Centre for Development and Enterprise in Johannesburg, and has published a wide series of studies on African economic development. She is the author of *Migration and Refugee Policies* (with M. Weiner), *Business and Democracy* (with Peter Berger), and *Policy Making in a New Democracy*. She has also served on the board of the Development Bank of South Africa.

Peter Boettke, the BB&T Professor for the Study of Capitalism, University Professor of Economics at George Mason University, and Deputy Director of the James M. Buchanan Center for Political Economy has authored numerous books and articles. His most recent work, *Challenging Institutional Analysis and Development: The Bloomington School* (Co-authored with Paul Dragos Aligica), analyzes the ascendancy of the New Institutional Theory movement. He is also the author of several volumes on the history and transition from socialism in the former Soviet Union, including *The Political Economy of Soviet Socialism: The Formative Years, 1918–1928*; *Why Perestroika Failed*; and *The Economics and Politics of Socialism Transformation*. Boettke has also served as the editor for the *Review of Austrian Economics* since 1998.

Lawrence E. Harrison is Director, Cultural Change Institute at the Fletcher School at Tufts University. He is the author of *Underdevelopment is a State of Mind: The Latin American Case; Who Prospers? How Cultural Values Shape Economic and Political Success; The Central Liberal Truth; The Pan-American Dream*; and co-editor, with Samuel Huntington, of *Culture Matters: How Values Shape Human Progress*; with Jerome Kagan of *Developing Cultures: Essays on Cultural Change*; with Peter Berger of *Developing Cultures: Case Studies*.

Robert W. Hefner is Professor of Anthropology and the newly appointed Director of CURA at Boston University. He is also currently President of the Association of Asian Studies. He has been the director of several major research projects, including a Ford Foundation project called 'Southeast Asian Pluralisms: Social Resources for Civility and Participation in Malaysia, Singapore, and Indonesia' (1998–2000). His most recent book is *Civil Islam: Muslims and Democratization in Indonesia*, and he is currently directing a CURA-sponsored cross-national study of moderate Islam.

János Mátyás Kovács is Permanent Fellow at the *Institut für die Wissenschaften vom Menschen*, Vienna. He teaches history of economic thought at the *Eotvos Lorand University*, Budapest. His publications include *Reform and Transformation in Eastern Europe; The Communist Legacy in Eastern Europe;* and *Small Transformations: The Politics of Welfare Reform—East and West*.

Christopher Marsh is Associate Professor of Political Science and Director of Asian Studies at Baylor University. He is the author of *Russia at the Polls*, and he is currently directing a CURA-sponsored study entitled 'Orthodoxy and the Construction of Civil Society and Democracy in Russia'.

Stephen Rule runs a research consultancy in Johannesburg. He has previously been director of surveys at the Human Sciences Research Council, director of research for the Minister of Social Development and taught geography at what is now the University of Johannesburg. Amongst others, he has authored *South African Social Attitudes: Changing Times, Diverse Voices* (with Pillay and Roberts) and *Electoral Territoriality in Southern Africa.*

Rebecca Samuel Shah is an analyst of the relationship between religion and economics and an expert on the statistical assessment of development projects in the global South. She currently serves as a Fellow with the Oxford Centre for Religion and Public Life. She holds a Bachelor's of Science in Economics and Economic History and a Master's of Science in Statistical Demography, both from the London School of Economics. Shah served as a Research Analyst with the World Bank's Human Development Network from 1998 to 2002. She also served as Chief Research Analyst for the Ethnic Health Unit of the British National Health Service and as a Research Assistant for Harvard's Center for Population and Development. Shah authored a chapter for the volume, *Local Ownership, Global Change: Will Civil Society Save the World?* (MARC Publishers, 2002), entitled "Faith, Community, and Development: Christian Micro-Finance and Civil Society in South India," a field and analytical study of the impact of spirituality on micro-level economic performance in Bangalore, India. Her work has appeared in various journals, including *Transformation, Third Way, Society,* and the *Journal of Church and State.*

Timothy Samuel Shah is Senior Research Scholar with Boston University's Institute on Culture, Religion and World Affairs. Formerly, he served as Research Director for the Project on Evangelical Christianity and Democracy in the Global South, funded by The Pew Charitable Trusts, which produced an Oxford University Press series under Shah's editorial direction: Terence O. Ranger, ed., *Evangelical Christianity and Democracy in Africa* (2008); Paul Freston, ed., *Evangelical Christianity and Democracy in Latin America* (2008); and David Lumsdaine, ed., *Evangelical Christianity and Democracy in Asia* (2009). Shah's articles on religion and politics have appeared in *Foreign Affairs, Foreign Policy,* the *Journal of Democracy,* the *Review of Politics, Political Quarterly,* and the *SAIS Review of International Affairs.* He has contributed chapters to numerous edited volumes, including, most recently, *Church, State and Citizen: Christian Approaches to Political Engagement* (Oxford University Press, 2009), edited by Sandra Joireman, and *Blind Spot: When Journalists Don't Get Religion* (Oxford University Press, 2009), edited by Paul Marshall, Lela Gilbert, and Roberta Green Ahmanson.

Robert Weller, Professor of Anthropology at Boston University and Research Associate at CURA, is the author of several books on East Asia, including *Alternate Civilities: Democracy and Culture in China and Taiwan; Unities and Diversities in Chinese Religion;* and *Resistance, Chaos and Control in China: Taiping Rebels, Taiwanese Ghosts and Tiananmen.* He is currently conducting a CURA-sponsored study of civil society in Chinese cultures.

PREFACE

The idea that societies have economic cultures as well as aesthetic, literary, and artistic cultures is well-embedded in a number of major studies attempting to identify the origins of national wealth and progress. From Adam Smith's recognition of the role of moral sentiments, to the recent acknowledgement by Nobel prize-winning economic historian Douglass North that culture plays a key role in economic progress, there has always been awareness that it needed to be understood more completely. That it still is not speaks more to its complexity as a question than to the efforts devoted to its understanding.

Explanation in this field has to meet the challenge of the great number of factors in the equation, and the parallel challenge that many disciplines find culture hard to handle – too fuzzy, not visible or measurable enough, a residual perhaps after all the other more tangible things have been counted. Our aim here is to place it more centrally, not by further theoretical speculation, but by presenting evidence from several parts of the changing world about how the realm of the spirit affects the economy. The evidence comes from recent studies in Europe, Asia, Africa, Russia, and the US. The book is not entirely without theory, but its main intent is the presentation of new findings from the fields.

The initiative for this collection of work began with a collaboration between the Metanexus Institute, Pennsylvania, and the Institute on Culture, Religion and World Affairs of Boston University. The support of Metanexus for the project included the funding of a meeting in Washington, D.C. in 2006, at which the writers were able to present initial schema, and a later partial meeting in Paris at which the final shape of the project and the book was set. This generous support is gratefully acknowledged.

The editors would also like to express their gratitude to the staff of the CURA in Boston, and the Euro-Asia and Comparative Research Centre, INSEAD, for their helpful assistance. Most helpful assistance for the Paris meeting came from Philippe D'Iribarne and is gratefully acknowledged. Gordon Redding would additionally like to thank the HEAD Foundation,

Singapore, for its support. The assistance of Virginie Servant and Ross Thorne in final manuscript preparation was both timely and highly appreciated, as was also that of Janka Romero at Anthem Press. We also gratefully acknowledge the conference participants and especially as commentators Francis Fukuyama, Carina Lindberg, and Leslie Young. We editors also thank our author colleagues for their willingness to work through the drafts as the project reached its final shape.

Peter L. Berger, Boston University
Gordon Redding, INSEAD

Chapter 1

INTRODUCTION: SPIRITUAL, SOCIAL, HUMAN, AND FINANCIAL CAPITAL

Peter L. Berger and Gordon Redding

Explaining the role of religion in societal progress has for long remained a major challenge to thinkers observing the varieties of success and failure in the progress of societies towards wealth and a better life for their people. In the Western world, from the full analysis by Adam Smith two and a half centuries ago, and his insistence on addressing the question of 'moral sentiments', to more recent returns to the same issue by writers such as Deidre McCloskey, and Gertrude Himmelfarb[1], the question of *how such influence works* remains open to clarification. This is the terrain walked over in this book. In doing so, the walk is taken in the company of scholars who have dedicated years of enquiry into specific countries and religions, and each of them is well recognized in his or her specialism. They have in addition been encouraged to explain not just their theories, but the facts on the ground as they exist in China, India, Russia, Indonesia, South Africa, and Eastern Europe. They do so on the basis of current studies in the environments they observe. An overall guide to world trends is provided at the outset, as is also a statement of the setting of the core question: how does religion sponsor or otherwise a society's progress towards prosperity?

The religions considered here include Confucianism and Taoism as practised in China and Taiwan, charismatic Christianity in the form of Pentecostalism as practised in South Africa and also India seen more historically, Eastern Orthodox Christianity in Russia, Islam in Indonesia, and the swirling complex of spirits of capitalism in the cross-currents of Eastern Europe. These are described against their own societal contexts. This allows us to take into account issues of economics, politics, sociology, and psychology, as well as religion itself, and the work is consequently both inter-disciplinary and comparative. Above all it is designed to be alive with the realities of religion's current contribution to the complex flows of forces that make up any society.

We work with the notion of 'spiritual capital', seeing it as a set of resources stemming from religion and available for use in economic and political development. The word 'use' is of course to be interpreted loosely, as there are rarely instances where a conscious policy is adopted to apply such influences in a deliberate shaping of behaviour. Instead the influence process is extremely varied, and would encompass features such as the following:

(a) the adoption within a society of specific institutions stemming from religion, and initially developed within a religious context, examples of which would be shari'a law, at an earlier period double-entry book-keeping, or the concept of the corporation as legal person;
(b) the adoption of attitudes and values capable of shaping behaviour in the context of the economy, such as the 'Protestant ethic';
(c) the fostering of communal ideals that lead to behaviour within ideologically controlled limits such that the behaviour of others can be more easily predicted, this in turn leading to higher trust;
(d) the encouragement of the idea of the self as autonomous and self-reliant (with its opposite in the encouragement of fatalistic acceptance of one's lot in life);
(e) the stabilizing of a society's power structure by making it legitimate through an elite's borrowing of religious support, in turn permitting greater control and coordination of economic action, as with 'God bless America'.

Spiritual capital is a subset of social capital. The latter amounts to a society's ability to make the processes of social and economic exchange run smoothly and fully, by drawing upon norms about cooperation and about the public good. Its spiritual subset is that part in which religious beliefs exert influence. For example, the powerful and efficient business networks of the regional ethnic Chinese in Southeast Asia are at least partly explained by the 'glue' formed among people with shared Confucian ideals about reciprocal obligations. It is important also to see the workings of spiritual capital as possibly negative as well as positive. For instance the relative failure of many Islamic economies is influenced by inheritance traditions that prevent the passing on of business empires intact from one generation to another. For economic growth there is 'bad' spiritual capital as well as 'good'.

In looking for the connections between worlds of ideas and of action we are faced with both the complexity and the dynamism of societal systems. Stable economic systems that work efficiently are miracles of balance. The fact that they are capable of being unbalanced and thrown into temporary states of disorder such as recessions, downturns, overheatings, currency crises, strikes and mass protests, is a reminder that their components normally work together in an achieved equilibrium, perhaps one that can re-establish itself. This is not to say that the equilibria are fixed and unchangeable as they may transit to a newer state of balance containing different features, but in essence when they work well they remain internally cohesive and consistent, and their parts fit together well enough to keep the total running. These long-term equilibria are achieved only if they contain three subtly invisible elements that keep them capable of maintaining their balance: they have to be efficient in how they treat the resources at their disposal; they have to be able to sponsor innovation; and they have to be capable of adapting without losing the equilibrium. The more the world's systems of equilibria interact and compete, the more crucial do such conditions become. Religion can play a significant role in a society's meeting of these three requirements, but it will share influence with a long list of other features.

The other features in the list might be thought of as the other forms of capital available for use, in simple terms *financial, human,* and the wider form of *social* capital. For each of these it is possible to identify subsidiary components, and in doing so to list a whole series of institutions – those stable patternings of rules of behaviour that bring order to the potential chaos of social interaction. Whether the end result is a rock-solid building or a swaying edifice that nevertheless holds itself together, without those institutions nothing orderly can be achieved and nothing will serve to act as a platform on which progress might continue.

Financial capital is like water in agriculture. Without it nothing happens, and with it what happens depends on how much is available, in what ways is it accessed. What makes societies different in their use of capital is primarily the amount of it available, but it is not just that. Its availability is usually conditional. If you go to the stock-market for it there will be pressures for the return of dividends – the expected percentages varying between societies. If you go to the bank, there might well be assumptions about capital growth, but perhaps more patience about returns. If you go to your family there will be expectations about control, about moral obligations, about the distribution of profits. If you use retained earnings you may have more say in determining what is expected. If you bring in private equity or venture capital you will perhaps have a lot less say than you had before. Capital is not a single unit of input, and it is not used in isolation from other features of the context. It may appear to be a purely 'economic' factor, given the rational calculations that normally surround it, but it is in reality a very 'social' component.

Human capital is what executives are talking about when they say – as they do regularly – 'this business is all about its people'. This is at one level a truism; you cannot have economic exchange without people to do it. But the regular acknowledgement of the significance of such a form of capital goes beyond that. It implies that what matters are peoples' talents, attitudes, willingness to cooperate, creativity, and commitment to work. Two large features of a society play important parts here: the education system in stimulating and channelling the talent; and the way the labour market is organized, for its ability to foster (or otherwise) the matching of talents with their use.

Social capital, when available in high quantity, delivers trust into the workings of the system, like oil to the workings of a machine. It is common to see two kinds of such lubrication. Trust can be institutional or interpersonal, and societies work differently according to the proportions of each available. Institutional trust is most visible in law, accounting, the use of professional standards, the richness and reliability of information. Personal trust is visible where business is conducted over networks of reciprocal, often informal, obligations. Both can be at work and can feed off each other. Some societies have more of one than the other, and there is a clear difference in how long it takes to establish them, with personal trust being highly fluid and reactive to opportunity, as in the cases of China or Russia today. Institutional trust can take centuries to accrete, as it depends so much on the historical construction of reputation and the slow seeping into society of procedures that become traditions. The essential dilemma always faced by developing societies, and solved by the developed, is the constructing of a system of exchange in which people can trust strangers.

The place occupied by religion within the category of social capital comes from its value in stabilizing and clarifying the purposes around which people can build their willingness to cooperate. To understand this we need to go beyond institutions to examine the realm of 'meaning' that underpins both social action and institutions. For a society to function, its design needs first to be agreed upon in a way that its members can understand and accept. In this a primary agreement is needed about three questions. As symbolized in Gaugin's great painting on the theme, they are: 'Where do we come from? Why are we here? Where are we going?'. The role of religion is to answer these questions, and in doing so to provide the 'sacred canopy' under which people can shelter from the chaos of the unknown. It is the second of these questions – why are we here? – that comes into play when analysing how religion plays a part in shaping the workings of an economy. When people go to work they implicitly accept that what they do has 'meaning'. It is part of the workings of society. Whether it is simply that they need the money and this is a way of getting it, or they like the sense of companionship, or they feel their work is 'worthwhile' in a wider sense, they do not normally work in a vacuum of meaning. Their purposes may not be consciously analysed, but they exist.

No organization can exist without a purpose. It would be too confusing for people as they would not know what behaviour took priority. So organizations are purposive by design. They have strategies, plans, targets. They also have leaders, or groups in charge, and they in turn have purposes, more or less overlapping with the publicly visible ones that guide action. The power of an individual business leader – at least in a free society – is based on whether subordinates 'go along with' what they perceive as that leader's deeper intentions. If an organization adopts purposes that go against the ideals of the society it is in, then it will be seen as an illegitimate organization, and may be attacked by the society. Obvious examples are visible in the punishing of corporations for fraud, or pollution, labour abuse, or fattening the innocent population. Less obvious processes of influence are visible when companies change policy and adopt new purposes, as when those most guilty of polluting spend money to appear the most green, or when they are taken over and changed forcibly to become more appealing to their customers.

Studies of the institutional fabrics of various societies reveal two laws at work. First, the institutions of a society tend to reflect the fundamental structures of meaning established within the culture. If, for instance, individualism and competitiveness are ideals within the culture, then firms will be forced to compete and people will be judged individually. The institutions will reflect the culture, and will historically emerge from it in a never-ending reciprocal process.

Second, when an institutional fabric in turn sponsors a particular form of economic behaviour, as for instance visible in particular forms of enterprise, then the success or failure of that response compared to responses in other societies, will depend on the extent to which that societal system can display the three key features described earlier: efficiency, innovation, and adaptiveness.

The contributors to this book have all looked at specific societies with such issues in mind, and have described how religious influences penetrate the economic arena. We begin with an overview by Lawrence Harrison of the world's successes and relative failures (so far) in achieving economic progress. This setting of the scene is a necessary prelude to what follows, as it places the facts before us, and challenges us to find reasons behind them.

The Global Context

Harrison presents findings from a study of 117 countries, each with at least a million people and each containing populations where a majority identify with one of eight broadly defined 'religions'. These are the clearly defined Buddhism, Hinduism, Islam, Judaism; Christianity seen in three forms – Protestant, Catholic, and Eastern Orthodox; and the secular ethical code of Confucianism. He rates the countries by religious category against ten indicators widely accepted as measuring progress towards a modern condition of prosperity. His conclusions are summarized as follows:

1. Protestantism has been far more conducive to modernization than Catholicism, above all in the Western Hemisphere.
2. The Nordic countries are the champions of progress.
3. Confucianism (a surrogate for Chinese culture, which includes several other currents including Taoism and ancestor worship) has been far more conducive to modernization than Islam, Buddhism, or Hinduism.
4. The most advanced Orthodox country, Greece, was the poorest of the European Union members prior to the 2004 accessions. There are some parallels between the Orthodox Christian and Catholic countries. But there are also some apparent residues in Orthodox countries from the Communist experience.
5. Islam has fallen far behind the Western religions and Confucianism in virtually all respects. There are some significant differences between Arab and non-Arab Islamic countries.
6. Hindu India's democratic institutions have held up well, and it has experienced rapid economic growth during the past two decades. But it has been very slow to educate its people, particularly its women, and it does poorly in the Corruption Perceptions Index.
7. It is difficult to generalize about Buddhism, but the data suggest that it is not a powerful force for modernization.
8. Traditional African religions are an obstacle to progress.
9. Close parallels among the values propagated by Protestantism, Judaism, and Confucianism suggest the existence of a universal culture of progress. All three promote the values of control of destiny, achievement, education, diligence/work ethic, merit, saving, and social responsibility, albeit in different degrees. And those values tend to persist even in the face of secularization, as the Nordic countries demonstrate.

Peter Boettke presents a complementary analysis to that of Lawrence Harrison. The 'what has happened?' is thus followed by the 'why?' and 'how?'. His paper is an overview of the shifts in analysis by political economists over time. He shows how development economists have turned in the post-Communist period from an initial focus on the straight application of economic logic – *getting the prices right* – to a more contextualized second phase of *getting the institutions right*, and more recently to the deeply contextualized problem of *getting the culture right*.

In this latter field, religion plays a central part as the focal point for the coordination of a society's mental models. Working through both formal doctrines and informal beliefs and spirituality, religion shapes and legitimates institutions, its contribution being two-fold as the economic exchange processes unfold and intensify. Firstly a population that has internalized the informal and formal rules of social intercourse needs fewer policemen and preachers, and so provides more free space for action. Secondly when cooperation among anonymous actors is possible, at low transaction costs, then the gains from trade, and from productive innovation, are higher. The evidence for these two benevolent processes runs through the book.

These findings and stages of analytical progress challenge us to explore many versions of the core question 'Why?' And in doing so we acknowledge the great complexity faced in tracing the effects running between a religious belief and a national economic outcome. Our aim is not so much to re-visit the grand theories that already exist in the work of Weber, North, Eisenstadt, Landes, and others, but rather to offer a view from the ground level, so that understanding may be gained from that immediacy, rather than from the necessary use of abstracts and formal rationales. We want in simple terms to bring the question to life, and to bring life to the question.

China

We begin empirically with China, for the last two decades the most compelling of economic miracles, and Robert Weller describes how the traditional systems of Chinese ethics are currently playing a part in that miracle. Drawing on his knowledge of both Taiwan and China, Weller sets out to connect religion with other cultural features typically associated with economic growth and also democratization, seeing these as including individualism, a work ethic, respect for education, civility, limitations on the power of leaders, and trust. His first important contribution is to clarify what is happening. By far the most common form of worship in China is village temple and ancestor veneration, practices that are only loosely connected with the named traditional religions of Buddhism and Taoism. It is of course arguable that the veneration of ancestors is an expression of the Confucian centrality of family, but it is worth noting also the parallel presence of Chinese pietistic traditions, Christianity, and new forms of Buddhism. The religious scene is more complex than commonly thought.

As in all societies the spiritual domain's encouragement of individualism needs to be balanced by a concern with broader social concerns, and Weller reviews a number of historical attempts to reconcile the two. He raises the interesting – and currently unanswerable – question as to whether the 'network capitalism' built on Chinese social ethics of reciprocity, and conducive to the adventurous entrepreneurial organizations that now dominate both the Chinese and Taiwanese economies, is an alternative to the rational western bureaucracy, or a pre-modern form that will change as it evolves. Attached to this question is the implicit contrast with what Weber described as the 'distinct and peculiar rationalism' of the Protestant west.

The local nature of most Chinese religious practice is well described here, and so too its flexibility, as there is no monolithic superstructure to seek permission from. As Weller points out there is very little institutional inertia standing in the way of new interpretations. Local temples, at least in Taiwan, have helped to consolidate democracy and to mobilize for civil liberties. In a similar way, in this relatively free and open social space in Taiwan (but not China) new religious sects have fostered other forms of coordination within the community, as exemplified by the Confucian-oriented Way of Unity, a grouping of two million members containing a 'disproportionate number of successful businessmen'. The Way of Unity, the Eighteen Lords, forms of Christianity, all foster shared values and the penetration into the economy of moral virtues.

In China, Christianity is at least legally recognized, unlike some groupings, but it works under severe constraints, and has adapted by becoming a weak component of a limited civil society. The Buddhist revival in many Chinese societies outside China, with its charitable social activism, has not yet penetrated the mainland. But the real contribution of religions in these societies may well be to act as reservoirs for key societal values through times of authoritarian government control.

India

The Dalit class, or the 'untouchables' of an earlier time, account for 45 percent of India's 24 million Christians, and in the historical study reported here by Rebecca and Timothy Shah, these relatively unfortunate people are seen as escaping from their caste-defined lowly fate by changing the way they see themselves. Indian society also sees them differently in consequence. The detailed and comprehensive study dates from the 1930s when the caste system was in full operation, and so we have an insight into what is possible when a marginalized group finds a way out of an apparent cul-de-sac. The relevance for groups in other countries is obvious, but here the vehicle was Pentecostalism, and its phenomenal growth requires understanding as to the source of its effectiveness.

Why does the evangelical version of the religion account for the lion's share of global Protestantism today? And within that why is Pentecostalism so powerful? We see here – as we do also in the next chapter on South Africa – the workings of the new ways of sense-making that religion can bring, and how such a change in perception can redefine a person's place in society, not just for the convert but also for surrounding others. Protestantism in its traditional European homeland was overwhelmed by the Modernism of the early twentieth century, and the sciences, wars, and new philosophies that coincided with it. Its dramatic 'comeback' in the developing world is then intriguing. The form that that took in India included the relatively rare feature of mass conversions – a sign of the clustering in the society. But it is the changes in behaviour that are most revealing of the new spirituality at work: the conquest of evil spirits; better marital conduct; resistance to alcohol; access to credit; but above all a sense of self-worth that acts to underpin the taking of initiative.

South Africa

The rise of the Pentecostal form of Christianity is a global phenomenon of impressive power, sweeping regions like Latin America and Africa, and countries such as South Korea, often offering to nominal Catholics an alternative source of guidance. In Africa the numbers of Pentecostal and Charismatic Christians rose from 94 million in 1990, to 150 million in 2005. In this fine-grained study, Ann Bernstein examines a current South African version of the Protestant ethic at work. Other studies suggest that the new values encouraged include individualism, education, a work ethic, and participation. Outcomes are a new middle class, new roles for women, higher mobility, and a protective social capsule for the disadvantaged. It also appears to sponsor very high levels of capacity for organizing, an effect of some significance in the context of concern here.

A key to understanding the obvious welcome given to a religious form such as this is that it provides a bridge between traditional African conceptions of morality and selfhood and the new rules of urban life needed in an environment where many black people can still feel uncomfortable away from their rural origins. The theme of self-worth as an antidote to earlier supernatural beliefs is reported from interviews, as is also the escape from perceived racial inequality. The 'mending of the social fabric' that results from membership also leads to incentives and supporting features for entrepreneurship. Ann Bernstein and Stephen Rule report their surprise and obvious pleasure at finding such a world of activity, energy, and entrepreneurship operating discreetly in a society in need of it.

Eastern Europe

Janos Kovacs sits at the interface between what used to be eastern and western Europe. Those labels contain worlds of meaning represented in the German popular discourse as the *Ossi* and the *Wessi* – two types of people. His interest here is in describing the extent to which the *Ossi* have absorbed new ideas from outside, and especially from the *Wessi*, in forming the successful new capitalisms of eastern Europe. He examines entrepreneurship, state governance, and economic science, as arenas in which effects may be seen. As with China, such post-Communist transformations can be revealing of both the forces of change and the resistance of earlier institutions to the discomforts of adjustment. Given that the eastern context was Communism, the question addressed is not so much how *religion* might have been re-shaped, but how spiritual capital more broadly defined has played a part. Religion is thus only one of the forms of spirituality, this latter while containing religion also containing what was the proto religion of Marxism, perhaps the ultimate opiate of the people.

What now is the spirit of capitalism in Eastern Europe, and what are the sources of any spirituality it may contain? In the background to these questions is the east–west 'secular cleavage' between two dominant mentalities. The interpenetrating of the two systems leads to complex effects: partial borrowings from the market system; the creation of cultural hybrids; and the transformation of what is transferred. In each of these processes in Eastern Europe both national identity and spiritual heritage are being re-asserted. This is then a focussed version of the larger debate over the 'Americanization' of Europe and the countervailing but less coordinated European 'social' response. Despite globalization the past continues to matter.

A little-acknowledged feature of the changing scene here is that Communism was in reality also a school of capitalism, as a side effect of its particular form of modernizing. It led to responses by entrepreneurial organizations that have served them well as comparative advantages in the global arena. These rest on a large stock of spiritual capital quite different in nature from that associated with Protestantism, Confucianism, or Pentecostalism. The resulting flexibility, improvisation, capacity for risk, and informality, may work better than the professional rationality that tends to be the flavour of the imported systems.

János Kovács presents findings from a detailed study of what is in effect the importing of spiritual capital via new managerial systems in multinational banking. In comparing the results in Poland, Slovenia, the Czech Republic, and Bulgaria, he identifies the highly diverse and essentially profane nature of the process, but observes that at the same time it is capable of mobilizing not just the intellect but the soul of the participants, and in fact needs to if it is to persist. The new norms and values – including trust, cooperation, and self-discipline – become spiritual assets that accumulate, and that in turn can be reinvented, exchanged, and transformed – even perhaps wasted. This emergence of a 'surrogate religion', embedded in rational practices and without a cosmic overlay or a God, seems able to sponsor a faith community providing life with meaning, a sense of belonging, and moral cohesion. Spiritual capital can come into being without a religious underlay. But its penetration varies from country to country and that depends on the fertility of the pro-capitalist seeds planted historically. History matters.

Russia

In his study of spiritual capital within Russian Orthodoxy in the current reforms, Christopher Marsh begins with a danger warning. The combination of Russian Orthodoxy and revived Russian nationalism might prove a more difficult obstacle to reform than the legacy of central planning. To examine this, it is first necessary to clarify what Orthodoxy means in a situation where although about two thirds of people are now nominally Orthodox, only around 6 percent attend church regularly. The habits of the seven decades of enforced secularism seem to have prevented the wholesale re-emergence of the thousand-year-old religion into the conduct of daily life. The society's social and moral fabric may for some time carry the scars from the onslaught it suffered.

An assumption among several observers is that to be culturally Orthodox does not require regular church attendance. Marsh suggests, from his data, that in fact the truly Orthodox community of churchgoers exhibits some troubling tendencies – anti-Semitism, Islamophobia, xenophobia, and general intolerance. The broader community has ideals that in some respects support market-driven capitalism, for instance a great respect for work and for achieved differences in income, but at the same time there is strong support for state involvement. Clearly the straight emulation of the market-driven model is not likely.

Trust in Russia is notoriously weak at either the institutional or the personal level, even though progress is now visible in the former as the strong government sponsors law and order. The Church is the most trusted institution but appears to be hampered in moving the society towards greater civic engagement and political participation. Strong leadership is universally appreciated in this society, by both the religious and the non-religious, with all that that implies for the economy's evolution.

Indonesia

Robert Hefner applies here his long experience of Islam in Indonesia, the country with the largest Moslem population, and considers how the 'soft' version of Islam found in this avowedly secular state might be supportive of its economic progress. He begins with some of the questions implicit in Lawrence Harrison's data. Why can one associate Protestant faith with democracy in the US, but not Catholic faith with democracy in Italy? In what ways is fundamentalist Islam anti-democracy, whereas in Indonesia the gentler version is pro-democracy? What is the nature of faith-based social capital and how does it work in this unusual, but very large case.

Defining spiritual capital as the cultural and ideological content that flows through networks, cooperation and trust, Hefner reminds us that it can be negative as well as positive. Indonesia's record of ideologically-based violence needs no recapitulation. But here we have a huge society that made the transit from military dictatorship to full democracy with quite remarkable smoothness, and is now engaged in extensive decentralization of decision powers in a way that is transforming the business scene away from its accustomed dependence on co-opting support at the centre to courting partnership in the local areas.

Asking how the spiritual capital he defines is evident now in Indonesia, Hefner reports that 'modern Islam produces great volumes of the stuff'. Over four decades there has been a vast resurgence of Muslim piety, schooling, and associational life – a mass production of spiritual capital. At the same time internal debates are still unresolved as to what to do with it. There are two main types: the radical version adopted among para-militaries; and the gentler, more cosmopolitan form instilled in the vast education system of private and public Islamic schools.

A disturbing insight is presented in describing how impervious is the radical mindset to alternative perceptions. The duty to command right and punish wrong, each defined prior and unquestioned, admits of no debate. But we are assured by supporting data that of Indonesia's 46000 Islamic schools only 1 percent are radical in this way. So, despite the drama of occasional radical acts, a vast majority of the form of spiritual capital available here is at least amenable to considering the alternatives presented by modernization. The crucial debating ground is the tension between *shari'a* law and democracy, and Hefner takes us into the finer points of this debate in reporting his surveys of key holders of influence such as teachers.

Given the fast-growing population of the Islamic world, and the tensions associated with the clarity and power of the religion, adjustment in the Indonesian case is of great potential significance. The process is at an early stage, but there are few countries as well suited as Indonesia to the job of finding a way to resolve the dilemmas posed.

Integrating the Ideas

The book closes with an integration of the ideas and the data. This places spiritual capital in a wider framework and proposes a number of themes illustrated in the specialist reports from individual societies. Three integrating ideas are proposed. Firstly there are certain catalysts within societies that have been economically successful. They may not be all required but enough of them need to be present to allow economic exchange to flourish. Secondly, the catalysts work to stimulate the complex reactions in economic life only if there is 'room to manoeuvre', to experiment, to innovate, to allow variety. Spiritual capital plays a significant role in introducing and supporting such catalysts and in encouraging a society to provide such room. Thirdly the 'meaning' of economic action, the purposes adopted by the key players and bought into by their employees, is itself a main channel through which flow some of the key influences on economic behaviour.

Notes and References

1 Himmelfarb Gertrude. (2004) *The Roads to Modernity*, New York, Alfred A. Knopf.
Mc Closkey Deidre. N. (2006) *The Bourgeois Virtues*, Chicago, University of Chicago Press.

Chapter 2

DO SOME RELIGIONS DO BETTER THAN OTHERS?

Lawrence E. Harrison

There exists today a widespread presumption that all religions must be regarded as of equal worth, and in any event are not to be the object of comparative value judgments. That presumption – let's label it religious relativism, a corollary of cultural relativism – is the dominant one in the West, and surely in our universities. However, when it comes to the relationship between religion and human progress, I find compelling evidence that some religions do better than others in promoting the goals of the UN Universal Declaration of Human Rights: democratic politics, social justice, and prosperity.

Figure 2.1 at the appendix of this chapter is the summary of an idealized typology of 25 cultural factors that are viewed very differently in cultures prone to progress and those that resist it. As you will appreciate, religious doctrine and practice influence virtually all of these 25 factors.

As an example of a religion that is highly resistant to progress, consider Voodoo, the dominant religion of Haiti and a surrogate for the many traditional religions of Africa, the birthplace of Voodoo. Haiti is by far the poorest, least literate, most misgoverned country in the Western Hemisphere. Voodoo is a religion of sorcery in which hundreds of spirits, very human and capricious, control human destinies. The only way to gain leverage over what happens in one's life is to propitiate the spirits through the ceremonial intervention of the Voodoo priests and priestesses. Not only does Voodoo involve sorcery and nurture irrationality; it also nurtures a sense of impotence and fatalism and discourages the entrepreneurial vocation. It focuses on the present, not the future. Voodoo is without ethical content and, consequently, a major contributor to the high levels of mistrust, paranoia, sense of helplessness, and despair noted in the anthropological literature about Haiti. The insight of Placide David, a Haitian in exile writing in 1959, is particularly poignant: 'our souls are like dead leaves. We live in indifference, are silently malcontent...the most flagrant violations of our rights and the most outrageous abuse of authority provokes among us merely submission'.[1]

Voodoo's roots are in the Dahomey region of West Africa – today the country of Benin. The indicators of income, child malnutrition, child mortality, life expectancy and literacy are virtually identical for Haiti and Benin. The roots of much of the population of Barbados are also in Dahomey. But unlike Haiti, which won its independence from France in 1804 through an uprising of the slaves, Barbados gained its independence from Britain in 1966, at which time the descendants of the slaves dominated politics and the economy. During three centuries, they had so acculturated to British values and institutions that they are sometimes referred to as 'Afro-Saxons' or 'Black Englishmen'. The dominant religion is the Church of England. Today, Barbados is a prosperous democracy, number 30 on the 2005 UN Human Development Index, ahead of the Czech Republic, Argentina, Poland, and Chile. It is approaching First World status.

I believe that Voodoo has made a major contribution to the socio-political pathology, including extremely low levels of trust, and poverty that have plagued Haiti's history. I also believe that, as Daniel Etounga-Manguelle argues in *Culture Matters*, traditional African religions have similarly impeded progress in many countries in the region.

I have examined the performance of 117 countries, each with a million or more people of whom a majority identify with one of six religions – Buddhism, Catholicism, Eastern Orthodox Christianity, Hinduism, Islam, and Protestantism – and one secular ethical code – Confucianism. I also include one small country – Israel – that is predominantly Jewish.

I have located the position of each of the 117 countries in ten indicators or indices and have then grouped these data by predominant religion (see Figure 2). I present the data in both weighted (for population) and unweighted averages, with separate calculations for Protestant, Catholic, and Confucian countries in the First World. Within Islam, I have also grouped Arab countries separately. The ten indicators or indices are:

1. The UN's Human Development Index
2. UN data on literacy
3. UN data on female literacy
4. UN fertility data
5. Freedom House's Annual Survey of Freedom in the World
6. The chronology of democratic evolution
7. World Bank per capita income data
8. World Bank income distribution data
9. World Values Survey data on trust
10. Transparency International's Corruption Perceptions Index

I acknowledge the considerable scientific limits to the analysis. The data derive from respectable sources, but some distortions are inevitable. For example, while I have generally held to the line that a majority of a country's people subscribe to the religion in which that country is grouped, there are wide variations in the religious composition of many countries. Although India is predominantly Hindu, it has one of the largest Moslem populations in the world. Indonesia, by contrast, is overwhelmingly Moslem, but its small Chinese, mostly Christian, minority has made a vastly disproportionate contribution to the country's economic development. Although South Korea is treated as a Confucian country, many Koreans practice religions, Christian religions prominently among them. And the label 'Confucian' is itself oversimplified: it would be more accurately described as Chinese culture, also embracing aspects of Buddhism, Taoism, and ancestor worship, among others. Finally, I have classified Germany, the Netherlands and Switzerland as Protestant, although there may today be more practicing Catholics than Protestants in each country. I have done this on the same grounds that the World Values Survey has, because, to quote Ronald Inglehart, '…historically, Protestantism has shaped them'.

Moreover, within a given religion, there are divisions, cross-currents, and national variations that are not reflected in Figure 1. For example, several of the generalizations that follow about Catholicism do not apply to the Basques, who have a centuries-old tradition of entrepreneurship, creativity, and cooperation, and who are very Catholic (the Society of Jesus was founded by a Basque). Islam is quite different in Indonesia and Saudi Arabia. And our analysis does not disaggregate Sunni, Shia, and Kurdish Muslims.

I want to stress that religion is not the only influence on a country's performance with respect to the indicators, or on its culture. Geography, including climate, topography, and resource endowment, clearly plays a key role as do the vagaries of history – for example, wars, colonial experiences, geopolitical forces, economic models chosen or imposed. The level of prosperity powerfully influences performance. Leadership matters: that Singapore is among the most affluent and least corrupt countries in the world surely reflects the vision and influence of Lee Kuan Yew.

But culture also matters, and culture is profoundly, although not exclusively, influenced by religion and/or an ethical code like Confucianism. While I am unable to quantify 'profoundly' with any precision, the patterns that will appear as we examine the data tend to confirm the conclusion that some religions are more conducive to modernization than others. But these patterns must be considered approximations. Narrow differences could too easily be explained away by shortcomings in the data or by the intrusion of non-cultural factors. So we have to be looking for patterns that involve significant contrasts.

Seven broad conclusions derive from the data:

1. Protestantism has been far more conducive to modernization than Catholicism, above all in the Western Hemisphere.
Predominantly Protestant countries do substantially better than predominantly Catholic countries on the UN's Human Development Index. The Index is the most comprehensive of the ten. It combines life expectancy, adult literacy, school enrolment, and GDP per capita. On a scale on which number one is best and number 162 is worst, the weighted average of all Protestant countries is 9.2, that of all Catholic countries 58.3. To be sure, the majority of Protestant countries are in the First World, while the majority of Catholic countries are not. But a significant difference is also found when comparing First World countries: the weighted average for the Protestant countries is 8.5, for the Catholic countries 17.4.

Some other salient contrasts:

- The average date for the commencement of democratic continuity in the Protestant countries of the First World is 1852, of the Catholic countries 1934.
- Trust, as measured by the answers to the World Values Survey question, 'Can people in general be trusted?', is much higher in Protestant countries than in Catholic countries generally, and while the gap narrows when one considers only First World countries, it is still substantial: a weighted average of 42% trust others in the First World Protestant countries, a weighted average of 24% in the Catholic countries.
- A comparably large gap exists with respect to corruption. On a scale where the cleanest is number 1 and the most corrupt number 91, the weighted average for the Protestant countries is 14.9, for the Catholic countries 45.6. For First World countries, the Protestant advantage is 14.7 to 24.4.

Of the ten least corrupt countries in the 2001 Transparency survey, eight were Protestant, one Confucian (Singapore at number 4), and one (Luxembourg, with a population of fewer than 500,000) Catholic. The data on trust and corruption evoke Weber's contrast of the rigor of the Protestant insistence on 'a life of good works' and 'the very human Catholic cycle of sin, repentance, atonement, release, followed by renewed sin'.

2. The Nordic countries are the champions of progress.
The Nordic countries – Denmark, Finland, Iceland, Norway, and Sweden – all of whose evolution was profoundly and apparently indelibly influenced by Lutheranism ('indelibly' because a large majority of contemporary Nordics do not attend church) and all of which are relatively homogeneous, get high marks

across the board. Interestingly, a recent assessment of social capital in the United States finds Americans of Scandinavian and British descent at the top.[2]

3. Confucianism has been far more conducive to modernization than Islam, Buddhism, or Hinduism.

The data for the Confucian countries are, of course, dominated by China, which drives all of the indicators down, particularly when we weight for population. The averages for the Confucian First World societies – Japan, South Korea, Taiwan, Hong Kong, and Singapore – are similar to those of the Catholic First World countries in (1) the UN Human Development Index; (2) literacy, including female literacy; (3) per capita GDP; and (4) income distribution. Trust is substantially greater in the Confucian countries than the Catholic countries, while corruption is about the same – with the noteworthy exception of Singapore, which tied with Iceland as fourth cleanest.

4. The most advanced Orthodox country, Greece, was the poorest of the European Union members prior to the 2004 accessions. There are some parallels between the Orthodox Christian and Catholic countries. But there are also some apparent residues in Orthodox countries from the Communist experience.

The Orthodox Christian and Catholic countries come out in the same position on the UN's Human Development Index with weighted averages of 58 in the rankings, and they are fairly close in per capita GDP and trust. Greece is the only First World country that is Orthodox, but it is the poorest. Reflecting the Communist emphasis on education, the Orthodox countries enjoy First World literacy levels. Their worse showing on the Corruption Perceptions Index than the Catholic countries might be explained in part as the consequence of the widespread corruption nurtured by the Communist system.

5. Islam has fallen far behind the Western religions and Confucianism in virtually all respects.

The data for the Islamic countries reveal a strong resistance to modernization, in striking contrast to the vanguard role of Islam during its first several centuries. The Islamic countries are far behind the Confucian countries and even further behind the Christian First World countries on the UN Human Development Index; in literacy, particularly female literacy; in per capita GDP; in the World Values Survey data on trust (except the Catholic countries); and in the Corruption Perceptions Index.

Particularly noteworthy are the low levels of female literacy: below 50% in Egypt, Morocco, Pakistan, and Bangladesh, among others, reflecting the subordinated position of women in the Islamic religion.

Also noteworthy are the data on fertility. The Islamic countries had the highest fertility rates in the world according to the UN 1995–2000 estimates. While they continue to present the highest rates among the various religious groups in the UN estimates for 2000–2005, we note a recent across-the-board decline.

The Islamic countries are less free according to Freedom House than any other group except the Confucian countries, where the numbers are overwhelmed by China's authoritarianism. Trust is low in the Islamic countries, and corruption is high.

6. *Hindu India's democratic institutions have held up well, and it has experienced rapid economic growth during the past two decades. But it has been very slow to educate its people, particularly its women, and it does poorly in the Corruption Perceptions Index.*

Hindu India scores better than any other religious grouping except the Protestant countries in the Freedom House rankings. British political institutions have taken root.

India's continuing economic surge is among the most encouraging development trends of the early years of the twenty-first century. But the literacy data for India are surprisingly low – more than half of Indian women are illiterate – reflecting, as in the Islamic countries, the subordination of women in Hinduism as well as the large numbers of Muslim Indians. And India does not do well on the Corruption Perceptions Index.

7. *It is difficult to generalize about Buddhism, but the data suggest that it is not a powerful force for modernization.*

The seven countries where Buddhism has had predominant influence include, in order of population size, Thailand, Myanmar, Sri Lanka, Cambodia, Laos, Mongolia, and Bhutan. Mongolia is among the freest countries in the Third World; Myanmar is among the least free. The Gini data on Mongolia, Cambodia, and Thailand are typical for Third World countries, but Sri Lanka does much better, in fact better than the United Kingdom and the United States. The only Buddhist country to have experienced sustained high rates of economic development is Thailand, but, as in Indonesia, Malaysia, and the Philippines, the Chinese minority has made a vastly disproportionate contribution to that growth.

***

The problem of generalizing is further complicated by the diversity of Buddhism: major divisions, numerous sects, and sectarian variations over time. What is clear, however, is that no predominantly Buddhist country is close to joining the First World club, which up until now includes only Protestant, Catholic, Jewish, and Confucian members.

Religious reform is a key element in the final chapter of *The Central Liberal Truth*, 'Guidelines for Progressive Cultural Change'.

1. Islam

Islam is the chief source of values, beliefs, and attitudes for many of its believers. In this respect, Islam is unique: no other religion today so powerfully influences the culture of its faithful. In the West, with the exception of the United States, the influence of religion has declined in favour of secularism – a secularism, to be sure, that has been profoundly influenced by earlier religiosity, as in the Nordic countries. But the cultural power once exerted by religion in Scandinavia is very much a reality in the Islamic world today. And whereas Lutheranism was a force for progress, e.g. with respect to universal education, a rigorous ethical code, in the Nordic countries, Islam today, with a few exceptions, is not. Unlike medieval Hellenized Islam and even the nineteenth century Islam of reform and liberal thought, contemporary Safist-Wahhabi and Islamist Islam reject learning from others.

While there are numerous factors that lie behind the slow progress of the Islamic countries, a major contributor has been clerical interpretations of the Quran that have (1) transmitted fatalistic dogma; (2) permitted adoption of science and technology advances from outside but closed the door to the liberalizing cultural forces that have made these advances possible; and (3) perpetuated the subordination – and illiteracy – of women. This condition is not uniform throughout the Islamic world as Turkey and Indonesia demonstrate. But it is the predominant condition, and as Islam has steadily slipped from its early leadership in the arts and sciences, and with the subsequent collapse of the once-omnipotent Ottoman Empire, most Muslims today are constantly reminded of how far behind the West and East Asia they have fallen. This insistent insult to self-respect is central to the motivation of Osama Bin Laden and his followers.

Bassam Tibi's Culture Matters Research Project (CMRP) papers on Islam and Egypt, Robert Hefner's papers on Islam and Indonesia, and the four UNDP Arab Human Development Reports are crystal clear: reform of Islam is indispensable for accelerated progress toward the goals of democratic governance, social justice, and prosperity. Among the key elements of reform: openness to the values, ideas, and institutions of the non-Islamic world; tolerance of other religions; a broad commitment to excellence, education, and gender equality.

2. Roman Catholicism

As Michael Novak points out in his CMRP paper, the number of people who identify themselves as Catholics is growing with many new adherents in Africa. But in Europe and Latin America, the number of practicing Catholics is declining, and in the case of Latin America, tens of millions of Catholics have converted to Evangelical and Pentecostal Protestantism. It is also highly significant that the transformations of Italy, Spain, Ireland, and the Province of Quebec have all involved substantial loss of influence by the Church.

As I documented earlier, Catholic countries are generally outperformed by Protestant countries in most of the ten indicators that measure democracy, prosperity, social justice, trust, and corruption. That is substantially also true when assessing only the advanced democracies. But the most compelling evidence of the need for reform in the Catholic Church is the condition of Latin America. Although the Church can take some credit for the advance of democracy, at least in the electoral sense, in the region in recent decades, it must also assume some responsibility for Latin America's most troubling problems:

- With the exception of Chile, economic growth rates have been insufficient to offer hope of real transformation.
- Distribution of wealth, income, land, and opportunity is among the most inequitable in the world.
- Levels of trust are among the lowest in the world.
- Levels of corruption are high (Chile being a salient exception).
- Levels of criminal activity, including violent crime, are high, symbolized by the current epidemic of kidnappings, many of short duration and involving petty ransoms.

Michael Novak makes a compelling case for an unqualified commitment by the Church to democratic capitalism. (We are reminded of the title of Miguel Basáñez's CMRP paper on Mexico – 'The Camel and the Needle'). Minority elements of the Church support Novak's views, but there are also influential Church leaders driven by utopian socialist ideology who are among those attacking 'neo-liberal' (read 'capitalist') economic policies in Latin America. The irony is that while the Church continues its preference for the poor, Catholic Latin America has produced vastly more poor people than Protestant Canada and the United States, testimony to which is the heavy flow of poor Latinos *al norte*. It is a further irony that tens of millions of poor Latin Americans have been drawn to Protestant religions that preach a message similar to that of Deng Xiaoping: 'To get rich is glorious'.

But there is another important aspect of Latin America's problems for which the Church must also assume some responsibility and for which new approaches by the Church could be extremely helpful: the ethical issues underlying Latin America's generally dismal performance with respect to social justice, trust, corruption, and crime. At the root of these phenomena is an elastic ethical code, a failure to inculcate the Golden Rule. To be sure, there are other factors in play besides religion, American pop culture among them. But that the Church bears some responsibility is underscored by the Latin Americans, predominantly poor and female, who convert to Protestantism not only because they identify it with prosperity but also because they believe that it will keep their men out of the bars and bordellos and provide a measure of family stability in which their children will stand a better chance for a better life.

Were the Catholic Church to take a leadership role in a campaign to promote a rigorous ethical standard in Latin America and elsewhere, it could make a huge contribution to progress as well as to its own relevance and credibility.

3. Orthodox Christianity

Orthodox Christianity, an offshoot of Roman Catholicism that became fully independent of Rome in 1054, is the dominant religion in Russia, Greece, Ukraine, Belarus, Romania, and several smaller countries in eastern Europe and western Asia including the Republic of Georgia. In his CMRP paper on Georgia, Irakli Chkonia lists a number of progress-resistant characteristics often associated with Orthodox Christianity:

> ...submission to authority, discouragement of dissent and initiative, discouragement of innovation and social change, submissive collectivism rather than individualism, emphasis on ethnic cohesion rather than supranational relationships, isolationism and particularism, spiritual determinism and fatalism. Also embraced in the pattern is the aversion of Orthodoxy to the non-Orthodox Christian West and the Islamic World, political rivals of the past and the present.[3]

But the CMRP papers by Chkonia, Archie Brown on Russia, and Georges Prevelakis on Greece emphasize both significant national variations in Orthodoxy as well as a considerable diminution in its influence and practice over the past century, consistent with secularizing trends in Europe more generally. Brown observes, 'The Orthodox religious legacy is almost certainly of less political significance in contemporary Russia than the seven decades of Communist rule, followed by some fifteen years of political pluralism...'.[4]

As in other religions, both reformist and conservative currents are found in Orthodoxy, and the two vie with one another for dominance, particularly in Russia. Nikolas Gvosdev concludes his paper on Orthodox Christianity with the observation, 'The foundation for reform exists, but it is not yet clear that construction will begin'.[5] He subsequently elaborated that view: 'Orthodox Christianity today is in a pre-Vatican II state; perhaps on the verge of reforms designed to make relevant its ancient traditions—but not yet clear that it will move in that direction'.[6]

The circumstances are similar to those of Roman Catholicism. The influence of the church is generally in decline. Reform of Orthodox Christianity aimed at support of democracy and market economics could help reverse the erosion of both in Putin's Russia at a crucial moment; have similar positive effects in other Orthodox countries; and enhance the relevance and credibility of the religion.

4. Hinduism

Hinduism has been labelled 'anti-progress' by, among others, Max Weber and Gunnar Myrdal. Fatalism, the caste system, and the subordination and exploitation of women are the chief characteristics of Hinduism that critics have highlighted. But, as Pratap Bhanu Mehta stresses in his CMRP essay on Hinduism, the religion is a good deal more flexible and diverse than many critics appreciate, and it has demonstrated a considerable capacity for change. Moreover, India's democratic politics have played a powerful corrective role with respect to Hindu doctrine, for example in breaking down the caste system.

Nonetheless, Hindu leaders might ponder the CMRP typology with a view to doctrinal modifications that support India's quest for modernity. The caste system is still a disturbing, if diminished, force in India.

5. Buddhism

Although Buddhism is an extremely diverse religion, Jay Garfield observes, '...Buddhist theory for the most part remains resolutely a theory about individual life and practice. In a strictly formal sense, Buddhism and democracy are mutually independent. Buddhism neither precludes nor entails liberal democracy; liberal democracy neither precludes nor entails Buddhism'.[7] Yet there are elements in Buddhist doctrine and practice that are clearly compatible with democracy, above all the egalitarian nature of the *sangha*, the ideal Buddhist community in which seniority matters but not class, caste, wealth, or prestige.

Similarly, Gregory Ornatowski argues that notwithstanding Buddhism's focus on 'an individualistic pursuit of enlightenment...Buddhist economic ethics...play a significant role as a part of overall Buddhist philosophy regarding social life and even enlightenment itself'.[8] But Ornatowski concludes that, on balance, Buddhism is not a dynamic force for either economic development or social justice, although it is not necessarily an obstacle, either.

There is, of course, a major question as to the extent of contemporary Buddhist influence on politics and economics, with so many other forces, globalization prominently among them, in play. It seems reasonable to conclude that 'reform' of Buddhism is unlikely, if for no other reason than its diversity – and unlikely to have that much influence on the paths followed by the countries in which the religion predominates.

6. Confucianism, Judaism, Protestantism

These are the three 'religions' (once again, Confucianism is not a religion but an ethical code) whose value systems most correspond with the progress-prone column of the CMRP typology – the 'universal progress culture' described in Figure 1. All three promote the ideas/values of control of destiny, achievement, education, diligence/work ethic, merit, saving, and social responsibility, although in different degrees. And those values tend to persist even in the face of secularization, as the Nordic countries demonstrate.

All three will confront sooner or later the costs of success in terms of the erosion of the traditional values. This is the dilemma posed by the founder of Methodism, John Wesley, who believed that those values produce so much success, so much wealth, that they would undermine themselves, for example diluting the work ethic, frugality, the quest for achievement. As David Martin suggests in his CMRP 'Note to Mainstream Protestants', success and affluence may also produce disdain for those poorer coreligionists who dedicate themselves to the old values, the old religion.

To be sure, the largest – by far – Confucian society, China, remains a one-party dictatorship lacking in political legitimacy and sustaining itself in power largely through the success of its economic policies that have liberalized markets, encouraged foreign investment, and maintained stability, policies normally associated with the capitalism that was once its most-despised enemy. And Singapore has thus far avoided the democratic transition experienced by its fellow-'dragons' South Korea and Taiwan. Not to mention North Korea. But I believe that Francis Fukuyama was right in his prediction that high rates of economic development will produce a populace accustomed to the freedom of the marketplace, inevitably leading to demands for political freedom.

But the general lesson is clear: these cultures share values that work in very different settings. Lagging societies must find ways of strengthening those values.

7. Traditional African Religions

In his chapter in *Culture Matters*, Daniel Etounga Manguelle says, 'A society in which magic and witchcraft flourish today is a sick society ruled by tension, fear, and moral disorder. Sorcery is a costly mechanism for managing conflict and preserving the status quo, which is, importantly, what African culture is about'.[9] Animist religions, in which what happens in life is determined by a pantheon of capricious spirits, present an extreme case of progress-resistant culture, as we have seen in Haitian voodoo, the roots of which are in Africa. Animist religions are most widely practiced in Africa, although they are also found in the western hemisphere in Haitian voodoo and Brazilian Santería.[10]

The guideline with respect to animism is: encourage conversion of those practicing animist religions to more progress-prone religions.

***

Religion is not the only fount of cultural values, beliefs, and attitudes, but it is surely one of the most influential. Religious relativism is an obstacle to the reform of those religions associated with slow movement toward democracy, social justice, and prosperity. Reform of those religions could significantly accelerate progress toward these goals.

On further reflection, I have concluded that "spiritual capital" is a flawed concept not only because some religions – e.g., Protestantism – are clearly more nurturing of progress than others – e.g., Voodoo – but also (1) because the values that nurture progress can be promoted by non-religious/non-spiritual factors such as environment or historic vagary; and (2) a major source of values, beliefs, and attitudes for more than a billion people is Confucianism, which has no spiritual dimension – Confucius may well have been an agnostic.

I consequently have concluded that *"cultural capital"* is a far more useful concept. By focusing on the values, beliefs, and attitudes widely shared in a society, *"cultural capital"* can illuminate both the sources of human and social capital and, most importantly, the avenues that offer the possibility of progressive cultural change.

Appendix: Figure 2.1

Typology of Progress-Prone and Progress-Resistant Cultures

Based on the original structure of Mariano Grondona with inputs from Irakli Chkonia, Lawrence Harrison, Matteo Marini, and Ronald Inglehart.

Factor	Progress-Prone Culture	Progress-Resistant Culture
Worldview		
1. Religion	Nurtures rationality, achievement; promotes material pursuits; focus on this world; pragmatism	Nurtures irrationality; inhibits material pursuits; focus on the other world; utopianism
2. Destiny	I can influence my destiny for the better.	Fatalism, resignation, sorcery

(Continued)

Factor	Progress-Prone Culture	Progress-Resistant Culture
3. Time orientation	Future focus promotes planning, punctuality, deferred gratification	Present or past focus discourages planning, punctuality, saving
4. Wealth	Product of human creativity, expandable (positive sum)	What exists (zero-sum)
5. Knowledge	Practical, verifiable; facts matter	Abstract, theoretical, cosmological, not verifiable; debate matters
Values, Virtues		
6. Ethical code	Rigorous within realistic norms; feeds trust	Elastic, wide gap twixt utopian norms and behavior=mistrust
7. The lesser virtues	A job well done, tidiness, courtesy, punctuality matter	Lesser virtues unimportant; love, justice, courage matter
8. Education	Indispensable; promotes autonomy, heterodoxy, dissent, creativity	Less priority; promotes dependency, orthodoxy
Economic Behavior		
9. Work/ Achievement	Live to work: work leads to wealth	Work to live: work doesn't lead to wealth; work is for the poor
10. Frugality	The mother of investment and prosperity	A threat to equality
11. Entrepreneurship	Investment and creativity	Rent-seeking
12. Risk propensity	Moderate	Low; occasional adventures
13. Competition	Leads to excellence	Aggression; A threat to equality—and privilege
14. Innovation	Open; rapid adaptation	Suspicious; slow adaptation
15. Advancement	Merit, achievement	Family, patron, connections
Social Behavior		
16. Rule of law/ corruption	Reasonably law abiding; corruption is prosecuted	Money, connections matter; corruption is tolerated
17. Radius of identification and trust	Stronger identification with the broader society	Stronger identification with the narrow community
18. Family	The idea of 'family' extends to the broader society	The family is a fortress against the broader society
19. Association (social capital)	Trust, identification breed cooperation, affiliation, participation	Mistrust breeds excessive individualism, anomie

(Continued)

Factor	Progress-Prone Culture	Progress-Resistant Culture
20. The Individual/ the group	Emphasizes the individual but not excessively	Emphasizes the collectivity
21. Authority	Dispersed: checks and balances, consensus	Centralized: unfettered, often arbitrary
22. Role of elites	Responsibility to society	Power and rent seeking; exploitative
23. Church-state relations	Secularized; wall between church and state	Religion plays major role in civic sphere
24. Gender relationships	If not a reality, equality at least not inconsistent with value system	Women subordinated to men in most dimensions of life
25. Fertility	The number of children should depend on the family's capacity to raise and educate them	Children are the gifts of God; they are an economic asset

Notes and References

1 Placide David, *L'Heritage Colonial en Haiti* (Madrid: publisher unknown, 1959).
2 Rodger Doyle, 'Civic Culture', *Scientific American* (June 2004): 34.
3 Irakli Chkonia, 'Timeless Identity versus Another Final Modernity: Identity Master myth and Social Change in Georgia', pp. 7–8.
4 Archie Brown, 'Cultural Change and Continuity in the Transition from Communism: The Russian Case'. P. 9.
5 Nikolas Gvosdev, 'Re-imagining the Orthodox Tradition: Nurturing Democratic Values in Orthodox Christian Civilization', p. 12.
6 E-mail of 8 February 2005.
7 Jay L. Garfield, 'Buddhism and Democracy', http://www.buddhistinformation.com/buddhism_and_democracy.htm, p. 1.
8 Gregory K. Ornatowski, 'Continuity and Change in the Economic Ethics of Buddhism: Evidence From the History of Buddhism in India, China and Japan', http://www.appropriate-economics.org/materials/ethicsofbuddhism.html, p. 1.
9 Op. cit., 'Does Africa Need a Cultural Adjustment Program?', p. 73.
10 Animism also finds some adherents in Asia–see, for example, Robert Weller's CMRP paper on Taiwan.

Chapter 3

SPIRITUAL CAPITAL AND ECONOMIC DEVELOPMENT: AN OVERVIEW

Peter J. Boettke

Introduction

One of the most startling empirical puzzles in modern political economy is the lack of convergence between the rich and poor countries in terms of per capita income over time. The East Asian countries grew rapidly in recent decades, but Africa stagnated. Why would development not follow, especially when countries in the so-called third world have received both financial and technical assistance from the rich countries of the West? The 'great divergence' does not easily fit into the intellectual framework that economists developed after WWII to explain economic growth and development.

The last twenty years have seen a vibrant debate emerge among economists and political economists concerning this issue. At a conference at Princeton honoring P. T. Bauer in 2004, Amartya Sen was asked what the biggest difference was between the state of the art in development economics in 1964 and in 2004. He replied that the most obvious difference is that in 1964, the market was viewed as a source of exploitation while in 2004 the market was seen as the arena of mutually beneficial exchange and as a source of liberation. From Hernando de Soto[1] to C K Prahalad[2] it is now common-place to hear intellectuals extol the virtues of the small scale trading and beginnings of capital accumulation that P T Bauer[3] emphasized in his work, as opposed to foreign assistance programs. Two books by William Easterly[4] have documented this divergence between the West and the rest and the failed efforts by the West to aid the rest.

The transition from subsistence to exchange and wealth creation is only thwarted by government actions that either directly confiscate the property of the poor, or create an environment where others can easily predate on the poor. Exchange and production, and the institutions within which exchange and production take place, determine whether economies develop or fall behind.

In short, the intellectual agenda has been transformed over the last two decades to move away from the Keynesian-inspired questions of investment gap and the vicious circle of poverty to one that looks to institutions (rules of the social game and their enforcement). Claiming that poor countries are poor because they are poor no longer has the persuasive power it once incorrectly had. Instead, it is now recognized that all countries at one time started out poor, and yet some were able to transition to become rich and that the explanation of that can be found in the informal and formal rules that govern social interaction. Rich countries are rich because the rules in operation permit wealth creation, while poor countries are poor because the rules discourage wealth creation. Adam Smith once put it: "little else is requisite to carry a state to the highest degree of opulence from the lowest barbarism but peace, easy taxes, and a tolerable administration of justice."[5]

But we must admit that unless we unpack this Smithian claim, it begs the question as to why some nations are able to follow this formula whereas others seem to resist its teachings despite the clear evidence to support it. Why is economic development so elusive and near impossible for us to orchestrate by grand plans? Here I think it is important to recognize the shifts in market-oriented development thinking over the post-socialist experience.[6]

During the first phase of the post-communist experience, I believe it is accurate to say that a significant number of economists thought the problem was merely one of *getting the prices right*. The problem with socialist economies was that they were shortage economies and their administered prices were set below market clearing levels. Human betterment would be achieved by allowing free pricing so that market-clearing levels were obtained and shortages were eliminated. However correct this position was (and remains), it is an incomplete picture because prices only work within a context of established private property rights and freedom of contract (including the absence of legal restrictions on entry and exit).

In other words, getting the prices right implied the second phase of thinking about transition, that of *getting the institutions right*. Privatization is a critical component to realizing improved economic performance, but it is not sufficient. Privatization without eliminating legal and political barriers to entry simply transforms monopoly power from state enterprise to the private enterprise supported by the state regulations and legal privileges. The politicization of economic life remains intact. Privatization, however, was supposed to minimize the influence of politics on economic life. The reality of the methods of privatization in East and Central Europe and the former Soviet Union, for example in post-communist Russia, often reinforced political ties with business enterprises rather than broke those ties. The continuous complaints one heard during the 1990s of a rising new class of Oligarchs in post-communist Russia reflected this reality of privatization without the necessary institutional reforms to ensure a depoliticized economic structure.

In addition to the problem of getting the correct institutions in place, scholars increasingly turned their attention from stating in the abstract the necessary institutions for a vibrant market economy (such as private property rights, freedom of contract, and the rule of law) to asking how in concrete form institutions were established in any given society through transference from abroad, indigenous evolution, or some combination. As the 1990s turned into the 2000s and the 'getting the institutions right' mantra was echoed throughout the former socialist and into the developing world, it became evident that the transfer of institutions from the West to the rest was perhaps more difficult than previously recognized. Saying you need a rule of law and a set of governing capabilities is not the same thing as establishing those fundamental political and legal institutions in a country. In the West, many of these institutions took centuries to evolve (e.g., the common law). And more importantly for our purposes, these institutions found core support in various mores and habits of the heart and mind that evolved in western culture over a thousand years. The third phase in our post-communist intellectual framework on economic development thus inevitably shifted focus from 'getting the institutions right' to *getting the culture right.*

In many ways political economy has returned from the long detour of the 20th century where the belief was that a technical science of economics could replace the often vague and philosophical discipline of political economy. The beginning of the 21st century has witnessed economists returning to the questions of Max Weber and R H Tawney. Not only are economic/financial and political/legal institutions examined as determinants of growth, but social/cultural institutions are sought as explanations for economic processes of development and social change. In particular, religious beliefs and practices are once again being explored as potential explanations for why some nations are rich and others are poor.

With this in mind, one way to characterize the chain of causation in economic analysis of comparative historical development is as follows:

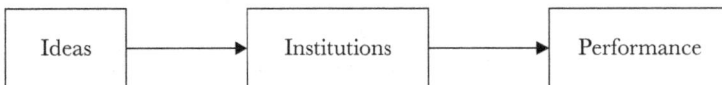

Ideas → Institutions → Performance

Ideas can be studied through an examination of the shared mental models that people exhibit and the belief systems that are in operation in any given society. Religion (both in terms of *formal* doctrine and organizational tradition, and *informal* belief and spirituality) is perhaps the leading carrier of deep cultural beliefs and serves as the focal point for coordination of mental models of a people. Institutions impact social interaction by structuring incentives and providing for a flow of information to individuals in terms of critical feedback and rewards for the efficient use of existing resources as well as the discovery of new opportunities for improvement in the human condition. Another way to think about the impact of institutions on the economy is to consider how alternative institutions impact the mechanisms of 'social epistemology' that are effectively in operation in any given society. Some institutional environments are more conducive to economic learning than others, just as some classroom settings are more effective for the conveyance of existing information from teacher to student and the mutual learning of new knowledge. Improvements in social interaction are measured in economic terms by improvements in material well-being.

Most of my work has focused on how comparative political/legal institutions affect economic performance in the context of transition and developing economies.[7] However, what I want to focus on here is the first stage in the logical chain of causation I have just laid out – the role of ideas in shaping and legitimating the institutions that are in place in society – and then turn to how the recognition of the role of ideas in society may transform our understanding comparative institutional analysis.

The basic punch-line of my paper is that a free society works best when the need for policemen and preachers is least because the population has internalized the informal and formal rules of social intercourse to such an extent that external enforcement of the rules will be little required. In such an environment, the transaction costs associated with pursuing the gains from trade and the gains from productive innovation will be minimal and cooperation among the multitudes of anonymous actors that constitutes a modern society will be realized. We must learn to live in the company of strangers if we want to reap the benefits of modernity[8].

Scarce in a lifetime, Adam Smith remarked, do we have time to make but a few friends, but in a modern society we rely on the cooperation of thousands of others we do not know (and never will come to know) to secure the breakfast we eat, the clothes that keep us warm, and the shoes than cover our feet. Wealth creation results from the adoption of rules that enable social cooperation under the advanced division of labour. Without these rules that promote peaceful association among strangers, the Smithean process of the virtuous circle of markets (the generalized increasing returns associated with 'the division of labour is limited by the extent of the market') will fail to be realized and instead the Malthusian trap of subsistence will result.

The stating of 'good' rules and writing them down in the books does not mean that the rules will be respected and enforced. In analyzing the rules governing society, we must focus not only on the content of the rules adopted, but their enforcement by the formal institutions of police and courts and professions, and the informal institutions of norms and conventions. Rules that do not resonate with the population would require formal enforcement through legitimated force, whereas rules that have the consent of the population behind them are predominantly self-enforcing and require formal enforcement only at the margin. Without self-enforcement, the costs of formal enforcement might be so high as to be prohibitive and thus the rules on paper will not be binding.

From Social Capital to Spiritual Capital

During the 1990s it became commonplace for social scientists to discuss social capital under the influence of Robert Putnam's *Making Democracy Work*[9]. The concept of social capital was introduced in the sociological literature by James Coleman[10] and the basic idea is how membership in certain groups or networks yields economic benefits. Various civic associations are often the primary unit of examination as the vehicle through which individuals obtain valuable social capital. In Putnam's work, this last point was transformed into an infamous lament at the decline in civic association in America in his *Bowling Alone*[11]. We have supposedly lost the art of association that defined the America of Tocqueville's observations in the 19th century.

In building his narrative, Putnam distinguishes between bonding and bridging social capital. Bonding social capital enables us to work closely with our intimate associates, while bridging social capital enables us to work with others outside of our intimate group. Bonding social capital can turn ugly when it eschews bridging and focuses instead on mechanisms of exclusion. Freedom of association would suggest that not all efforts at exclusion are universally bad, only those that take a particularly ugly turn in terms of violence toward outsiders. In waging war, soldiers must develop bonding social capital. Gangs, war lords, the KKK, etc. all rely on mechanisms for building strong bonding social capital among members for the purpose of imposing their will on others outside the membership. This is the dark-side of social capital. But on the bright side, social capital of the bonding variety is also an input into building the sort of bridging social capital that enables individuals and groups to realize mutually beneficial gains from trade with anonymous others.

Spiritual capital is a particular form of social capital that is associated with religious membership and the internalization of certain religious mores. In John Mueller's *Capitalism, Democracy and Ralph's Pretty Good Grocery*[12], we read of how immigrant shopkeepers would often hang symbols of Christian beliefs on the door to their shops in the 19th century to signal to visitors that their association with Christianity implied a trustworthiness in trading that otherwise might be doubted by strangers. In order for a signal to be credible it cannot be just 'cheap talk'. Larry Iannaccone, for example, has explained the logic behind extreme religious sects – since they provide more public (or club) goods to their members they cannot allow low cost ways to access the benefits of group membership[13]. But extreme religious beliefs are not necessarily correlated with high levels of material production. Rachel McCleary and Robert Barro have found that while religiosity is positively correlated with economic growth, religious attendance is actually negatively related to economic growth[14]. In other words, if the population expresses belief, but doesn't waste much time in the 'non-productive' activity of attending sermons, then the benefits of religious belief (e.g., honesty and trustworthiness) are realized without having to spend time away from the activity of exchange and production. Religious adherence to certain core beliefs enables individuals to expand their social network to anonymous others and realize the gains from trade.

Spiritual capital as I would define the term refers to the deep culture beliefs that underlie the ideas of association in any society. And as I said earlier, religious beliefs are the most dominant carriers of these deep cultural belief structures. The basic idea as it relates to economics, is that the greater the stock of spiritual capital (that promotes honesty, trustworthiness, the respect for property, the appreciation of talent, and the recognition of universal humanity and the need for forgiveness and hope for the future), then the lower the transaction costs will be in adopting institutions that promote wealth creation and with it economic development. If instead, religious ideas preach envy and hatred of others, then don't expect those societies where those ideas are dominant to realize generalized prosperity.

The basic human predicament is that while there are many ways that individuals and societies can choose to live, there are very few ways they can live prosperously. But the moral codes of behaviour required to live in accordance with prosperity are not communicated in many religions. A high stock of spiritual capital does not in itself dictate lower transactions costs associated with adopting the basic institutions of private property and freedom of contract that are in turn positively correlated with economic growth and development. It has to be a high stock of a certain type of spiritual capital. But this also is tricky because religious ideas are malleable to a considerable extent. The bottom-line, *religious beliefs must possess complementarities with the general public ideology that legitimates and reinforces the institutional practices of private property, freedom of contract, trustworthiness and honesty in dealing, prudence in decision-making and future orientation, in order to see a positive link between the stock of spiritual capital and economic development.*

Of Fallen Angels and Risen Apes: Transforming Spiritual Capital into Public Capital

For the relationship between spiritual capital and the institutions of a free and prosperous commonwealth to be established, we have to specify the mechanism by which the spiritual capital that resides at the level of the individual or in the community of believers is transformed into the public institutions of governance. James Buchanan in *The Limits of Liberty* introduced the term 'public capital' to describe the rule of law and the basic institutions of governance that exist in any society that provide the basic framework of social interaction[15]. As this public capital declines (which Buchanan feared was the case in the 1960s and early 1970s), then the possibilities of realizing the benefits of peaceful social cooperation under the division of labour (specialized production and exchange) would be diminished.

Following this line of reasoning, the critical question is how the stock of social capital translates into public instruments of constraint. Our natural proclivities as fallen man, must be bound. Just as social capital can be divided into bonding and bridging, it may be useful to divide public capital into binding and enabling. James Madison understood the dilemma when he said in *The Federalists* that if men were angels there would be no need for government and if government was to be run by angels than there would be no need to constrain, but precisely because men are being asked to rule over other men we must first empower and then constrain[16]. Just as bonding social capital has a positive role but can turn dark, so can enabling public capital cut against itself and destroy a society's institutions of governance. The founding fathers were in possession of a certain philosophical anthropology which fuelled their rhetoric in the search for effective mechanisms of binding government from abusing its power. If man is a fallen creature, he is inherently untrustworthy unless appropriately constrained. But as the fallen nature of man was increasingly called into question by the intelligentsia in the late 19th and beginning 20th century, this justification for constrains on using the power of the government to right social ills lost its persuasive power. If man is not fallen, but instead a risen ape, then anything is possible and binding man is merely a consequence of religious superstition that must be rejected by the modernist mind. Socialist experiences with social planning are the most obvious manifestation of this shift in the content of our spiritual capital, but it is also evident in the shift from constitutional democracy to social democracy.

My argument is quite simple – the way we envision ourselves determines how we constrain ourselves, and how we constrain ourselves will determine how we interact with one another. In an ironic twist, the more we distrust our unconstrained proclivities due to our fallen nature the more we will seek to establish effective bindings to limit our ability to engage in predator behaviour. To the extent we trust the public capital of the binding institutions of governance, the more trust we will place in our social interactions. Our spiritual capital may provide legitimacy to the public capital that constrains power. As that spiritual capital declines, the legitimacy of the public capital that constrains democratically elected governments declines and government discretionary powers are unleashed. The result, unfortunately, is the increased opportunity for public predation in the name of the 'public interest' which often merely masks the private interest group logic that underlies political machinations.

Andrei Shleifer, and a series of co-authors in a variety of papers, has explored the various mechanisms of warding off predation by both private and public actors[17]. Shleifer's basic result states that in situations where regulators and judiciary are incompetent, the most effective means to ward off predation is to rely on market mechanisms of self-governance, and in situations where the judiciary is effective and regulators are either incompetent or competent, then freedom of contract enforced by the rule of law (again the market mechanism) will be the most effective means of limiting predation. However, in those empirical situations (and only those) where regulators are competent, but the judiciary is incompetent will reliance on state regulation outperform the mechanism in limiting the social losses to predation. Whatever we may think of Shleifer's empirical claims, the framework he developed in these papers is extremely relevant to the current discussion. Only those institutions of governance which minimize the threat of predation from both private and public actors are consistent with wealth creation. The poor countries of the world lack these institutions and thus their people live in fear of predation from either private or public actors, while the rich countries of the world can trust that predation will be limited – something that they will not have to deal with in their daily transactions or if they do will be dealt with either by the parties to the transaction or others within the market place or through the system of governance.

The Moral Consequences of Economic Growth

As Peter Berger so forcefully argued in *Pyramids of Sacrifice* and *The Capitalist Revolution*, economic growth and development are not neutral processes[18]. Modernity does threaten traditional forms of life. A significant component of the critique of the attempt in 20th century economics to reduce the discipline of political economy to a technical science, and yet also provide policy advice for social change, was that the moral element was inexcusably pushed aside. In the positivistic picture of the discipline all questions of meaning must be relegated to non-scientific discussions and as such were not to intervene in the serious business of scientific planning of economic development. This social engineering vision of economic policy failed miserably to the detriment of billions in the second and third world.

Berger argues that a moral responsibility falls on those who impose public policy on developing societies, especially when the imposition of unproductive and inefficient economic arrangements are often introduced in situations already defined by hunger, disease and degrading poverty. We cannot look to governments to orchestrate economic development in accordance to the grand plans of economists. Instead, as Berger put it in *The Capitalist Revolution*, 'it is quite clear that the state as such is not the bearer of development. At best, states can institute policies that leave room for the real agents of development – enterprising individuals, families, clans, compadre groupings, and other traditional units, and more modern associations such as cooperatives or credit unions'. It is this sort of small-scale trading and rudimentary capital accumulation that fuels economic growth and is the vehicle for transforming lives from subsistence existence to one characterized by surplus.

Modernity, in other words, as Berger put it in the *Pyramids of Sacrifice* cannot be viewed only as a threat to traditionalists. Instead, it must be appear 'as a great promise – of longer and better life, of a plenitude of material goods (the 'cargo'), but also of individual liberation and fulfilment'. We do not advocate economic growth for economic growth sake, but for the package of possibilities that enhanced material conditions of life provide for the individuals in the societies we are examining. The Index of Economic Freedom demonstrates in a clear way that many of the results desired from modernity (better sanitation, higher education, more equality between the sexes, better health) are all positively correlated with higher levels of economic growth. The various measures of enhanced human capabilities that Amartya Sen and Martha Nusbaum argue should be the primary focus of any discussion of economic development are in fact correlated with the growth enhancing policies of economic freedom (secure property rights, freedom of contract, rule of law, low taxes, low regulation, fiscal responsibility, low inflation, and free trade)[19]. Economic freedom generates economic growth, and economic growth provides the material means with which we are able to satisfy a wide variety of demands for enhanced capabilities to improve human well-being.

Conclusion

I have argued that modern political economy has come full circle back to the great debates of the late 19th and early 20th century concerning the underlying cultural foundations of capitalism and economic development. I have suggested that the literature on social capital (and trust) give way to a deeper discussion of the spiritual capital that resides in our deepest cultural beliefs about who we are as humans, and how we should relate to one another. Religious beliefs are the most effective carriers of deep culture. Following the work of James Buchanan, it was argued that the stock of existing spiritual capital either legitimates the public capital we rely on to govern our social intercourse and ward off predation, or it cuts against these efforts and delegitimizes the effort at constraint. Without effective and binding constraints, economic growth cannot be realized and without economic growth the struggle for survival dominates and curtails efforts to live flourishing human lives. If on the other hand, the stock of spiritual capital lowers the transaction costs of establishing effective binding arrangements on our proclivity to predate at both the private and public actor level, then economic growth miracles can and will take place. And with that economic growth the lives of billions will move from a life of subsistence to one of surplus as they realize the gains from trade and engage in rudimentary capital accumulation which enables them to continually improve their lot in life. Once they are on this path of the Smithian virtuous cycle rather than the Malthusian trap of subsistence existence, then the move from barbarism to opulence will, as Adam Smith put it, take place in the natural course of things.

Notes and References

1 De Soto, H. 2000. *The mystery of capital: Why capitalism triumphs in the West and fails everywhere else*. New York: Basic Books. De Soto, H. 1989. *The other path: The invisible revolution in the Third World*. London: Tauris.
2 Prahalad, C. K. & Ramaswamy, V. 2004. *The future of competition: Co-creating unique value with customers*. Boston, Mass.: Harvard Business School Pub.
3 Bauer, P.T. 2004. *From subsistence to exchange and other essays*. Princeton, NJ: Princeton University Press.
4 Easterly, W. 2006. *The white man's burden: Why the West's efforts to aid the rest have done so much ill and so little good*. New York: Penguin Press. Easterly, W. 2001. *The elusive quest for growth: Economists' adventures and misadventures in the tropics*. Cambridge, Mass.: MIT Press.
5 Smith, A. 1976. *Wealth of Nations. Vol. I*. Chicago: University of Chicago Press, p. xl.
6 Boettke, P., Coyne, C., Leeson, P. & Satuet, F. 2005. 'The New Comparative Political Economy', *Review of Austrian Economics*, 18 (3–4): 281–304.
7 Boettke, P. 2002. *Calculation and Coordination: Essays on Socialism and Transitional Political Economy*. New York: Routledge.
8 Seabright, P. 2004. *The company of strangers: A natural history of economic life*. Princeton, N.J.: Princeton University Press.
9 Putnam, R. D., Leonardi, R. & Nanetti, R. 1994. *Making democracy work: Civic traditions in modern Italy*. Princeton, N.J.: Princeton University Press.
10 Coleman, J. 1988. 'Social Capital in the Creation of Human Capital', *American Journal of Sociology*, 94: S95–S120.
11 Putnam, R. D. 2000. *Bowling alone: The collapse and revival of American community*. New York: Simon & Schuster.

12 Mueller, J. E. 1999. *Capitalism, democracy, and Ralph's Pretty Good Grocery*. Princeton, N.J.: Princeton University Press.
13 Iannaccone, L. 1992. 'Sacrifice and Stigma', *Journal of Political Economy*, 100 (2): 271–297.
14 McCleary, Rachel M. and R.J. Barro. 2006. 'Religion and economy', *Journal of Economic Perspectives*. 20, 2, 49–72.
15 Buchanan, J. M. 1975. 'The limits of liberty: Between anarchy and leviathan', in *The collected works of James M. Buchanan*, Vol. 7. Indianapolis, IN: Liberty Fund, 2001.
16 Madison, J. [1788] n.d. 'The Federalist No. 51'. In *The Federalist*. New York: Modern Library.
17 Djankov, S., E. Glaeser, R. La Porta, F. Lopez-de-Salines, and A. Shleifer. 2003. 'The New Comparative Economics', *Journal of Comparative Economics*, 31: 595–619.
18 Berger, P. L. 1991. *The capitalist revolution: Fifty propositions about prosperity, equality, and liberty*. New York: Basic Books. Berger, P. L. 1975. *Pyramids of sacrifice: Political ethics and social change*. New York: Basic Books.
19 Sen, A. & Nussbaum, M. (eds.). 1993. *The Quality of life*. New York: Oxford University Press.

Chapter 4

THE POSSIBILITIES AND LIMITATIONS OF SPIRITUAL CAPITAL IN CHINESE SOCIETIES

Robert P. Weller

At the time of my first field research in the late 1970s, relatively uneducated Taiwanese villagers used to chastise me with their response to imported ideas of religion. 'Don't you people know', I heard over and over, 'that all religions are really the same? They urge people to do good'. They meant this as a critique of the missionary message of monotheistic Truth, and it reflected the flexibility of their complex, pluralistic, and relatively uninstitutionalized religious context. I agreed with them at the time: religions do share some similar moral messages, and they also generally share a deep involvement in social bonding that can have important implications beyond religion.

Yet, in some ways those villagers were wrong. Moral messages across religions do indeed overlap, but they are not identical. Religions do intertwine with social bonds, but not all in the same ways. Spiritual capital, in brief, cannot be reduced to social capital, especially if we want to understand religion's broader influence on social, political, and economic change. Instead, we have to understand both crucial differences among traditions – levels of institutionalization, forms of socialization, messages and media –and the social contexts in which they evolve.

In this chapter I will discuss the ways that various religions have contributed importantly to Taiwan's market success and eventual democratization, and the evidence that they may play as important a role in the rapidly evolving situation in the People's Republic. Chinese spiritual capital will continue both to shape and be shaped by these changes, but I also conclude that the religious contribution to something like Taiwan's democratization was by no means a foregone conclusion or an automatic extension of the inherent qualities of any religious tradition. The traditions themselves, as I will discuss, have aspects both favourable and unfavourable to democracy and to market success, and which potentials are realized depends much on how the tradition reacts with broader social conditions.

A second and related point that comes out of the Chinese and Taiwanese material is that not all spiritual capital is necessarily good for the society as a whole. At one extreme, it can foment massive violence, as in China's Taiping Rebellion of the nineteenth century, or the Boxer Rebellion of the early twentieth. More commonly in the Chinese context, however, it can simply cement local groups together at the cost of broader ties, leading to limits of scale on spiritual capital's contributions to the creation of a civil society.

This essay explores how spiritual capital can influence some of the cultural features that are typically associated with market success or democratization. These include individualism, a work ethic, a high valuation to education, civility, limitations on the power of leaders, and trust with its associated social capital. I will begin with local religious practice – the village temple and ancestor worship that has only loose associations with named religious traditions like Buddhism or Daoism, but that is by far the most common form of worship in China. Later sections will take up the very different kinds of organization in congregational and voluntary religions, including Chinese pietistic traditions, Christianity, and new forms of Buddhism.

Local Practice

Most popular religious practice in Chinese societies, especially in rural areas, focuses around worship of ancestors and spirits of various sorts at community altars and temples. Important features include community ownership of temples through management committees, widely variant deities sometimes known only locally, worship generally by individuals rather than congregations, a strong emphasis on votive requests, widespread use of spirit mediums, and hiring of priests usually only for major events[1]. There were no sacred texts comparable to the Bible or the Buddhist and Daoist canons.

Chinese religions during the late imperial period fostered at least two major attitudes toward market morality. On one side, the official state cult left little room for market culture. Both its funding and its cosmology depended on a political ideology that gave little prestige to markets. Merchants were the lowest of people in imperial Confucian thought, and at some periods they were not allowed to take the imperial examinations. On the other hand, the state in late imperial times allowed an enormous free space for other forms of worship. Local community temple cults were by far the most widespread form of worship, and here the attitude toward the market was very different. Typically run as share-holding corporations, these temples raised funds from a combination of donations, informal taxation, and selling services. They hosted votive cults that resembled the Roman Catholic ones (or similar traditions in Indian temples), with repayment to the gods typically taking the form of gold medals for the gods to wear or sponsoring operas for them to watch. The comfort with the market is especially clear in the use of paper 'spirit money' (*mingqian*) which pervaded all aspects of contact with the spirit world. The form of this money varied widely, but it could include everything from paper imitations of gold and silver ingots to copies of currency saying 'Bank of Hell' (in English) in the British colony of Hong Kong.

As an aspect of market culture, this side of Chinese religion tended to expand and respond during periods when the commodity economy grew rapidly, even well before the world capitalist system fully entered China in the nineteenth century. One such period occurred in the sixteenth century, at the end of the Ming Dynasty. At that time a set of five deities called the Wutong metamorphosed into gods of wealth by combining the first Ming Emperor's attempt to rationalize worship across the country with an aspect of the cult that saw the five deities as amoral spirits with an intemperate interest in sex and cash. The story itself shows the complex possibilities of Chinese religion, but the details are less important here than the general flow of the cult, toward an acceptance of market profit as an appropriate goal of worship[2]. Something similar, but a bit more sinister, happened again two centuries later, in the same lower Yangzi area. This had long been China's most commercially developed region, and the commodity economy was again booming in the eighteenth century. This time an epidemic of accusations of soul stealing rocked the area, as rumour told of people murdered in order to provide profit through occult means[3]. Far from being the remnant of some kind of premarket mentality, such amoral or immoral cults had intimate ties to market expansion.

Taiwan saw a version of something similar in the late 1980s, with the rise of a set of temples to ghostly spirits that would do anything at all in exchange for payment – pure fee-for-service religion with no morality in the way. This period saw Taiwan's transition to a developed economy by most standard measures, but its earlier growth based on cheap labour was ending, the thousands of small enterprises that powered the economy did not have sufficient capital to move into other kinds of industry, and the government still limited investing abroad or in China. The result was a lot of money invested in unproductive possibilities like land speculation and the stock market, or an illegal lottery that boomed during the period. Getting rich appeared for the moment more as the product of luck and opportunism than intelligence and hard work.

One result was a boom in temples to spirits that would grant any request, mostly ghosts of people who died by violence or without descendants and low-level gods with a reputation for mischief. Most gods in community temples also provided votive services, but requests had to be in keeping with moral standards.

These newly popular temples would help gamblers, prostitutes, pickpockets and speculators – the beneficiaries of unearned wealth. The most popular included one to the ghost of an executed bank robber (Liao Tianding) and especially one to the ghosts of seventeen unidentified dead bodies and one dog (jointly called the Eighteen Lords *Shiba Wanggong*), who were washed ashore in a fishing boat[4]. The Eighteen Lords became one of the most popular temples in Taiwan at the time, bringing in thousands of supplicants every night, when the ghosts were at their strongest. Like the illegal lottery in which it aided so many patrons, this temple combined carnivalesque play with a sense of risk from the petty thieves said to worship there frequently. It spawned a movie, a television serial, and at least one fake temple intended to draw customers away (and so very much in the spirit of the original).

A decade later, Taiwan's economy was already quite different, mostly because the possibility of overseas investment had massively changed the situation for many people. Taiwan's entrepreneurs became some of the most important drivers of the Chinese and Vietnamese economies, as they opened new factories abroad. The Eighteen Lords and similar deities did not disappear, but they certainly faded from the limelight as the kind of Wild West capitalism they highlighted became less salient to most people's experience.

Ghosts like the Eighteen Lords show the two faces of individualism. Chinese ghosts do offer an image of individuals unfettered by social ties, whose relationships are above all based on market and contractual exchanges. On the other hand, they also tend to be malevolent and unreliable exactly because they lack the control of broader communal and social ties. In the same way, individualism is an important underpinning of market success, but also paves the way for self-serving behaviour – greed, corruption, crime – that undermines the market system. Individualism may be a key to a thriving market economy, but only an individualism somehow embedded in the broader society. Even in the United States an ideologically rooted individualism in economic behaviour has broader social supports, as Granovetter and others have argued[5].

The key then is less having the cultural resources to develop a Western-style individualism than having the resources to combine an ethic of individual achievement with broader social values. It may well be that thriving market economies are compatible with a wide range of such combinations. Indeed, a kind of networked capital seems to have developed in most Chinese societies, including most recently the People's Republic under the economic reforms. This is a form of social capital built around interpersonal relationships – *guanxi*[6]. These relationships overlap with but are not identical to the ascribed and particularistic ties that Weberians saw as an obstacle to market development. They include ties of kinship and neighbourhood, but even these are fundamentally socially constructed in China. Beyond the immediate family, such ties create an easier path for the development of *guanxi*, but there are no guarantees. Trustworthiness (*xinyong*) is as important a consideration as blood, and even kinship networks are thus selective. Other kinds of ties, like classmates or just friends (both accepted Confucian relationships with a long history), are even more obviously constructed.

Numerous studies have now documented the importance of such ties in Chinese business arrangements in Hong Kong, Taiwan, and overseas Chinese communities in Southeast Asia[7]. More recent studies show the same kind of thing developing now that the market economy is opening up in China itself[8]. While some have suggested that this reliance on interpersonal ties discourages the development of very large companies, the evidence is nevertheless now overwhelming that this particularly Chinese adaptation to capitalism has worked very well. Even if it is true that large corporations are more difficult to organize under this system, it is no longer clear that large corporations are necessarily superior in the current economy dominated by innovation and market flexibility.

If we turn now to the political implications of temple worship, perhaps the most important difference from other traditions is the absence of any strong institutional ties above the very local levels of village and small town. Every rural hamlet and many urban neighbourhoods in Taiwan, for instance, have their own temples to the local Earth God (Tudi Gong *miao*). The neighbourhoods themselves build and maintain these shrines, and each local household in turn takes responsibility for making daily offerings there. These small temples were the first to be rebuilt across southern China in the 1980s, as part of the significant increase in local freedoms that followed on the economic reforms[9].

Other kinds of deities mark off somewhat larger communities. Temples to such deities often centre in market towns. The gods mark their turf by making the rounds of their villages on major festival days, and by parading around in processions that consciously recollect imperial magistrates touring their counties. Community contributions build and support these temples, which often intermix with the most local levels of politics. Some had the ability to tax households to raise funds for rituals or reconstruction, and many in Taiwan serve as the power base for a political faction. Such temples continue to be vital in Taiwan, and have been rebuilt rapidly in the People's Republic.

Some deities are worshipped on a much larger scale, sometimes across the entire country. Even then, however, the actual social organization of religion remains strictly local. Community temples are not parts of large hierarchies, in spite of the implications of the imperial metaphor that their deities' iconography and official titles imply. These temples are the financial, social, and symbolic creations of their local communities. They typically have no resident priests that would tie them into broader clerical hierarchies, and answer to no authorities beyond the community. Both Taiwan and the People's Republic have temple registration requirements, but both are enforced spottily now, and neither claims any authority over the religious details of the temples.

When temples link up, the connections are almost always economic and historical, but not directly tied to official political authority. The most frequent relationship among temples is called 'incense division' (*fenxiang*), and typically occurs when immigrants to a new area bring some incense ash from their old temple to found a new daughter temple. They will return through periodic pilgrimages to renew the tie. Many temples in Taiwan have such ties with old temples in Fujian Province. Taiwanese have gone streaming back to these mother temples in the opening up of the last few years, partly to enhance their (and their temple's) prestige at home, partly to open the way for economic investment in China, and partly to express their own devotion. This broadest level of religious organization typically helps shape expanded social communities formed through historical ties.

Worship of ancestors also roots people locally. Ancestral tablets themselves can be copied and moved, but lineage halls are rooted to localities, and so are burial sites. The ritual cycle marks these localities clearly. Children living far away return home for the lunar new year; descendants of a common ancestor come together for major lineage hall rituals; and the annual grave cleaning ritual (*Qingming Jie*) can come close to tracing out the lineage on the ground as descendants begin the day at the grave of their earliest ancestor, and gradually work their way down the kinship diagram from grave to grave. Grave cleaning was the first form of public worship to return throughout China as things loosened up after the Cultural Revolution.

Popular worship embedded people in social worlds as well as localities. This had both hierarchical and egalitarian aspects. Ancestor worship, as one would expect in a place where Confucius was so important, marked generation, gender, and age seniority in all its rituals. Families made offerings to ancestors and aged parents or grandparents in strict generational order at the lunar New Year, and descendants marked their exact relationship with the deceased through mourning dress at funerals. God temples also established hierarchies among the gods themselves and between gods and humans. The Chinese term for worship, *bai*, captures this dynamic by referring equally to acts of hierarchical respect for spirits or living superiors.

At the same time, however, temples are among the most important symbols of local solidarity. Lineages and local temple communities, for example, offer potential social resources that people can mobilize to raise capital or garner political support. These ties are not just reiterations of hierarchy, but also shapers of new social relationships. Events like funerals bring together wide ranges of kin, and weddings create new groups of ties between families. Sworn brotherhoods, which always have a religious dimension, cement horizontal ties among peers. Incense division networks also maintained useful social connections, which are currently easy to see as Taiwanese revive these old connections as routes to investment in China.

The low level of institutionalization in popular worship has been one of the keys to its continued success in all modern Chinese societies. The very lack of sacred texts, catechisms, priests, schools, and broad religious organizations has allowed this kind of temple religion to react easily to changing times. Very little institutional inertia stands in the way of new interpretations. Its close integration with local society does not directly make it democratic, of course, but its inherent flexibility allows it to adapt easily. Temple management committees in Taiwan, for example, are now chosen by popular election instead of by divination. Moreover, the social capital that temples embody has proved important in the local consolidation of democracy.

Let me give just a few examples of ways that this sort of religious practice has been important as both the economic and political situations have changed. First, local temples have been increasingly important as local communities mobilize for civil protest. This happened earliest in Taiwan, and became clear first in some of the large environmental protests of the 1980s, just as Taiwan was about to end martial law and one-party rule.

Given their intimate symbolic and organizational ties to local authority, it is no surprise that relatively wealthy, politically conservative community leaders control most major community temples in Taiwan. It is thus often difficult to acquire their support for protests. Yet when temples can be won over, they offer the movement a powerful moral sanction in local terms, alongside a ready-made organizational network and a stockpile of funds. One of the first large-scale mobilizations of temple ties occurred in protests against Taiwan's fifth naphtha cracker. This plant was to be built in a neighbourhood of Kaohsiung City by China Petrochemicals, in a large refining complex already there[10]. Protesters had blockaded the west side gate to the compound soon after the new plant was proposed in 1987. The blockade continued through the next two years.

Cai Chaopeng, one of the main leaders of the movement, was a religious specialist with an intimate understanding of the potential power of religion. Liu Yongling, another top leader, told me that they had asked one of their major local gods – Shen Nong, the god of agriculture – for support at the very beginning. They used the simplest method of divination, throwing two curved pieces of bamboo root (poe), which can come up 'yes', 'no' or 'laughing'. Defying the odds, he says it came up 'yes' nine times in a row. When the government tried it, he says, the result was always 'no'. Probably more critically, Cai managed to garner financial backing from this temple in August 1987 – it offered two million NT (nearly US $100,000) to the self-help committee, as life insurance for anyone killed in defence of the community.

The most creative use of local religious practice came in December of that year. As Cai Chaopeng and Liu Yongling told it, the protesters had left a handful of people to keep watch over the banner that represented their blockade of China Petrochemical. Plainclothes police came by late at night, bringing alcoholic gifts. When the sentries finally passed out, the police removed the banner, symbolically ending the blockade. Expecting trouble the next day, a thousand riot police were out in force to prevent a renewal of the blockade. When the protest organizers discovered this in the morning, they used the temple public address system to call people together. Religion provided an ideal mechanism to re-establish the blockade, because religious parades, unlike other forms of public demonstration, usually receive rubber-stamp official permission. The police backed down after the parade arrived, and the blockade went back up.

The final crucial religious intercession occurred on 5 May 1990. This was the eve of a local referendum on building the plant. Everyone expected a victory for China Petrochemical; eighty-one percent of people polled nationally supported building the plant. The forces most adamantly opposed to construction gathered people to worship the God of Agriculture and ask his preference in the referendum. The crucial moment came when the goddess Guanyin suddenly possessed an older woman. Putting her fingers into the lotus mudra, the goddess/woman began chanting that the neighbourhood would be doomed if the plant were built. Such spirit possession is not at all unusual in Taiwan, and provides a powerful possibility for mobilizing religious power, since the normally conservative authorities who manage temples cannot control what their god says through a medium. After the fact, many people credited this single event with the results of the next day – people voted to oppose the naphtha cracker without compromise. In the end, the government ignored the referendum and approved construction, but the long protest did succeed in pushing the company to set up a 1.5 billion NT (about US $60 million) foundation to benefit the neighbourhood, and to promise extensive investment in pollution control.

Such protests are still politically risky in Mainland China, but even there we have examples of temples taking a similar role. Jun Jing, for example, shows the important role a set of fertility goddess temples took in environmental protests in Gansu Province[11]. As protectors of community welfare, and often as symbols of community opposed to national or other interests, local deities provide easy cultural opportunities for social movements. Popular worship, in addition, offers an established social network that can be mobilized. Indeed, temples and political factions together (and sometimes kinship) provide the main lines through which leaders can normally mobilize local people. They are too communal and locally based to be classic civil society organizations, but they provide exactly the kinds of informal political sector ties that can become important in the construction of a new civil society under conditions like Taiwan's lifting of martial law in 1987.

As a very different kind of example, local gods also play an important role in rotating credit associations. In both China today and Taiwan until recently, it was very difficult for small entrepreneurs or consumers to obtain credit from banks. One result was that many people turned to rotating credit associations (*biao hui*), even though they lacked any legal standing. Such groups have traditionally been set up as religious organizations (*shenming hui*), worshipping a shared deity. Indeed, in late imperial times, nearly all local social organizations took the form of such religious groups, from guilds to philanthropic groups.

Western scholars have tended to ignore communal, particularistic, and informal ties like those of Chinese popular worship when looking for significant political activity or to explain market behavior. Yet such ties empirically have had an important civic and market potential, and will continue to do so. Paul Katz has suggested that the introduced concept of *shehui*, 'society' (from Meiji-era Japanese *shakai*, which was coined as a translation for the Western term), is less salient for understanding China than the older meaning of the term *shehui*, the community created around the shrine to the god of the locality[12]. Limiting our vision only to the most modern-looking sectors of society runs the danger of blinding us to some of its most powerful social forces. Popular worship in Taiwan, and again now in many parts of the People's Republic, fosters the kinds of community ties that ultimately influence both politics and market behaviour.

Salvationist Groups

Most Chinese distinguish the local worship I have been discussing from 'teachings' (*jiao*). Nearly everyone paid respect (*bai*) to various kinds of spirits by offering incense, but only a minority followed a teaching like Buddhism, Confucianism, Daoism, or Christianity. Unlike temple religion, this was the realm of texts and commentaries, and of masters and disciples. Allegiance was voluntary – unlike the geographic or kinship base of local worship – and people tended to form something like congregations around a teacher or member of the ordained clergy. In most cases people did not see this as an alternative to popular worship; following a teaching was a separate category of behaviour. In the rest of this essay I will briefly examine some of the larger groups of this type, beginning with salvationist groups (from pietistic sects to Christians), and continuing in the next section with new forms of popularizing Buddhism[13].

By the late Ming Dynasty (16th–17th centuries), China had developed a strong tradition of what Overmyer calls 'pietistic sects', which did not require the priestly virtuosity of the Buddhist or Daoist clergy, but did have a much stronger voluntaristic and congregational structure and a stronger textual emphasis than popular worship[14]. This is roughly the same time that Jesuit missionaries also began to preach in China. While those early missions eventually ended, they founded communities in parts of China that continue into the present. Pietistic sects and Christians are very different in many ways, of course, but they share enough important features that I will combine them here. Both kinds of religion are voluntary and congregational, with a much stronger emphasis on doctrine and belief than we see in temple worship. They share an eschatological concern with the eventual (or imminent, in some versions) demise of the world. Finally, especially if we concentrate on the more Pentecostal forms of Christianity that have been especially successful in China in recent years, both tend to develop charismatic leaders, and to have a strong potential to divide into new sects.

In modern times, the most important period of growth for such groups began in the 1970s in Taiwan, and about a decade or so later in China. Taiwan legalized the largest pietistic sects after its democratization in 1987, leading them to come above ground with claimed memberships of over two million people. These groups are also active on the mainland, but remain illegal and repressed (especially in the wake of the Falun Gong demonstrations). Christianity is probably about 4–5 percent of the population in both places, but this figure disguises relative stagnation in Taiwan and rapid growth, especially among Pentecostals, in China[15].

Let me begin with the pietistic sects, which grew rapidly throughout the period of authoritarian rule in Taiwan, in spite of sometimes heavy-handed repression. Unlike temple religion, these sects were built of voluntary members who got together for regular meetings, often featuring texts revealed by spirit possession. Many of these texts describe a world-creating goddess (the Eternal Venerable Mother, Wusheng Laomu), and her disappointment at the poor behaviour of her creation.

The most important of these groups was the Way of Unity (Yiguan Dao), which was illegal because the KMT accused it of collaboration with the Japanese in Mainland China during World War II. In addition, all the pietistic sects trace a loose intellectual kinship with the White Lotus and other groups that had fostered large-scale rebellions in the late imperial period. In fact, however, whatever political messages appeared in their spirit writing texts during Taiwan's authoritarian rule were quite conservative, but the government apparently perceived a large potential for trouble anyway. The current situation in Mainland China is similar, but this has also made direct research on these groups impossible, and my comments will thus concentrate mostly on Taiwan.

Like some similar groups in China and Taiwan, the Way of Unity expects its members to give a stern and thorough moral accounting of their lives. These groups typically require the active management of moral capital, with an emphasis on self-discipline, work, and the good management of property and relationships[16]. While the Way of Unity stresses its retention of conservative Confucian values, it places them always in the context of practical concerns, especially health and wealth. By the late 1980s, when the Way of Unity was finally legalized in Taiwan, their huge following included a disproportionate number of successful businessmen.

Their most prominent example is the shipping and airline tycoon Chang Yung-fa (Zhang Rongfa), who attributes his own spectacular success to membership in the sect. No systematic research has been done to examine this, but journalistic accounts suggest some element of truth. They point to the unusually clean and orderly workplaces, neat dress and clean speech from workers, and efficient use of resources. Chang's Evergreen Shipping has a reputation for an anti-union and authoritarian leadership style, but also for paying high salaries with excellent benefits[17]. We know that this group frequently recruits through business, as some members set up companies explicitly as recruitment tools, using the organization to proselytize as well as to make a profit[18]. Like worshippers of the Eighteen Lords, members of such sects fully welcome the market, but unlike the Eighteen Lords group, they also see this as a market completely consistent with conservative moral values.

Chang's claim that membership in the Way of Unity encourages market success suggests indirect social benefit from this kind of religion, where ties of trust that such groups create can offer economic benefits[19]. Followers of a particular temple or teacher often come from scattered areas, and form a new kind of achieved community through a shared commitment to the teaching. This process bears a certain resemblance to the way Max Weber described Protestant sects creating generalized trust, because followers knew that fellow sectarians shared a similar set of values, even if they were strangers[20]. The belief systems themselves had no necessary resemblance to Protestantism, though, nor did such structures always fit under the Western rubric of religion. Organizationally, such groups need not look very different from other ways of passing on learning, like martial arts traditions. Their essentially voluntary nature, however, makes them resemble civil society organizations more than the ascribed communities of popular worship.

Christianity itself, of course, is quite different in many ways, but it shares with the pietistic sects a similar kind of voluntary and congregational organizational structure, an interest in moral behaviour related to a future transformation of the world, and what Weber called an 'elective affinity' for market capitalism. In some cases, whole villages have been Christian for several centuries; in others churches attract mixed groups from various neighbourhoods and have expanded rapidly only in recent years. There are also significant differences between Catholics and Protestants in China. Catholics have tended to be connected more through kinship ties or locality (usually the entire family or entire villages were Catholics), while the Protestant groups have more mobile connections, for instance, based on conversion among university students.

If we accept the hypothesis that the pietistic sects and Christianity fill similar niches – offering morality in an apparently amoral world, hope for salvation a new world to come, social networks for uprooted people, and so on – then it seems easier to understand why the sects have grown so rapidly in Taiwan while Christianity has stagnated, and why the situation is apparently reversed in China. In Taiwan's more open political system, the indigenous alterative has been more welcome, while repression of sects in China has tilted the playing field toward Christianity, which at least has some legal recognition.

We still have very few ethnographic studies of Christians in China, and especially of the many new converts. It may well be true that Christians do very well in the market, as has been asserted for other parts of the world, but no reliable data exist yet. Certainly it seems safe to assert at least that neither Christians nor sectarians offer ideas that would stand in the way of market success.

Politically, Christians seem to function best in China as a sort of semi-civil society. That is, they appear to have a strong ability to mobilize their own resources to benefit their communities, but their beliefs often limit their ability to work with other groups. Ironically, village temples in the mainland (which have no legal standing) seem to do very well at mobilizing political resources, while Christian churches (some of which have legal recognition and protections) usually do not[21].

The politics of Christians in Taiwan have been more studied. Kuo Cheng-tian, for example, found that Christians scored the highest of all religious groups in his survey of democratic values and behaviours. Yet his data also reveal internal differences within Christianity that are just as great as the variation across the whole society. Presbyterians in Taiwan show much more democratic behaviour than other Christians (primarily Baptists, some Pentecostal groups, and Catholics), who generally scored lowest. Kuo attributes this to Taiwan's history, where the Presbyterians were leaders of the opposition to the authoritarian government, while other groups were cooperative or isolationist[22]. In internal organization, however, the Pentecostals are more democratic than the others.

With the exception of Taiwan's Presbyterians, Chinese Christians have not been at the forefront of democratization, but they have been important in building spiritual capital in ways that can improve people's lives. This can be an indirect contribution to creating a civil society, just as I have argued for popular worship. Much the same is true for the pietistic sects, whose claims about economic success are not matched by claims of political progressiveness. Rather like the Baptists or Pentecostals in Taiwan, they learned to keep their heads down under authoritarian rule, and they still carry that legacy. What we see for both kinds of groups is the creation of strong ties that cross-cut the local ties of temple worship. These have the potential to be mobilized toward democratic ends, but networks can of course also be used non-democratically. The importance of charismatic leaders in both sorts of groups may help keep the scale small (as new leaders break away with their groups) and also limit the potential for broader democratic development.

New Buddhists

Chinese societies have long clerical traditions of Buddhism and Daoism. Beginning in the late twentieth century, Buddhism has enjoyed an enormous revival throughout the Chinese world, most spectacularly beginning with several Taiwanese movements. These groups are dedicated to the humanitarian aims of building a 'Pure Land on Earth'. They had already grown huge by the 1980s and 1990s[23]. Three of these groups now have massive global followings, with each accounting for millions of people. Much more than either temple worship or the pietistic sects, these groups have an explicit social mission, building hospitals, founding universities, bringing aid to the poor, and providing emergency relief around the world. They have not yet established independent branches in China, due to the political sensitivities, but they are active in delivering aid there, and some mainland monasteries are beginning to emulate them.Here I will discuss primarily the largest of these groups, generally called Compassion Relief (Tzu Chi).

Compassion Relief began in 1966 on Taiwan's poor east coast[24]. The founder was a nun named Zhengyan, who still provides charismatic leadership for the group. Beginning in a small temple near Hualian, she aspired to create a this-worldly Buddhism centred on charity, and above all on providing medical care for the poor. As the group tells it, her main inspirations for this were the sight of a miscarriage of an aboriginal woman who could not afford the hospital registration fee, an argument with some Catholic nuns about Buddhism's failure to care for society, and the earlier example of the monk Yinshun, who had tried and failed to create a movement for 'humanistic Buddhism' in the 1950s[25]. Yinshun himself had ordained Zhengyan.

The group began with thirty housewives and five disciples of Zhengyan. The housewives contributed a few pennies a day, and the clergy made baby shoes for a little additional income. From these very modest beginnings, the group gradually grew through the 1970s. In 1979, Zhengyan announced plans to build a state-of-the-art hospital in Hualian, which was completed in 1986. In the process the group burst onto the national scene, gaining both political support and a surge in membership. By the early 1990s (after which they stopped releasing figures), they claimed about four million members (making them the largest civil association in Taiwan), and had branches in dozens of countries.

This extraordinarily rapid expansion beginning in the 1980s had several interlinked causes. Taiwan's lifting of martial law in 1987 freed up all kinds of social organizations to grow outside the corporatist framework; Compassion Relief became the largest such organization. This was also the decade when Taiwan joined the ranks of the wealthier countries of the world. The late 1980s in particular were a period when a lot of wealth was chasing very few investment opportunities. People had money they could afford to contribute, and philanthropy appealed as a moral alternative to the perceived greed and selfishness of Taiwan's market economy[26].

Although the top leaders are nuns, this is essentially a lay movement that does not push people toward monastic vows. Followers make contributions, and the biggest donors are rewarded with special uniforms and titles as 'commissioners'. Zhengyan's main emphasis, however, is on action rather than donation. She urges followers to volunteer their time to Compassion Relief activities like visiting the sick, identifying and delivering relief to needy families, or organizing recycling programs. Followers also attend regular meetings, which provide some entertainment, testimonials about how activists' lives have changed, and often sermons from Zhengyan, either in person or by videotape. Sutra recitation plays only a small role, and the movement over all has little concern with Buddhist philosophy. Its appeal instead lies in the effort to change the world through charity.

Compassion Relief comes much closer to standard definitions of a civil association than traditions of Chinese popular worship. It is fully voluntary, based on shared interests and beliefs rather than ties of locality and kinship. Its values are universalistic rather than based in local society. And while it relies on charismatic leadership, it also exists within a formally defined legal realm, with an internal structure that is becoming increasingly rationalized.

In many ways like the Christians and the pietistic sects, Compassion Relief offers a morality to ameliorate the perception of a heartless market and the empty lives of modernity. They draw on both the Bodhisattva ideal of helping all sentient beings before achieving nirvana and on a very conservative set of Chinese values, especially those associated with women, like nurturance. It is not a coincidence that most of the followers are women, typically from families that have done very well in the market[27]. Their success has also encouraged numerous other religious groups (including the Way of Unity, mentioned above) to emulate their non-religious activities, like founding universities or giving out medical aid. Compassion Relief is not a prosperity cult – it offers happiness rather than wealth and promotes action outside a market context. It accepts capitalism and relies on wealth generated through markets, but its primary goal it to create a world of alternate values and actions, and it works primarily in the non-market economic world of charity.

Politically, just like the sectarians and many of the Christians, this group (and all the other large Buddhist groups) relies on charismatic leadership and has little democracy in its internal structure. Compassion Relief itself (here unlike some of the other groups) refuses to take political positions – it will neither endorse candidates nor allow its core members to lobby or campaign. Yet as a major reservoir of social and spiritual capital, politicians cannot stay away. Constant delegations of politicians and candidates come to pay their respects, even though they know there will be no endorsement. The indirect political effects are thus quite significant, as I have also argued for the other kinds of groups, even without any explicit political agenda.

Conclusions

Groups like Compassion Relief, Christians, or sectarians appear more like 'civil society' than popular worship. They foster ties of trust through the new social communities they create, and they can mobilize those ties for social action. They are voluntary associations based on individual choice, rather than aspects of a particularistic world of local society and kinship. Their divorce from the local ties of popular worship has allowed some of these organizations to grow huge, encompassing millions of people in dozens of countries.

Yet I do not wish to imply that large, voluntary, globalizing associations like these are necessarily better than the scattered localisms of popular worship for democratic transitions or even just building a public sphere. Their very scale makes them more vulnerable to control by an authoritarian state. The new Buddhists in Taiwan, for example, rarely take on the really controversial issues, like nuclear power, that local movements with religious ties can tackle[28]. The political conservatism of the pietistic sects and some of the Christians in Taiwan is also the result of long years of cooperation and caution toward the state.

On the other hand, the social tendrils of popular worship can feed into local social movements in Taiwan, and they are now parts of rebuilding community life in the People's Republic. They can accomplish this exactly because of the localist and particularist roots of these practices. Religion has allowed Chinese and Taiwanese under authoritarian control to retain active reservoirs of values and social relations relatively insulated from government control. While attempts to push this on to a large scale have happened – like China's Falun Gong or Taiwan's Way of Unity – the large religious institutions have generally contributed less to this than local popular worship with its base in particularistic ties of kin and community. The larger institutions either entered into intimate relations with the government or were forced underground. Large, independent, universalizing religious institutions thrived in Taiwan only after martial law was lifted, and they were built in part on the thick social ties that already existed thanks to popular worship and other local forms of civil association. The disaggregated and flexible nature of popular worship made it both more difficult to repress and more likely to remain beneath the active attention of these governments.

I do not want to claim too much here. Neither local worship nor large belief-based associations were the primary forces that moved Taiwan to democratize, nor do I think they are likely to play that role in China. The spiritual capital that all these forms of religion foster may have been important in market behaviour, but it is worth remembering that Chinese in general have had little problem adapting to the market. Certainly there was nothing in any of these traditions that actively stood in the way of the new economy, and many features that proved helpful. Popular worship, with its management committees, contractual relationships with deities, paper spirit money, and karmic accounting system has much to offer a market economy, even as other aspects (like the feudal hierarchy of gods) refer to older social worlds. Its very lack of institutionalization has been one of the keys to its rapid adaptation.

Politically, Chinese popular worship provides one of the major building blocks of local society, and it will play a role in the realization and consolidation of any democratic opening. Chinese popular worship is not, of course, the usual stuff of civil society theory. To oversimplify a bit, its values are localist and not universalist, its social basis is particularistic and not voluntary or individualistic, and its organization is informal and not based on clear rules. Popular worship seems, in short, just too pre-modern for theories that tie civil society clearly to modernity.

In fact, however, there is nothing remarkably pre-modern here – the problem lies more in theories of modernity than in Chinese religious practice. The very lack of institutionalization in popular worship has allowed it to adjust easily to all kinds of changes. Its rapid growth as the economy has boomed in both China and Taiwan is further evidence of just how compatible it is with modernity. On the other hand the more 'modern' looking religious institutions, with their universalist ideologies and rationalized organizations, have played a more minor role. The kind of authoritarian corporatism that Taiwan once practiced, and that China is today emulating, has been quite successful in keeping such groups under control. Local religion provided a crucial seedbed that allowed an independent society to grow once martial law was lifted in Taiwan. The People's Republic appears to be following a similar path.

Chinese spiritual capital, as we have seen, flows through many different forms, all of which have adapted rapidly over the last century. Its resources have been important in maintaining social and spiritual worlds independent of sometimes overwhelming state power. Like any resource, though, it is open to new uses. Politically, these run the full range of resistance, avoidance, participation, and cooptation. Economically, they run from affirmation of the market to the creation of a philanthropic alternative to market distribution. Rather than seeing spiritual capital as an undifferentiated whole, the Chinese and Taiwanese cases lead us to see it as something adaptable, but also as something whose fundamental qualities can differ importantly from one religious traditions to another.

Notes and References

1 For a general overview of the development of this field, see Meir Shahar and Robert P. Weller, 'Introduction: Gods and Society in China', in *Unruly Gods: Divinity and Society in China*, ed. Meir Shahar and Robert P. Weller (Honolulu: University of Hawai'i Press, 1996), 1–36. For a very useful review of the literature on Taiwan, see Hsun Chang, 'Guangfu Hou Taiwan Renleixue Hanren Zongjiao Yanjiu Zhi Huigu [A Review of Anthropological Studies of Han Chinese Religion in Taiwan, 1945–1995]', *Bulletin of the Institute of Ethnology, Academia Sinica* 81 (Spring 1996): 163–215.

2 See Qitao Guo, *Exorcism and Money: The Symbolic World of the Five-Fury Spirits in Late Imperial China* (Berkeley: Institute of East Asian Studies, 2003); Michael Szonyi, 'The Illusion of Standardizing the Gods: The Cult of the Fiver Emperors in Late Imperial China', *Journal of Asian Studies* 56, no. 1 (1997): 113–35; Richard von Glahn, *The Sinister Way: The Divine and the Demonic in Chinese Religious Culture* (Berkeley: University of California Press, 2004).

3 Philip A. Kuhn, *Soulstealers: The Chinese Sorcery Scare of 1768* (Cambridge, Mass.: Harvard University Press, 1990).

4 I discuss this in some detail in Robert P. Weller, *Resistance, Chaos and Control in China: Taiping Rebels, Taiwanese Ghosts and Tiananmen* (London: Macmillan, 1994), 113–83.

5 Mark Granovetter, 'Economic Action and Social Structure: The Problem of Embeddedness', *American Journal of Sociology* 91.3 (1985): 481–510.

6 The most detailed studies of *guanxi* in China include Andrew B. Kipnis, *Producing Guanxi: Sentiment, Self, and Subculture in a North China Village* (Durham: Duke University Press, 1997); Yunxiang Yan, *The Flow of Gifts: Reciprocity and Social Networks in a Chinese Village* (Stanford: Stanford University Press, 1996); Mayfair Mei-hui Yang, *Gifts, Favors and Banquets: The Art of Social Relationships in China* (Ithaca: Cornell University Press, 1994).

7 Examples include S. Gordon Redding, *The Spirit of Chinese Capitalism* (Berlin: Walter de Gruyter, 1990); Gary G. Hamilton, 'Culture and Organization in Taiwan's Market Economy', *Market Cultures: Society and Morality in the New Asian Capitalisms*, ed. Robert W. Hefner (Boulder: Westview, 1998) 41–77.

8 Jiansheng Li, *Network Families: Kinship and Economic Change in Tianjin*, Ph.D Dissertation, Boston University (1999).

9 For other kinds of examples of increases in personal freedoms, see Jean C. Oi, 'Realms of Freedom in Post-Mao China'. In *Realms of Freedom in Modern China*, ed. William C. Kirby (Stanford: Stanford University Press, 2004), 264-84.

10 This summary is based on newspaper reports for the period, interviews with some local residents, and interviews with Cai Chaopeng and Liu Yongling, two of the top leaders of the protest, in July 1992.

11 Jun Jing, 'Environmental Protests in Rural China'. In *Chinese Society: Change, Conflict and Resistance*, edited by Mark Selden and Elizabeth J. Perry. New York: Routledge, 2000.

12 Paul R. Katz, 'Local Elites and Sacred Sites in Hsin-Chuang: The Growth of the Ti-Tsang An During the Japanese Occupation', paper presented at the Third International Conference on Sinology (Taipei, June 29–July 1, 2000), 31.

13 Daoism as a teaching has so far not creating organizations on the same scale, and so I will give it less attention here.

14 Daniel L. Overmyer, *Folk Buddhist Religion: Dissenting Sects in Late Traditional China* (Cambridge: Harvard University Press, 1976); David K. Jordan and Daniel L. Overmyer, *The Flying Phoenix: Aspects of Chinese Sectarianism in Taiwan* (Princeton: Princeton University Press, 1986).

15 Presbyterians, who have the longest missionary history in Taiwan, played an important role in oppositional politics, and Christians continue to be an important political force there See Murray A. Rubinstein, *The Protestant Community of Modern Taiwan: Mission, Seminary, and Church* (Armonk, NY: M. E. Sharpe, 1991).

16 For an earlier historical example of such a group, see Judith A. Berling, 'Religion and Popular Culture: The Management of Moral Capital in *The Romance of the Three Teachings*', in *Popular Culture in Late Imperial China*, ed. David Johnson, Andrew J. Nathan and Evelyn S. Rawski (Berkeley: University of California Press, 1985), 208–18.

17 'Shenmi Jiaopai Chongshi Tianri [A Secret Sect Sees the Light of Day Again]', *Yazhou Zhoukan*, 5 August 1990, 28–39; Dingjun Zhao, 'Yiguan Dao Caili Shen Bu Ke Ce [The Immeasurable Wealth of the Yiguan Dao]', *Wealth Magazine* 121 (April 1992): 131.

18 This is based on unpublished field research by the sociologist Wu Hsin-chao.

19 Haiyuan Qu, *Minjian Xinyang Yu Jingji Fazhan [Popular Beliefs and Economic Development]*, Report to the Taiwan Provincial Government (N.p.: Taiwan Shengzhengfu Minzhengting, 1989).

20 Max Weber, 'The Protestant Sects and the Spirit of Capitalism', in H.H. Gerth and C. Wright Mills, eds., *From Max Weber: Essays in Sociology* (New York: Oxford, 1946), 302–22.

21 Tsai, Lily Lee. 'The Informal State: Governance and Public Goods Provision in Rural China'. Ph. D. diss., Harvard University, 2004.

22 Cheng-tian Kuo, *Religion and Democracy in Taiwan* (Albany: SUNY Press, 2008).

23 Hwei-syin Lu, 'Taiwan Fuojiao 'Ciji Gongdehui' de Daode Yiyi [The Moral Significance of Taiwan Buddhist 'Ciji Merit Association']', paper presented at the International Conference on Chinese Buddhist Thought and Culture (Shanxi University, July 12–18, 1992); Benxuan Lin, 'Zongjiao Yundong de Shehui Jichu — Yi Ciji Gongdehui Wei Lie [The Social Base of a Religious Movement — the Example of the Compassion Merit Society]'; C. Julia Huang, *Charisma and Compassion: Cheng Yen and the Buddhist Tzu Chi Movement* (Cambridge: Harvard University Press, 2009).

24 See Hwei-syin Lu, 'Women's Self-Growth Groups and Empowerment of the 'Uterine Family' in Taiwan', *Bulletin of the Institute of Ethnology, Academia Sinica* 71 (1991): 29–62; Hwei-syin Lu, 'Taiwan Fuojiao 'Ciji Gongdehui' de Daode Yiyi [The Moral Significance of Taiwan Buddhist 'Ciji Merit Association']', paper presented at the International Conference on Chinese Buddhist Thought and Culture (Shanxi University, July 12–18, 1992); Chien-yu Julia Huang and Robert P. Weller, 'Merit and Mothering: Women and Social Welfare in Taiwanese Buddhism', *Journal of Asian Studies* 57 (1998): 379–96; Wei'an

Zhang, 'Fuojiao Ciji Gongde Hui Yu Ziyuan Huishou [The Buddhist Compassion Merit Society and Recycling]', paper presented at the Workshop on Culture, Media and Society in Contemporary Taiwan (Harvard University, June 12, 1996).
25 For more detail on Yinshun, see Charles Brewer Jones, *Buddhism in Taiwan: Religion and the State, 1660–1990* (Honolulu, 1999).
26 For an expansion of this argument, see Huang and Weller, 'Merit and Mothering'.
27 For more on this, see Chien-yu Julia Huang and Robert P. Weller, 'Merit and Mothering: Women and Social Welfare in Taiwanese Buddhism', *Journal of Asian Studies* 57, no. 2 (1998): 379–96.
28 As a parallel, big businesses in Taiwan or Hong Kong were also not particularly active in the push for democratization. Small firms, which did not have the close governmental ties of the big firms, were far more active. See Alvin Y. So, 'Hong Kong's Problematic Democratic Transition: Power Dependency or Business Hegemony?' *Journal of Asian Studies* 59 (2000): 359–81; Hsin-Huang Michael Hsiao, 'Formation and Transformation of Taiwan's State-Business Relations: A Critical Analysis', *Bulletin of the Institute of Ethnology, Academia Sinica* 74 (1993): 1–31.

Chapter 5

HOW EVANGELICANISM – INCLUDING PENTECOSTALISM – HELPS THE POOR: THE ROLE OF SPIRITUAL CAPITAL

Rebecca Samuel Shah and Timothy Samuel Shah[1]

Introduction

The idea that Evangelical Protestantism – including in its Pentecostal variants – can generate resources for promoting economic and political development is nothing new. In 1958, Edward Banfield argued in his classic study, *The Moral Basis of a Backward Society*, that the underdevelopment he observed in a southern Italian village resulted primarily from an ethos of 'amoral familism' – an exclusive concern for one's sib over and against the common good (Banfield 1958). This ethos consisted of an extreme distrust of individuals and groups outside of one's family and virtually guaranteed that those in its grip would refuse to undertake joint activities or form wider associations to better themselves[2].

Banfield concluded his book by reflecting on how this 'amoral familism' might be overcome. One possibility lay in the region's religious and spiritual transformation. 'The change in outlook that is needed', Banfield surmised, 'might conceivably come as the by-product of Protestant missionary activity' (Banfield 1958: 162). As a basis for this suggestion, he cited a 1955 article by anthropologist Emílio Willems, 'Protestantism as a Factor of Culture Change in Brazil'. According to Banfield's summary, Willems found that '[i]n Brazil Protestantism is reported to have created among its adherents an unprecedented participation in group affairs and to have reduced illiteracy, dishonesty, and gambling' (Banfield 1958: 162 n. 8)[3]. The type of Protestantism largely responsible for these profound transformations,

Willems, observed in more than a decade of field work in the 1950s and 1960s, was fervent Evangelicalism, especially Pentecostalism.

However, use of the term 'spiritual capital' to articulate the idea that religion can effect pro-developmental change *is* new. The term is not the only way to capture this idea, of course, but it has merit. As in the terms 'social capital' and 'human capital', the 'capital' part of the term 'spiritual capital' connotes resources that are fungible in the sense that, though they are accumulated in one domain, they can be leveraged or 'spent' in another. In the work of James Coleman and Robert Putnam, for example, 'social capital' connotes relational networks and norms of trust and cooperation that are accumulated in private associations, but which can nonetheless be leveraged to advance public goods, such as economic development and effective governance (Coleman 1987; Putnam, Leonardi, and Nanetti 1993; Putnam 2000). The 'spiritual' part of the term 'spiritual capital' refers to such fungible resources that are accumulated in the religious domain by specifically religious means, but which can be 'spent' or leveraged to advance non-religious purposes in non-religious domains like governance and the economy.

The purpose of this chapter is to provide an analytical overview of Evangelical Protestantism's contribution to the accumulation of spiritual capital in developing societies. Evangelicalism[4] is a revivalist and theologically conservative strain of Protestantism, characteristically stressing biblical authority, the atoning death of Christ as the indispensable source of salvation, personal conversion as the indispensable means of appropriating salvation, and the duty of all believers to communicate to others the message of salvation (Bebbington 1989; Freston 2001). Pentecostalism is one member of the Evangelical family – no doubt the heftiest and most voluble member. In large part because of the explosive growth of Pentecostalism, Evangelicals are the lion's share of global Protestantism today, which few would have predicted when liberal Modernism overwhelmed the major Protestant denominations in Europe and America in the late nineteenth and early twentieth centuries (Sandeen 1970; Marsden 1980). Indeed, no religious movement has grown more dramatically in the last hundred years in the developing areas of the 'global South' – Africa, Asia, and Latin America – than Evangelical Protestantism, particularly in its Pentecostal forms (Shah 2008; Woodberry and Shah 2004; Barrett, Kurian, and Johnson 2001). Evangelicalism's growth and distinctive qualities make its potential contribution to spiritual capital in developing societies a vital and promising subject.

In our research, we reviewed numerous studies of Evangelicalism and its social and political consequences in numerous developing societies across space and time. From 'mass' conversions to Evangelicalism in India to the spread of Pentecostal Evangelicalism in Brazil and Guatemala, many scholars from many disciplines have closely examined Evangelicalism's impact on individuals, communities, and cultures. Despite the importance of their studies, many of them have received little systematic attention. Taken together, they present a coherent and compelling picture of Evangelicalism's characteristic tendency to produce various forms of spiritual capital, which have at least the potential to facilitate the economic and political betterment of developing societies.

The present paper focuses on forms of Evangelical Christianity in India that are highly revivalistic and conversionistic, though they are not particularly Pentecostal or Charismatic. Specifically, it clarifies how conversions to Evangelical Christianity among Dalits (the 'broken', referring to 'untouchables' or 'outcastes') in India have historically generated socially and economically consequential forms of spiritual capital. We offer a typology that specifies the distinct kinds of spiritual capital that are characteristically generated by Evangelical conversion among the poor (and to some extent among the non-poor as well).

However, we hasten to add that our reading of numerous studies of Pentecostalism's impact on the poor throughout the developing world – particularly studies by Emílio Willems, David Martin, Sheldon Annis, David Maxwell, Cornelia Butler Flora, Rowan Ireland, Elizabeth Brusco, and many others – persuades us that the core spiritual dynamic is the same across Pentecostal and non-Pentecostal forms of Evangelical Christianity. In other words, we believe that our analytical typology, which specifies distinct types of Evangelically generated spiritual transformation among the poor and how they translate into social and economic betterment, is as applicable to fervent Pentecostal converts in the *favelas* of Brazil as it is to non-Pentecostal Evangelicals in southern India. An important implication of this is that what is developmentally significant about Pentecostalism has little or nothing to do with its distinctive beliefs and practices concerning the Holy Spirit, but everything or almost everything to do with what it shares with other forms of Evangelical Protestant Christianity. Among the poor, at least, Pentecostal and non-Pentecostal Evangelicalism generate much the same 'spiritual capital'.

We conclude that Evangelicalism's contributions to spiritual capital go well beyond Max Weber's classic linkage between Protestantism and capitalist development through a pattern of moral self-restraint he termed 'inner-worldly asceticism' (Weber 1992 [1904–1905]). Evangelical beliefs and practices have a demonstrated capacity to generate spiritual capital insofar as they often give individuals in a wide variety of contexts a new sense of self, a new family structure, and a new relationship to the wider world – all of which can be conducive to at least modest forms of social, economic, and political improvement. This conclusion runs counter to two widespread characterizations of Evangelicalism: that it is a substitute for 'real' developmental progress; or that it represents a direct attack on or obstacle to such progress. In fact, where Evangelicalism appears to have negative developmental consequences, it is usually because Evangelicalism has proven too weak to thwart the negative consequences of wider cultural or social forces, not because Evangelicalism itself generates the negative consequences in question.

Evangelicalism and Spiritual Capital in India

Perhaps the clearest way to identify what forms of spiritual capital Evangelicalism can generate is to observe what happens when individuals and communities in entirely non-Christian contexts convert to Evangelical Christianity. A dramatic though under-studied class of such cases comes from India, where numerous instances of 'mass conversion' to Evangelicalism have occurred in the last hundred and fifty years. Indeed, such conversions continue to occur, and their tendency to generate distinctive forms of spiritual capital continues to be documented (Aaron 2007, 2008).

Yet these conversions are often ignored – for three reasons. First, it's assumed that they are a highly marginal and infrequent phenomenon. In part, this is because regulatory barriers to 'Dalit' (untouchable) conversions became high in post-independence India (with Dalits converting to Christianity losing an array of government benefits for which they would otherwise be eligible as members of 'scheduled castes'), but they were not so high in pre-independence India. Second, it's assumed that what few conversions did and do occur were and are artificially generated, as it were, by Western-operated and Western-funded missionary activity. In fact, however, by far the largest and most important cases of Evangelical conversion have occurred – and continue to occur – almost entirely outside the auspices of Western missionary endeavour. Third, it's assumed that whatever conversions do occur are material or instrumental, that converts are merely 'rice Christians'.

As we demonstrate in the course of this paper, all of these assumptions seriously misrepresent reality, and therefore Evangelical mass conversions in India deserve far more attention than they typically receive.

A Brief Historical Sketch of Christian Mass Movements in India

'The distinguishing features of Christian mass movements are a group decision favourable to Christianity and the consequent preservation of the convert's social integration. Whenever a group larger than a family, accustomed to exercise a measure of control over the social and religious life of the individuals that compose it, accepts the Christian religion (or a large proportion accept it with the encouragement of the group), the essential principle of mass movement is manifest' (Pickett 1933: 22).

To understand what mass movements were and to comprehend what their impact was, one must understand the context of India's caste system. The Indian caste system is a unique phenomenon that has created a social order that is unseen elsewhere in the world. A caste is an exclusive group bound by tradition, by a code of conduct, and by a body of customs that influence all social, economic and religious aspects of life. To say that the caste system is analogous to social orders or distinctions we see in other parts of the world is a common misunderstanding. In some cases, castes have traditional occupations, but in most cases very few members of any given caste are employed exclusively in a single occupation. Not all Brahmins can be priests, and yet Hindu scriptures declare that a Brahmin is to be regarded as having divine attributes, no matter what his occupation. A Brahmin man of the highest caste might be destitute, while a Sudra of the lowest caste might be an important social leader in the city.

'The man born in the outcaste village may as soon think of building his house in the other group as a pig may think of going to live in his master's front room' (Pickett 1933: 63). An outcaste is, as the name suggests, a person who is born in a caste that is denied the privilege of associating with 'caste' or 'respectable' Hindus. He or she is thus cast out or dismissed from social contact and lives beyond the fringes of respectable society. Caste rules and customs perpetuated by the upper caste groups assured that social contact with 'outcastes' – out of caste groups – were minimized. These included customs relating to marriage, food, residence, occupation and dress. 'Untouchability', based on Hindus laws of ritual purity and impurity, was applied to prevent contact with outcaste groups. Untouchables were relegated to occupations that exacerbated feelings of disgust because their traditional occupations involved 'unclean' work – with dead animals as leather workers, or as sweepers working with human refuse, for example. Untouchability, once proclaimed against a particular caste, continues for generations.

Background and Rationale for Pickett's Study

In 1871, the Indian census showed that the majority of Catholic as well as Protestant adherents in India were non-Brahmin and in particular were drawn from the lowest castes. By 1931, for example, a vast number of depressed classes in Andhra Pradesh had converted to Christianity. According to the historian Geoffrey Oddie, in some areas of the state there were converts in every untouchable hamlet (Oddie 1991: 95). In Guntur alone, 57 % of the districts were converted to Christianity. Malas and Madigas, the main untouchable caste groups, made up a majority of the converts in the state and by 1900 constituted an established and flourishing Christian community with ordained ministers and established churches.

Christian mission movements in India since the early 1800s were originally designed and geared to evangelizing the upper castes, and were based on the then popular notion of 'sanskritization', which presupposes that the lower sections of the community imitate the lifestyle of the higher, more dominant castes. It was believed that Christianity would percolate downward from the upper castes to the lower castes and therefore much effort was put into evangelizing the upper castes during the early 1800s.

The dramatic results of mass conversions of non-Brahmin, and in particular the lowest untouchable caste groups, to Christianity during the 1870s caused most mission societies, including the International Missionary Council, to question their accepted strategies for evangelizing Indians. In 1928, Dr. John Mott, chair of the International Missionary Council suggested that American Methodist Bishop and missionary to India, J. Waskom Pickett (then editor of the journal *Indian Witness*) conduct a rigorous study of the conversion movements taking place in India. Mott's motive was not enthusiasm for these mass conversions but rather the opposite: he feared that these movements would prove an obstacle to the evangelization of India. Previous studies of conversions typically included descriptive overviews of the mission field and, although informative on some level, were meant mainly to attract financial support for the mission. As chairman of the board of the Institute of Social and Religious Research (ISSR) in New York, Mott envisioned a study that would employ rigorous scientific methods to determine the validity and quality of the mass conversion movements sweeping the country. By the 1920s the American Social Survey movement had gained considerable recognition, and Mott wished to utilize emerging tools of social research to explain the phenomenal growth of outcaste converts in India.

Bishop Pickett conducted a seminal study between 1930 and 1931 in India in collaboration with (and with the generous financial backing of) the Institute of Social and Religious Research. The mass movement survey conducted by Pickett and his technical advisor Mr. Wilson was the earliest example of a household survey being conducted primarily to extract data on the religious, social and economic status of people in India. The survey developed separate schedules and was used to collect information from converts as well as from their non-Christian neighbours.

Data on the economic and social status of Dalit Christians were collected from the ten main areas where mass conversion movements of Dalits to Christianity took place. (See table below.) These areas included both northern and southern India.By the end of 1931, the survey staff completed 3,800 household interviews, making it the most ambitious survey ever to have been conducted outside of the West up until that time (McPhee 2005: 209). To date, it remains the single largest database amassed on Dalit Christianity and its social and economic impact.

Christian Mass Movement Study Areas (In Chronological Order)

Area/Geographical Center	Castes in the Mass Movement
Etah (Uttar Pradesh)	Sweepers
Vidyanagar (Andhra Pradesh)	Malas, Madigas and various Sudras
Nagercoil (Tamil Nadu)	Nadars and Sambavars
Govindpur (Orissa)	Mundas and Oraons
Vikarabad (Andhra Pradesh)	Madigas and Malas
Guntur (Andhra Pradesh)	Malas, Madigas and various Sudras
Cumbum (Tamil Nadu)	Malas, Madigas and various Sudras
Ghaziabad (Uttar Pradesh)	Charmars and Sweepers
Pasrur (Pakistan)	Churas
Barhan (Uttar Pradesh)	Sweepers

Source: J. Waskom Pickett, *Christian Mass Movements in India: A Study with Recommendations*, 1933.

Why Conversions Occurred

When the mass movements began in the late nineteenth century, Protestant, mainly Evangelical missionaries made contact with many outcastes in the towns and villages they worked in but made no deliberate effort to evangelize them. As noted previously, many missionaries believed that Christianity would filter downwards, and that the way to evangelize India was to concentrate on the elites in the hope that the lower castes would follow. In addition, some evangelistic methods adopted by missionaries working in India at the time were unconsciously 'elitist'. They included the distribution of tracts and attending religious festivals such as Christmas concerts and pageants. An outcaste could not hope to engage in, or to be part of, the target audience. Many missionaries became conscious of the elitist and exclusionary nature of their evangelistic methods only after a dramatic influx of outcastes took place as a result of the mass movement conversions. Some Protestant missionaries, like Bishop Clough who worked in Andhra Pradesh, engaged in evangelistic activities that targeted all castes. Evangelical Protestant missionaries, unlike their Roman Catholic counterparts, regarded the caste system as a religious institution that was integral to Hinduism, and thus chose to condemn it rather than to work within it. Numerous Evangelical missions pioneered efforts in mixing caste groups, including the outcastes, in schools and churches, and they were active advocates for the opening of public roads and public wells to outcastes and Muslims.

Were Dalits lured to convert by the promise of better education, food, healthcare, and other 'material' benefits, as some Hindus and missionaries charged? Was conversion the outcome of inducing unthinking and unfortunate people who were robbed of agency and became simply victims of cultural erosion and colonial subjugation? Was this a one-way street?

Missionaries did not pay special attention to outcastes, nor did they make any deliberate efforts at evangelizing them. Mass conversion movement of outcastes occurred primarily because the poorest and most depressed classes of people took the initiative to approach the missionaries. In fact, in 1909, Reverend Peachey, a Church Missionary Society missionary working in South India was cautious if not sceptical, suggesting that the 'movement was largely a social one. The chief desire seems to be to escape police worry and supervision'. In his view, the outcastes with a reputation for thieving became converts for 'mixed' or 'very mixed' motives.

Orientalists – who take their cue from Edward Said[5] – view conversion as a process in which the passive non-West is overwhelmed and the hapless native is subjugated and converted by the cunning and powerful West. Conversion, in this construction, accentuates the role of the missionary but fails to take into account the instrumentality and agency of the Dalit outcaste in actively seeking Christian conversion. Denied a dignified status, Dalits embraced Christianity because it could improve the quality of their life – which necessarily included better health, education and material prosperity. But material benefit was hardly the sole motivation for their conversion. It was that Dalits believed that Christianity embodied a life of dignity and hope for a future free of degradation and subservience. Bishop Pickett's household survey of converts revealed that Dalits saw that conversion offered them a social and religious identity rooted in a personal faith in a loving God rather than in an identity that was 'dependent on the recognition of higher castes' (Forrester 1980: 77). In the words of one of the converts: 'I wanted to become a Christian so I could be a man. None of us was a man. We were dogs. Only Jesus could make men out of us' (Pickett 1933: 36).

The notion that Dalit conversions were directed purely by instrumental reasoning ignores the fact that for centuries Dalits yearned for a personal experience of God that eluded them because of their caste and social position. Conversion to Christianity meant Dalits were able to realize their intrinsic and constitutive motivation to have a faith that was personal and inclusive and not alienating and exclusive. In the words of one missionary, Dalits, once they converted, 'learned that the powers of this world are under the control of a loving God of infinite wisdom who is their heavenly Father, and not subject to the caprice of evil spirits which have to continually propitiated' (Webster 1992: 187). Finally, the Dalits' intrinsic religious desires could be realized in

Evangelical Christianity; they belonged to a community where every aspect of their lives was dedicated to their faith and embraced by their faith.

How Conversions Occurred

The most expansive stage of the mass movement took place in the second part of the nineteenth century in the rural communities of India. During this period, new land revenue and legal systems were introduced and disrupted established rural life. It was at this time that Dalit leaders came into contact with missionaries and became the first converts. Missionary references to God's love 'even for the outcaste' made the message unique and appealing to these early converts. Early Dalit converts saw the gospel provide a new social and religious identity that they were determined to share with their family members and with other members of their caste. The leaders became the main evangelists in their villages, sharing the news about the Christian faith and encouraging people to get baptized. According to John Clough, a missionary working among the Dalits in Andhra, the movement sweeping over the Madiga community (an outcaste group in the region) picked up the best first – those who were ready to respond to the Christian appeal. The leaders had made the beginning. Then those followed who had been under their direct influence. The appeal, carried along with the impetus of clannish, tribal life, moved like an avalanche, gathering up as it went along.

As men of influence by virtue of their occupation or family connection, the new Christian leaders organized meetings and provided the audience when evangelists or teachers visited the villages. In the latter part of the 19th century when the missionaries discovered that there was a movement taking place in the villages they sent instructors and teachers to establish schools and churches and missionaries toured the areas preaching and supervising the new Christians. Working within the confines of the village and with the new indigenous leaders, the visiting missionaries trained and instructed the leaders of the rapidly growing mass movement. By 1912, the Anglican Mission in Andhra Pradesh conducted three thousand baptisms annually.

One of the reasons for the success of the mass movements was the willingness of wives and husbands to join each other in baptism. Their willingness to participate in conversion together helped preserve the family ties and protect each other in times of persecution and trouble. Family ties provided a channel to evangelize other members of the wider family and establish avenues of communication of the gospel, which was very important to the further spread of the movement. Baptismal registers show that relatives of a family baptized in one village were baptized in another.

In addition to the role of leaders of outcastes who took the initiative to bring their communities to the attention of the missionaries, dedicated mission workers such as John Clough and Rev. Panes working with the Church Missionary Society in Andhra Pradesh challenged the long-held vision and strategies of missionary organizations that focused on working with high-caste Hindus. Rev. Panes and Bishop John Clough set out to evangelize all castes but found that they had little success converting members of high castes, while at the same time they saw a surge of interest in Christianity from outcastes. Forced to make a choice between evangelizing the more influential higher castes and outcastes, Bishop Clough working in southern India was convinced from his reading of 1 Corinthians 26–29[6], that it was God's will that he respond to the urgent desire of the outcastes to become Christians.

Mission workers and teachers played a key role in instructing new converts in a new way of living. Bishop Clough made three requirements of his converts. These were to not work on Sunday, not to eat carrion, and not to worship idols. The instructions altered the new converts' work relationships and further ostracized them from the religious and social life of the village. These changes did not come without conflict, retribution, or persecution. It was also in this region that the largest number of conversions took place and the strongest church was built.

What Conversions did for Individuals

One of the most important qualitative assessments of religious commitment is whether an individual has an instrumental or constitutive religious commitment. As we have already seen, many were sceptical if not downright hostile towards the converts in the mass movements because, it seemed, these converts were too often motivated by the search for material advancement or for improved social status, or to escape authorities and to secure freedom from the bondage of oppressive caste rules. While in some cases, purely material or social benefits may have attracted converts, it is also undeniable that conversion almost always entailed at least some significant material and social costs. Dalit converts in particular faced serious persecution on becoming Christians. In the Khammamett district of Andhra, a major centre of mass conversions of Malas and Madiga outcastes, Bishop Whitehead wrote that while he saw that converts were persecuted more in this district, 'this only made them better and stronger as Christians than the converts in other districts. To some extent, therefore the conditions in the Khammemett district are more favourable to the growth of earnestness and spirituality than they are elsewhere'[7].

In terms of spirituality and spiritual development, Pickett's Mass Movement Study revealed a depth one would not expect to find in materially motivated converts. In areas of established and regular Christian instruction, for example, converts had acquired an understanding of God and in particular an understanding of their relationship to God. A belief in the love of God for them as outcastes had a powerful effect on their economic status, their conduct, and on their status in the community. Pickett also noted that in areas where worship and Christian instruction was not established, converts were less likely to want to change their lifestyle or their perception of themselves, which suggests that the changes generated were spiritually and religiously rooted.

Centuries of degradation and oppression in the caste system produced a deeply dysfunctional and pessimistic identity in Dalits. The Hindu doctrine of 'Karma', reinforced the notion that the outcasts' deprivation was a result of misconduct in their past lives and further strengthened their isolation from social and religious life in the village. Yet in areas of vibrant Christian worship and with careful instruction, Pickett noticed that converts, 'As they pray to God with the conviction that he is no respecter of persons, as they praise him for his infinite mercy to them, as they consider his call to render service in his name to other communities, they find release from the old inhibitions' (Pickett 1933: 129).

One of the most visible signs of transformation in the lives of converts was the willingness of Dalits to risk changing occupations. Breaking free from centuries of being relegated to menial occupations such as sewage disposal, new converts were found working as tailors, carpenters, gardeners and potters. Furthermore, non-Christian landlords and employers of outcastes who believed that their employees' conversion would disrupt their work, not only changed their opinion, but 'paid higher wages to Christian labourers because of their honest work' (Oddie 1991: 113).

Pickett discovered that parents with prolonged exposure to Christian worship and instruction were more likely to send their children to school. This included daughters as well as sons. It seems that as parents experienced one Christian institution, the church, they were more likely to want their children to experience another Christian institution, the church or mission school. Worship strengthened parents' hope for a better and richer life for their children.

In Pickett's eyes, one especially vivid feature of the transformation of outcastes into respectable converts occurred on Sunday mornings when Christians, washed and clean, entered the Church, knelt in quiet prayer, sang heartily, and seemed to be 'absorbed in the worship of God'. This change in their personal habits was noted by many high-caste Hindus, who observed that Christians converts were cleaner in personal habits and kept their homes cleaner than before they became Christians. In addition to personal cleanliness, many converts renounced eating carrion and even beef. As a result of their improved personal cleanliness, many Hindus allowed outcaste preachers and evangelist to enter their homes and were willing to let their children sit with Christians of outcaste origin in mission schools.

As Pickett discovered in his study of 1930s India, nothing troubled the outcaste more than the fear of encountering and offending an invisible evil spirit. 'Poverty is endured with less concern. Oppression by other humans worries them less, for they can do something to protect themselves against mere man, however powerful, or can find compensation in make-believe, but they are helpless before the attack of these powerful invisible spirits' (Pickett 1933: 186).

The fear of evil spirits and the practice of sorcery dominate the spiritual lives of people in India. It is not uncommon to see educated people carrying charms or drawing auspicious symbols on their homes to protect themselves from invisible evil spirits that are believed to lurk everywhere. Persons of the depressed classes, the outcastes, suffer the most as their misfortunes and sickness are attributed to the work of evil spirits. Ignorance and the lack of access to adequate medical care lead women to cling to sorcery and the use of charms, as this is the only way they know to protect the health and life of their children. In India, sorcerers are found in all castes, but outcastes who represent the oldest generations are assumed to have the best knowledge of the evil spirits that inhabit the villages.

A break with the past in renouncing a belief in evil spirits and the use of sorcery was extremely difficult for converts of the mass movements. Conversion did not automatically destroy all the Dalits' beliefs and fears concerning the unknown, but it did provide gradual relief. In areas where the Church was firmly established and where regular religious instruction was organized, converts were less fearful of evil spirits. Converts mentioned that evangelists who defied the wrath of evil spirits and ministered to people at inauspicious times and days and were still not attacked showed them that becoming a Christian was the best way to protect oneself against the spirits. Bible stories of Jesus casting out evil spirits contributed to the outcastes' belief that Christ was the only way to escape the fear of evil spirits. In 1932, it was the impression of Pickett and his team of interviews that less than ten percent of outcastes who became Christians practiced sorcery, and that in some Christian areas 'hardly a trace of a once universal belief in its efficacy survives' (Pickett 1933: 189).

What Conversions did for Families

Marriage involves the most established customs in any social group. Converts in the mass movements brought with them numerous customs – some of them antithetical to the teachings of the Christian church. Polygamy and divorce were common among outcaste Hindus. Removed from the regular practices and rituals of Hindu worship, most outcastes were ignorant of religious rites of Hindu marriage and divorce. Once outcastes became Christians, they were taught to abide by the obligations and duties of Christian marriage, which included pledges of permanent loyalty and love between man and wife.

The struggle for converts was that the Christian ceremony lacked the colour and excitement of the traditional marriage process. It was, in their words, 'unbearably dull and out of harmony' with their traditions. Bishop Azariah, the first Indian Anglican Bishop, in his diocese of Dornakal in what is now the state of Andhra Pradesh, started to introduce a new form of Indian Christian Marriage service that would meet the needs of new converts. Interviews of mass movement converts found that young men and women of Christian families wanted to marry by Christian rites.

The evidence of the impact of Christian marriage on the lives of converts was seen in the relationship between husbands and wives. Hindu and Muslim women interviewed said that in Christian homes husband and wife obey and respect each other. Divorce was less common among converts than among their non-Christian counterparts. 'Christian men are faithful to their wives, they give their wives their rights'. Wives said that since their husband's conversion they bring their earnings home and let the wives keep their own earnings.

In areas where Christian worship was established, interviewers found little evidence of children being married under the legal age. In areas where converts lived but where there was little organized Christian instruction or regular visits from mission workers the practice of child marriage continued with large numbers of children being married by Hindu rites who are below the legal age set by the law of the land and of the Church.

Pickett's team of interviewers found that converts of the mass movement had abstained from copious consumption of alcohol in southern India where it was available in large quantities and cheaply. Numerous observers when interviewed said that most of their Christian neighbours do not drink and that Christianity had led to a cessation or diminution of drink in the villages. A Brahmin official told the interviewers that one of the elders of the village church had been an opium addict before his conversion and had been 'miraculously saved from the habit'.

What Conversions did for Individuals' Relationship with the Wider Community

The mass conversion movement among the outcastes in Andhra Pradesh became one of the main engines of Christian growth in southern India. Other caste groups witnessed the vigorous growth and transformation of lives and the livelihoods of the outcaste converts in their own villages. By 1931, Christianity began to spread to higher caste groups, especially the prominent landlord and farmer communities. Most of the converts from high caste groups came from areas and villages where Christians from outcaste origins lived and worked. Nine out of ten high caste converts, when questioned, attributed their conversion 'wholly or in part' to the influence on them of the changes they witnessed in the lives of the outcastes, the Malas and the Madigas. In the words of one of the converts, '[W]e realized how much the outcaste Christians had advanced through the Christian religion. And we made up our minds to make no delay' (Oddie 1991: 111).

An outcaste convert's belief in the effectiveness of prayer and his willingness to help pray for higher caste neighbours during times of illness brought many higher caste members to Church.

In many areas where mass conversions took place and where churches were established, outcaste Christians benefited from lower interest rates and improved availability of credit. Mission organizations had set up cooperative societies to make credit available to converts at a rate below that charged by moneylenders and merchants. In addition to mission-based cooperative societies, Christianity had made converts better risks. Hindu money-lenders were more willing to lend money to church-going outcastes than to their Hindu counterparts. Prevailing interest rates were lower in areas where the churches were well established and where the improved character of converts was clearly known to all who lived in the area. In contrast, interest rates were higher and credit was less available to converts in areas where the church and the Christian character of its adherents was weak.

Clarifying the Linkages between Evangelicalism, Spiritual Capital, and Development

As the survey began, a young Dalit man we were interviewing was called away by the landlord about some incident for which he said he was not to blame. 'In my father's time', he said, 'The landlord would have struck him. He spoke roughly to me, but he didn't strike me, and I talked back to him. When my boy becomes a man, the landlord will write him a letter if he wants to make a complaint'. (From Pickett's Mass Movement Study)

In his work on identity and economics, Nobel Prize-winning economist George Akerlof (Akerlof and Kranton 2000) suggests that people have a concept of their own identity that determines how they choose to behave and who they want to be. In a world where there are vast social differences, different people in different social groups or categories have their own ideas about their identity. That is, they have ideas about who they want to be, how they should behave, and how others in their group should behave. The wealthy almost always have an opportunity to choose their identity. They get to choose how they behave and who they associate with, among other things. However, the poor and the socially excluded do not have the same level of choice, so much so that their identity is often chosen for them, by the wealthy and more influential persons in their communities. The poor are told how to behave, who to associate with, what jobs to perform, and where and how to live.

Akerlof believes that one of the most important economic decisions a person can make may be the decision about what kind of person he or she should be. In his view, in seeking to maximize their outcomes, individuals make economic decisions that maximize their utility as well as enhance and preserve their dignity. By being excluded from the opportunity to make decisions about their identity, the poor are also excluded from the opportunity to make choices to improve their lives and the lives of their families and communities. Decisions that affirm or deny a person's identity also affirm or deny a person's agency. Therefore a Dalit who is expelled from village life by Hindu laws of ritual purity, and hurled to the bottom of the material, social, and spiritual hierarchies, has a dysfunctional self-image and identity, shaped by the oppression of the past, and he develops fatalism and lack of hope about the future that robs him of any will to make choices to improve his circumstances.

Brown Univerisity economist Glenn Loury goes further than Akerlof in emphasizing the respects in which identity choice is a 'social event' (Fang and Loury 2005: 47). A person's identity is shaped by interacting with people within a community, not merely through the individual assertion of his or her values and experiences. People who interact frequently, who live in close proximity to each other, and who share similar social experiences and engage in similar activities may end up embracing similar identities. This strategy assumes that people embrace similar identities in order to collaborate effectively and deal better with conflict. To the extent, therefore, that a few members of the community may have a negative self-image or a negative identity, other members within the same and relatively closed community are likely to embrace and sustain a negative collective identity. Furthermore, people who are pessimistic about themselves and their circumstances and who are socially isolated tend to feel victimized, and are less willing or able to take risks to improve their lives.

A French ethnographer, Abbe Dubois, after studying the outcastes in India in 1906 wrote, 'The idea that he was born to be in subjection to other castes was so ingrained in his mind that it never occurs to the Pariah to think his fate is anything but irrevocable' (Webster 1992: 23). Dalit oppression and isolation from mainstream Hindu society created a dysfunctional collective identity that not only destroyed their sense of worth, but also robbed Dalits of the will to improve their lives and transform their circumstances. The concepts of an individual's will and sense of worth are distinct features, but they can also reinforce each other. The process can be conceptualized in terms of a negative feedback loop, in which a person's lack of worth or value reinforces his inability to act to change his life, which in turn lowers his sense of self, and he thus spirals downward into a destructive and vicious cycle of psychological and physical debilitation.

Evangelicalism promoted a radically positive sense of worth and will in Dalit converts, so that over time a virtuous cycle was created where the empowered and mobilized converts were able to transform their lives and the lives of their families and community. Conversion activated in the converts powerful new concepts of value and initiative through the generation of spiritual capital in two main ways: first, through the *attitudes and perceptions* of the converts towards themselves, and mutual attitudes and perceptions towards the family and the wider community, and second, through the *agency and capability* of converts, where individuals took responsibility before God to improve their lives, the lives of their families, and the lives of the wider community. Such a restoration of worth and will among Dalit converts was nurtured and reinforced through an enthusiastic adherence to Christian teaching and regular participation in Christian worship.

Our typology disaggregates the types of spiritual capital generated by conversion at the individual, family, and community level. We aim to illuminate the role Evangelicalism plays in bringing Dalits to encounter the reality of a personal and loving God and the rich and profound forms of spiritual capital that result from conversion. The two ways by which spiritual capital is generated – through attitudes and perceptions and through agency and capability – are interrelated partly because a higher sense of worth and stronger sense of will reinforce each other, but also because of the interactions between individuals and the lived faith of a community. For example, a positive sense of self promotes a desire to be an active agent of change, not only in one's own life, but also in the lives of one's family and the wider community.

Self-Assurance Capital

'Christ gave me a *pagri* [a turban, which is a symbol of respect], in place of dust' – Lal Begri, Dalit convert in Pasrur (Webster 1992: 23).

Most of the missionaries involved in the mass conversion movements in India regarded evangelism as their first duty, relying on regular Christian instruction among new converts and evangelistic missions to the surrounding villages to transmit the gospel message. Underlying their evangelistic efforts was the belief that the Dalits were completely ignorant of the true and one God of the Bible and they, like the whole world, needed salvation from damnation. Christian instruction was to be accomplished foremost, above all other tasks.

Evangelical Protestant missionaries set out to offer Dalits a new self-image as people whom God loves and whom He has already forgiven. Converts were to emerge as 'new creations' – as men and women who would throw off their material and spiritual bondage. Evangelicalism provided a powerful combination of a faith that gave Dalits a new identity as full human beings created in God's image and for friendship with Him and a hope of a life free of fear and full of possibilities. For the first time, Dalits received a new religious and social identity that was not dependent on the approval of higher caste Hindus. The gospel's inner transformation of the convert, in terms of their sense of self and their hope for the future, was significant enough to take subsequent generations of Dalit converts through the rigors of systematic discrimination and persecution.

In addition to gaining a new self-image as Christians, Dalit converts immediately became part of a new *jati* – a new community or new group. The convert's new Christian identity and membership was conferred immediately upon baptism, maintained by fellowship with other Christians, including Europeans, higher caste Hindu converts and with other Dalits in the surrounding villages. Converts forged strong bonds with fellow believers through regular participation in Christian worship and during festivals such as Christmas and Easter.

Evangelical mass conversion movements in India in the nineteenth and early twentieth centuries took place among the lowest and most depressed groups of people, whose self-image and identity were shaped by centuries of oppression. For Dalit converts, evangelicalism provided an opportunity to move away from the past and into a new faith and to reassess how they see themselves and how they wish to represent themselves to the world around them. Evangelical missionaries believed that a clear demarcation between the converts' past lives and their new existence was the only way for broken individuals to heal, to 'regain their manhood', and to emerge as people with a 'new moral fibre' (Webster 1992: 183). Conversion was meant to be socially and culturally disruptive and alienating. David Martin, writing about Pentecostal conversion in Latin America, perceptively notes that 'new converts to Pentecostalism become independent not by building up modest securities, but by the reverse: by the loss of all ties that bind, whether they be familial, communal or ecclesial' (Martin 1990: 197).

However, the type of social atomization recommended above is at odds with what most people today believe. From politicians to academics to social workers, most people believe that dysfunctional and economically backward groups must be helped within their contexts. In their view, contextualized assistance that is embedded within the social architecture of the group and within the person's own social environment is the only and best way to address issues of disparities.

Dalit conversions during the mass conversion movement in India took place in groups. Led first by a leader who heard about the Christian faith from a travelling missionary or evangelist, other outcastes followed and often converted as a group. As the group converted and whole villages followed suit, new practices and behaviours that destroyed old notions and assumptions about their personhood and worth were quickly adopted and put into action. Dalit converts – together as a group – instituted a radical form of social atomization that sought to destroy the old order and redeem themselves within the protection and safety of their new life. It was within their 'new society' that Dalit converts forged new patterns of behaviour, new concepts of self, new models of enterprise and initiative. Social atomization created a paradigm shift in the convert's self-perception and self-representation and released an optimism affirming of their dignity and humanity. It created a stock of self-assurance – or what one may call 'self-assurance capital'. This form of spiritual capital enabled Dalit converts to remain in their social milieu while ceasing to be of their social milieu.

Agency Capital – Am I Capable of Improving My Future?

'So I will be able to go to a shop and buy what I need just as other boys do. I don't like to stand outside while everybody else is being served, then have what I buy thrown to me or put down on the street for me to pick up'. – a young Christian Dalit boy talks about why he was so eager to study at the local mission school (Pickett 1933: 65).

Imprisoned in a caste system that oppressed them for centuries, Dalit Christians endured years of emotional and physical abuse from caste groups. Such treatment by the higher caste Hindus contributed to a traits and characteristics among Dalits which came to be formally known as the 'Depressed-Class mentality'. The Dalits' submissive acceptance of his status and his apparent indifference to suffering expressed itself in 'abject dependence, lack of ambition and initiative, carelessness, deceitfulness, extravagance, drunkenness, insolence, and harshness in dealing with others (Pickett 1933: 83). Physically assaulted and psychologically depleted, Dalits offered little resistance to the social patterns and norms imposed upon them by higher-caste Hindus.

In these circumstances, it was not surprising to see that the passive acceptance of ill treatment by higher caste Hindus so diminished the outcaste that he was unable to lift himself out of poverty either by improving his prospects through education or by organizing a movement of social or political liberation. The French ethnographer, Abbe Dubois, suggested that the prospects of freedom from their pathetic lifestyles was so bleak that outcastes had abandoned any desire to gain the public's goodwill, and had lost themselves 'without shame or restraint to vice of all kinds'.

Conversion to Christianity led to a process of transformation of the Dalit convert in a way that can be compared to the experience of a battered spouse being released from years of abuse in a violent marriage. Dalit converts were not going to be isolated; they opted to become agents of change and to reconstitute themselves spiritually, socially, and economically. In particular, conversion broke down longstanding inhibitions about movement and speech and cleared away the artificial occupation restrictions created by higher castes in order to preserve economic and social superiority over Dalits. Thus, Evangelical Christianity did more than instil a 'new morality' in Dalit converts; it did more than restrain destructive impulses or cause Dalits to internalize a socially and economically functional code of behaviour. Evangelical Christianity gave at least some converts the will to live lives of value and to have confidence in their abilities to transform themselves, their families, and their communities. This deep and profound transformation in the lives and outlook of people who converted was more portable, more fungible, and wider reaching than a moral change alone.

Armed with a determination to change their lives, Dalits in Nagercoil, for example, now part of Tamil Nadu in Southern India, ventured to work in different occupations. This was particularly difficult for the Dalit community called Nadars as they were traditionally relegated to the cultivation of Palmyra trees. Their primary occupation was to draw the juice from the trees, ferment it, and sell the toddy or palm wine. The mass movement survey discovered that upon conversion, the Nadars had entered any available work in the village and were pioneers in the introduction of new occupations. Survey staff reported that Christian converts in Nagercoil now earned twenty percent of their cash income from occupations that were not open to them prior to their conversion.

Familial Value Capital: What Attitude Do I Have towards My Family? How Does My Family Perceive Me?

'Before these people became Christians they bought and sold wives like we buy and sell buffalos. Now they choose one woman and remain faithful to her as long as she lives. The women have changed as much as the men have' (Pickett 1933: 129).

Conversion to Christianity laid down clear moral boundaries that had an absolute and non-negotiable quality. It did not invent moral boundaries; it drew on existing values and strongly sanctioned and promoted them as values of their new faith. Traditionally, a hardworking man might be a good provider, a good husband, and a good father, and yet his conscientious discharge of family duties might not be inconsistent with sporadic visits to the local brothel. Evangelical Christianity made it clear that these forms of behaviour were morally irreconcilable.

In the Dornakal Diocese of Southern India, Anglican Bishop Azariah strictly condemned a wide range of practices he considered to be un-Christian. Between the years 1914 and 1945, improprieties within marriage such as adultery resulted in more excommunications than any other transgressions. In the year 1941, seventy-two percent of the people who were excommunicated had been accused of adultery or other actions associated with sexual immorality (Harper 2000: 274).

No issue drew more animated discussion from non-Christian informants during the mass movement survey than the treatment of wives by Christian converts. In 1930, one hundred and sixty-five Dalit non-Christian women in Pasrur (now in Sailkot District in the Punjab province of Pakistan) were asked if Christian men treated their wives differently. One hundred and forty-three replied yes, twenty replied no, and two abstained. Christian husbands are less abusive, more loving, they bring their earnings home instead of squandering them on drink or women. Christian women related to their husbands with greater confidence than their non-Christian counterparts, and couples consulted each other on household matters.

A deeper consequence of the changed individual is the change in the family. The family now became a unit, a place where relationships were built and nurtured. No economic incentive or government program (we could imagine, anyway) could cause a man to change his inner attitude or disposition towards his family, to be less selfish in his spending patterns, to be more respectful of his wife, or to be more involved in his child's development. In numerous cases documented by Pickett's massive study, conversion to Evangelical Christianity brought about just these changes. A convert's spiritual commitment shapes his or her understanding of what it means to be a wife and mother, husband and father.

The orientation to intimate domesticity by Evangelical converts is nicely illustrated by the work of Cornelia Butler Flora, writing about the spending habits of new Pentecostals in Colombia in the early 1970s. Flora found that, in contrast to Roman Catholic respondents, the first and most costly item a Pentecostal family typically seeks to purchase after their conversion is a dining room table. Rather than a means to individual ends, family life and 'family solidarity' become ends in themselves (Flora 1976: 221; cf. Brusco 1986, 1995).

Familial Action Capital: Does My Family Have the Capability to Act Together to Improve Our Future and Our Lives?

Until the mass conversion movement of Dalits took place, neither the government nor Hindu reformers took much interest in the uplift of Dalits. It was in mission schools that the battle over whether Dalit children should be educated was fought. Frequently, it was the opening of a mission school to the children of Dalit converts that signalled the outbreak of persecution. Employers of Dalit converts and upper-caste Hindus were openly hostile to the opening of mission schools and took offense 'at the mere suggestion that the depressed classes aspire to any kind of schooling' (Pickett 1933: 273).

Dalit converts recognized that education was an important tool to harness the capability of their children and to secure a better future for them. The mass movement survey noted that almost always an individual's conversion to Christianity was accompanied by keen interest in schools. In fact, in some areas, it became a ritual that the opening of a school took place at the same time as groups of individuals in villages converted.

In 1930, 1880 families in ten of the key mass movement areas were surveyed to obtain data on the educational attainment of children aged eight. The survey selected age eight because it was understood, at the time, that normal eight-year olds attending regular school would achieve the minimum literacy[8] Children were divided into four categories *based on the length of time the parent professed to be Christian.* The categories were: A: Children whose parents were born in Christian homes; B: Children whose parents were converted before reaching the age of fifteen; C: Children whose parents were converted between their fifteenth year and the before their eldest child turned six-years old. Finally, D: Children whose parents had converted after the child had turned six-years old.

The survey found a strong, positive correlation between the length of time the parents professed to be Christian and the achievement of literacy of the child. In Guntur, now in present day Andhra Pradesh, 73 percent of the children whose parents were born in Christian homes were literate compared to 35 percent literacy rate for children born in homes where the parents converted only after the eldest child entered school at age six. The results of the survey illustrate that parents who were Christians for a long period of time, especially those born in Christian homes, conceived of themselves as God's stewards responsible before God for the lives and development of their children.

Given the widespread growth in education available for outcaste children and the absence of caste restrictions on occupational mobility among Dalit Christians in the Madras Presidency, the newspaper *The Hindu*, in 1905, observed that with 'these two advantages', 'it is probable they [Dalit Christians] will soon be the Parsis of Southern India; they will furnish the most distinguished public servants, barristers, merchants and citizens among the various classes of the Native community' (Oddie 1991: 112). Today, in fact, despite the large proportion of Indian Christians from Dalit or Adivasi (tribal) background, Indian Christians enjoy education and income levels that exceed the Indian average.

Reputational Capital: How Does My Community Perceive Me? What Kind of Attitude Do I Have toward My Community?

'In former times when a theft occurred, whoever might be the thief, the village authorities used to arrest us and put us in prison for some days. But since we have become Christians we are free from such troubles. No one is bold enough to touch us without the permission of our pastor. Besides that we are now worshipping the true God' (Oddie 1991: 115).

One of the most dramatic forms of 'capital' generated by Evangelicalism that emerges from our research on the mass movement conversions of Dalits is what could be called 'reputational capital'. Dalit converts accumulated reputational capital not only because they altered the conduct of their personal and family lives, but also because many non-Christians were persuaded that these changes were genuine and characteristic of Christians in general. Furthermore, non-Christians believed that the moral and ethical changes they observed in the lives of Evangelical converts made them more reliable partners in a variety of social enterprises, particularly in the economic domain.

'Fifteen years ago when they worshipped demons, there was only one honest man among them. Now half of them are honest' (Pickett 1933: 273). Non-Christian landowners and moneylenders, echoed the sentiments of the man quoted above and told Pickett's Mass Movement Study interviewers that they believed that conversion to Christianity would seriously affect and disrupt the Dalit laborers' ability to work. However, both landowners and moneylenders not only changed their mind about the new converts, but they paid Christian labourers higher wages because they were industrious and honest workers. In some cases, landlords granted Dalit Christian labourers permission to go to church on Sunday because they worked harder during the week. The mass movement survey interviewed one hundred and fifty non-Christians to assess the impact of conversion on the work habits of converts. Ninety-two of the informants said converts had become more 'industrious', while forty-seven said they observed 'no change'.

Similarly, numerous studies from the 1950s onwards have found that Pentecostals in a number of societies have enjoyed substantial stocks of 'reputational capital'. According to Willems, 'Protestants gradually acquired a reputation of being dependable, industrious, and efficient employees; fair employers; honest merchants; and proficient professionals with high ethical standards. None of our numerous informants thought or implied that such virtues could not be found among non-Protestants, but there was obviously a general expectation that Protestants did in fact live up to standards far from being collectively adhered to by non-Protestants' (Willems 1967: 176). Among numerous examples, Willems found that 'numerous local officials' testified to the regular adherence of Protestants to tax laws that others normally ignored (Willems 1967: 174).

It is noteworthy that such reputational capital can be a significant resource for politics and political mobilization. John Burdick's research in several small towns outside of Rio in the early 1990s found that Pentecostal leaders in local politics inspire trust because of the perception that they are more honest than others. 'The people around here believe a lot in us, they support us. They trust us'. Such expressions of trust are common whenever Pentecostals take on roles of political leadership. Non-Pentecostal smallholders who support a local Pentecostal as the leader of their peasant union, for example, spoke of his honesty. Elsewhere, non-*crentes* voted for Pentecostal candidates for assemblyman on the ground that 'they won't rob and steal' (Burdick 1993b: 26).

Furthermore, though Pentecostals often avoid involvement in militant forms of protest or political action, Burdick found that their reputational capital enhanced their influence and effectiveness when they did choose to get involved. 'When Pentecostals *do* participate…their conduct provides backbone to work stoppages and other actions. In some factories, Pentecostals represent up to a tenth of the work force. '*Crentes* are very firm in a strike', explained one non-Pentecostal organizer. 'They give credibility to the movement'. A Pentecostal confirmed this. 'We won't scab, we won't vacillate. When they want our support, we say, 'OK, but without any violence'. Indeed…organizers often rely on Pentecostals' support as a way of building legitimacy for the action, both among the workers and in negotiating with employers. '*Crentes* are very firm, honest', explained one organizer. 'Their example counts a lot' (Burdick 1993b: 32; emphasis in the original).

In the case of a strike of metalworkers in one plant, reported Burdick, 'the strike committee nominated a Pentecostal to approach the employer. Those with him clearly remember the effect this had on the climate of negotiations. 'He spoke calmly', one [organizer] recalled. 'He said, 'Look, we're not able to tolerate these wages'. He was right, because the salary was low. That gave the workers a real boost, and the manager got the rug pulled out from under his feet' (Burdick 1993b: 32–33).

Contributing to the enhanced reputation and image of Evangelical converts in India were significant changes in the hygiene and cleanliness of Dalit converts – which made an enormous impression on upper-caste Hindus. In an effort to improve the cleanliness of Christian villages in Southern India, as well as to improve the outcastes' chances for social mobility, Bishop Azariah of the Anglican diocese of Dornakal in Andhra Pradesh, developed various traditions including an annual 'house whitewash', in which the exterior of the house was cleaned and painted white using a mixture of slaked lime and chalk powder. Bishop Azariah urged Dalit converts to 'commend Christianity to Andhra by…a clean and well cared for body, home, and village' (Harper 2000: 266). Before conversion, upper-caste Hindus would not venture near the homes of Mala and Madiga outcastes, for example. Yet after conversion, Zamindars (landlords) 'do not hesitate to walk through the street; they even go into the court-yard and knock on the door of the teacher. [Azariah] when asked for the reason for this change replied, Cleanliness was the answer' (Harper 2000: 266).

Long restricted from growing flowers because of their low social status, twenty out of the twenty two first generation Dalit families said the they had become interested in flowers after their conversion. Prominent upper-caste Hindus initially objected to Dalits growing flowers, but the converts continued to plant flowers in front of their houses. In 1930, during the Mass Movement Survey, Mala converts appeared before the survey staff, washed, dressed, and ready to attend church. Almost all the women had neatly combed their hair and adorned it with flowers. One Muslim informant in Guntur, in Andhra Pradesh, told survey staff that, 'since they ceased to worship evil spirits and began to worship God, they have become clean' (Pickett 1933: 266).

An important area that offered the Dalit converts an opportunity to create reputational capital was with respect to carrion and meat (especially beef) consumption. In India, the eating of meat, and particularly the eating of beef and pork, is often associated with ritual impurity. Although any eating of meat is regarded as polluting, the eating of beef, which is the meat of the most sacred of animals, and the eating of pork, which comes from swine who eat excrement, is exceptionally repugnant to upper caste Hindus. Following conversion, the Pickett Survey shows that 80% of converts interviewed had voluntarily stopped eating carrion and beef, even though abstention was not required by the Church, because it was highly desirable for ritual purity and it offered them an opportunity to improve their social rank and reputation.

Widespread renunciation of meat eating along with improved cleanliness and personal appearance on the part of Evangelical Dalit converts had a radical impact on the attitudes of caste Hindus towards Dalit converts and towards Christianity in general. A Brahmin villager told survey staff, 'Christianity has brought a blessing to this village by saving a third of our population from these loathsome habits. What we Hindus failed to accomplish by boycott and abuse, the pastors have accomplished by instruction and kindness' (Pickett 1933: 203).

Another remarkable outcome of the converts' changed lives and character was the conversion of caste Hindus (non-Brahmin castes), especially in Southern India. The most remarkable and large-scale conversion of caste Hindus took place among the 'Sudras' in Andhra district and came to be known as the 'Telugu Sudra Movement'. The Sudras referred to caste groups who were middle-status non-Brahmins and included groups such as landlords, tenants, shepherds, and other agricultural communities. Improved attitudes towards work and a decline in drunkenness and violence among outcastes convinced many Sudras that if Christianity could improve the lives of people as 'degraded as the Malas and Madigas' it could help them and their communities.

Sudra converts were recruited by pastors, evangelists, and school-teachers drawn mainly from Mala and Madiga outcaste groups. Mala and Madiga evangelistic efforts served to revolutionize the ways in which outcastes were perceived and treated in many villages in Andhra during the mass conversion movement. While earlier, the very presence of Malas and Madigas would have been considered polluting, following conversion, upper-caste Hindus, especially Sudras[3], sat down to eat and study the Bible with outcaste preachers in open defiance of caste law. According to Bishop Pickett's mass movement study, in Dornakal diocese in Andhra, 170 out of the 187 villages in which Sudras were converted saw Mala and Madiga conversion take place *before* Sudras confessed their faith. One Sudra convert told Bishop Azariah that 'we realized how much the outcaste Christians had advanced through the Christian religion. And we made up our minds to make no delay' (Oddie 1991: 111). Many Mala and Madiga Christians put aside previous inhibitions and actively set out to evangelize their Sudra neighbours.

Collective Action Capital: Are Members of Our Community Working together to Improve Our Lives and Our Future?

'… Christians have acquired a new concept of themselves, and that this or a like concept has been accepted by their neighbours. Confirmation of this theory is provided by the decline of the use of the old term by which Christians in this area were known before their conversion.The term 'Chura' is falling into disuse. Hindu, Moslem, and Sikh informants told us that they seldom or never refer to the Christians in their villages by the old caste name' (Pickett 1933: 149).

Would a sweeper who works with human refuse choose to make pottery and sell it to his Hindu neighbours? Better still, would the Hindu neighbour buy the pottery from the outcaste Dalit? It is hard to imagine this taking place, yet, in areas where Dalit Christians had established strong Christian communities, members of outcaste groups earned a comfortable living making and selling pottery to their Hindu neighbours. Both the Dalit convert who redefined himself by working harder and living a cleaner, more acceptable lifestyle, and the upper-caste Hindu who strove to overcome his reservations about caste worked together to build networks of communication and trust and mobilized to create value for themselves by acting together so that both groups could realize the benefits of collective action. While opportunities for self-improvement existed before the outcastes were converted, it was only after conversion that they acquired the confidence to leverage their new identity into transforming their lives, their communities, and their reputation among their Hindu and Muslim neighbours.

A Hindu moneylender in Nagercoil, when interviewed by the mass movement survey staff, stated that a Sambavar (outcaste) who attends church presents a twenty-five percent lower risk than one who does not attend church. The moneylender said he would be twice as willing to lend money to a second-generation Nadar Christian than to the average non-Christian Nadar. In areas such as Nagercoil (present-day Tamil Nadu), where the Christian community was well established and where there was a regular and well-attended church, the interest rates were lower and moneylenders were more willing to lend to Dalit Christians. Furthermore, in areas where the church was securely established, Dalit Christians, with the help of the local mission, had organized cooperative societies to provide low-interest loans to church members. Survey staff reported sixty-eight societies in villages where there was a majority of Dalit Christians. Dalit Christians organized thirty-eight of the cooperatives, and only four of sixty-eight societies objected to the admission of outcaste members.

In many parts of southern India, Dalit women converts set out to become evangelists and became known as 'Bible women'. Dressed simply in white saris and without any jewelry or adornments, these women travelled around the villages instructing local women about the Bible, and about various aspects of domestic life such as nutrition, health, and hygiene. The activities of the Dalit Bible women in the early twentieth century presented opportunities for women and opened areas of activity that were once closed to them. Under the tutelage of women missionaries, Dalit Christian women cared for the sick and helped women from all castes, including those from higher castes. Dalit Bible women began to enter areas of public life in ways that opened doors for future generations. Subsequently, many Dalit girls and women went on to train as nurses and teachers and proved indispensable as numerous mission hospitals and schools sprung up around India. Even today, Indian Christians provide a disproportionate share of the nursing staff – not to mention the overall medical and healthcare infrastructure – around the country.

Conclusion

Evangelical Christianity did more than instil a 'new morality' in Dalit converts. It did more, for example, than teach men to stop drinking or womanizing. It gave them a new dignity and a new confidence to live better and more productive lives. In India, a convert's new dignity and self-assurance were best demonstrated by his ability to withstand severe persecution. In most villages in India, converts suffered immediate and prolonged oppression. Most converts of the mass movements in India during the late nineteenth and early twentieth centuries remained in their villages and towns after conversion. Since the new converts lived out their faith within their context, they were more vulnerable to widespread persecution from caste groups and people in authority. According to Bishop Clough, a missionary bishop working among recent converts in the late nineteenth century: 'The village washermen were told not to work for the Madiga converts; the potter was told not to sell pots to them; their cattle were driven from common grazing ground; the Sudras combined in a refusal to give them the usual work of sewing sandals and at harvest time they were not allowed to help and lost their portion of grain'.

In most cases the persecution of Dalits was more severe and included physical abuse, burning churches and chapels, and organized violence against the families of recent converts.

Pressure on Indian Christians, especially Dalit Christians, continues today – and to some extent with official legal sanction. Upon conversion, Dalit Christians, who account for over 45% of Indian Christians, lose their status as officially designated lower castes ('scheduled castes' in Indian legalese) and are singled out for exclusion from benefits with respect to jobs and education that are available to almost all other non-Christian scheduled castes and tribes (Muslim Dalits are the only other Dalit group that is similarly excluded from eligibility for 'scheduled caste' benefits and quotas). In 2001, the official Indian census form did not even allow Dalit Christians and Christian tribal groups to list Christianity as their religion. Recent years, particularly since 1998, have witnessed several waves of violence on Indian Christians in Gujarat, Orissa, and other states, almost certainly orchestrated by Hindu militant groups like the RSS (Rashtriya Swayamsevak Sangh) and the VHP (Vishwa Hindu Parishad), which are the vanguard of India's Hindu nationalist movement.

It is difficult to explain the ability of Indian Christians to withstand these ruthless and barbaric attacks unless one understands the role of the gospel in their lives. The best explanation for Christian stubbornness, and indeed the best explanation for continuing Dalit conversions to Evangelical Christianity, is not that Dalits are allured – via conspiratorial Western missionaries – by the prospect of immediate material rewards, as Hindu nationalist activists allege. Instead, the Dalits' embrace of Evangelical Christianity – like the conversion of millions of poor people to various forms of Evangelical Christianity all round the world, including in its Pentecostal expressions – releases types of spiritual capital that stamp them with an ineradicable dignity and empower them to realize substantial social and economic betterment.

Notes and References

1 Rebecca Samuel Shah, formerly a Research Analyst with the World Bank, is a demographer and independent researcher specializing in the relationship between religion and economic development. Timothy Samuel Shah is senior research scholar

with Boston University's Institute on Culture, Religion and World Affairs and adjunct senior fellow with the Council on Foreign Relations.

2 Though Banfield's field work was confined to a single village, which he analyzed under the fictional name 'Montegrano', subsequent research not only found a similar anti-associational tendency throughout southern Italy but also confirmed his claim that this tendency was a strategic factor in explaining the region's relative economic and political 'backwardness' (Almond and Verba 1963; Putnam, Leonardi, and Nanetti 1993).

3 Willems's article appeared in the still functioning journal *Economic Development and Cultural Change* (Volume 3, Issue number 4, pp. 321–333). Unfortunately for southern Italy's development prospects, Banfield concluded that such radical spiritual change is 'obviously impracticable' because '[t]here is little prospect...that Protestants will be permitted to proselytize in southern Italy' (Banfield 1958: 162 n. 8).

4 In this chapter, 'Evangelical Protestantism' and 'Evangelicalism' are used interchangeably.

5 Edward W. Said. 1978. *Orientalism*. New York: Pantheon Books.

6 1 Corinthians 26–29: 'Brothers, think of what you were when you were called. Not many of you were wise by human standards; not many were influential; not many were of noble birth. But God chose the foolish things of the world to shame the wise; God chose the weak things of the world to shame the strong. He chose the lowly things of this world and the despised things—and the things that are not—to nullify the things that are, so that no one may boast before him'.

7 G.A. Oddie, *Christian Conversion among Non-Brahmins in Andhra Pradesh*.

8 By 'minimum literacy', it meant they were able to read at a basic level and have basic numerical skills.

Select Bibliography

Aaron, Sushil J. 2007. *Contrarian Lives: Christians and Contemporary Protest in Jharkhand*. Asia Research Centre Working Paper 18. London: London School of Economics. Available at http://www.lse.ac.uk/collections/asiaResearchCentre/pdf/WorkingPaper/ARCWork ingPaper18SushilJAaron2007.pdf. Last accessed on July 23, 2008.

Aaron, Sushil J. 2008. 'Emulating Azariah: Evangelicals and Social Change in the Dangs'. In David Lumsdaine, ed., *Evangelical Christianity and Democracy in Asia*, pp. 87–129. Evangelical Christianity and Democracy in the Global South, edited by Timothy Samuel Shah. Oxford and New York: Oxford University Press.

Akerlof, George A., and Rachel E. Kranton. 2000. 'Economics and identity'. *Quarterly Journal of Economics*. 115.

Almond, Gabriel A., and Sidney Verba. 1963. *The civic culture; political attitudes and democracy in five nations*. Princeton, N.J.: Princeton University Press.

Banfield, Edward C. 1958. *The moral basis of a backward society*. Glencoe, Illinois: Free Press.

Barrett, David B., George Thomas Kurian, and Todd M. Johnson. 2001. *World Christian encyclopedia: A comparative survey of churches and religions in the modern world*. Oxford: Oxford University Press.

Bebbington, David W. 1989. *Evangelicalism in modern Britain: a history from the 1730s to the 1980s*. London: Unwin Hyman.

Brusco, Elizabeth E. 1986. *The household basis of evangelical religion and the reformation of machismo in Colombia*. Thesis (Ph. D.)–City University of New York, 1986.

Brusco, Elizabeth E. 1995. *The reformation of machismo: evangelical conversion and gender in Colombia*. Austin, Texas: University of Texas Press.

Burdick, John. 1993a. *Looking for God in Brazil: the progressive Catholic Church in urban Brazil's religious arena*. Berkeley: University of California Press.

Burdick, John. 1993b. 'Struggling against the Devil: Pentecostalism and Social Movements in Urban Brazil'. In Virginia Garrard-Burnett and David Stoll, eds., *Rethinking Protestantism in Latin America*, pp. 20–44. Philadelphia: Temple University Press.

Chan, Kim-Kwong. 2008. 'The Christian Community in China: The Leaven Effect'. In David Lumsdaine, ed., *Evangelical Christianity and Democracy in Asia*, pp. 43–86. Evangelical Christianity and Democracy in the Global South, edited by Timothy Samuel Shah. Oxford and New York: Oxford University Press.

Chesnut, R. Andrew. 1997. *Born again in Brazil: the Pentecostal boom and the pathogens of poverty*. New Brunswick, N.J.: Rutgers University Press.

Chesnut, R. Andrew. 2003. 'Pragmatic Consumers and Practical Products: the Success of Pneumacentric Religion among Women in Latin America's New Religious Economy'. *Review of Religious Research*. 45 (1): 20–31.

Coleman, James S. 1987. 'Social Capital and the Development of Youth'. *Momentum*. 18 (4): 6–8.

Fang, Hanming and Glenn C. Loury. 2005. 'Toward an Economic Theory of Dysfunctional Identity'. In Christopher Barrett, ed., *The social economics of poverty*, pp. 12–55. Priorities in development economics. London: Routledge.

Fernandes, Sujatha. 2008. 'Ethnicity, Civil Society, and the Church: The Politics of Evangelical Christianity in Northeast India'. In David Lumsdaine, ed., *Evangelical Christianity and Democracy in Asia*, pp. 131–153. Evangelical Christianity and Democracy in the Global South, edited by Timothy Samuel Shah. Oxford and New York: Oxford University Press.

Flora, Cornelia Butler. 1975. 'Pentecostal Women in Colombo: Religious Change and the Status of Working-Class Women'. *Journal of Interamerican Studies and World Affairs*. 17 (4): 411–425.

Flora, Cornelia Butler. 1976. *Pentecostalism in Colombia: baptism by fire and spirit*. Rutherford, N.J.: Fairleigh Dickinson University Press.

Forrester, Duncan. 1980. *Caste and Christianity: attitudes and policies on caste of Anglo-Saxon Protestant missions in India*. London studies on South Asia, no. 1. London: Curzon Press.

Freston, Paul. 2001. *Evangelicals and politics in Asia, Africa, and Latin America*. Cambridge: Cambridge University Press.

Harper, Susan Billington. 2000. *In the shadow of the Mahatma: Bishop V.S. Azariah and the travails of Christianity in British India*. Studies in the history of Christian missions. Grand Rapids, Michigan: Eerdmans.

Ireland, Rowan. 1991. *Kingdoms come: religion and politics in Brazil*. Pitt Latin American series. Pittsburgh, Pennsylvania: University of Pittsburgh Press.

Jayakumar, Samuel. 1999. *Dalit consciousness and Christian conversion: historical resources for a contemporary debate*. Oxford: Regnum International.

Lugo, Luis, et al. 2006. *Spirit and Power: A Ten-Country Survey of Pentecostals*. Washington, D.C.: Pew Forum on Religion & Public Life. Available at http://pewforum.org/publications/surveys/pentecostals-06.pdf. Last accessed on July 23, 2008.

Lumsdaine, David, ed. 2008. *Evangelical Christianity and Democracy in Asia*. Evangelical Christianity and Democracy in the Global South, edited by Timothy Samuel Shah. Oxford and New York: Oxford University Press.

Marsden, George M. 1980. *Fundamentalism and American culture: the shaping of twentieth century evangelicalism, 1870–1925*. New York: Oxford University Press.

Martin, David. 1990. *Tongues of fire: the explosion of Protestantism in Latin America*. Oxford: Basil. Blackwell.

Martin, David. 2001. *Pentecostalism: the world their parish*. Religion and modernity. Oxford: Blackwell Publishers.

Maxwell, David. 2006. *African gifts of the spirit: Pentecostalism and the rise of a Zimbabwean transnational religious movement*. Oxford: James Currey.

McPhee, Arthur G. 2005. *The road to Delhi: J. Waskom Pickett remembered*. Bangalore, India: SAIACS Press.

Oddie, G. A. 1991. 'Christian Conversion among Non-Brahmins in Adhra Pradesh: With Special Reference to Anglican Missions and the Dornakal Diocese, c. 1900–1936'. In G. A. Oddie, ed., *Religion in South Asia: religious conversion and revival movements in South Asia in medieval and modern times*, pp. 95–124. New Delhi: Manohar.

Pickett, Jarrell Waskom. 1933. *Christian mass movements in India: A study with recommendations*. New York: Abingdon Press.

Putnam, Robert D., Robert Leonardi, and Raffaella Nanetti. 1993. *Making democracy work: civic traditions in modern Italy*. Princeton, N.J.: Princeton University Press.

Putnam, Robert D. 2000. *Bowling alone: the collapse and revival of American community*. New York: Simon & Schuster.

Ranger, Terence O., ed. 2008. *Evangelical Christianity and Democracy in Africa*. Evangelical Christianity and Democracy in the Global South, edited by Timothy Samuel Shah. Oxford and New York: Oxford University Press.

Sandeen, Ernest Robert. 1970. *The roots of fundamentalism; British and American millenarianism, 1800–1930*. Chicago: University of Chicago Press.

Schlemmer, Lawrence. 2008. *Dormant Capital: The Pentecostal Movement in South Africa and its Potential Social and Economic Role*. Johannesburg, South Africa: The Centre for Development and Enterprise.

Sexton, James D. 1978. 'Protestantism and Modernization in Two Guatemalan Towns'. *American Ethnologist*. 5 (2): 280–302.

Shah, Timothy Samuel. 2004. 'The Bible and the Ballot Box: Evangelicals and Democracy in the 'Global South''. *SAIS Review*. 24 (2): 117–132.

Shah, Timothy Samuel. 2008. 'Preface'. In Paul Freston, ed., *Evangelical Christianity and Democracy in Latin America*, pp. vii–xix. Evangelical Christianity and Democracy in the Global South, edited by Timothy Samuel Shah. Oxford and New York: Oxford University Press.

Weber, Max. 1992 [1904–1905]. *The Protestant ethic and the spirit of capitalism*. Translated by Talcott Parsons, with an Introduction by Anthony Giddens. London: Routledge.

Webster, John C. B. 1992. *A history of the Dalit Christians in India*. San Francisco: Mellen Research University Press.

Willems, Emílio. 1955. 'Protestantism as a Factor of Culture Change in Brazil'. *Economic Development and Cultural Change*. 3 (4): 321–333.

Willems, Emílio. 1967. *Followers of the new faith: culture change and the rise of Protestantism in Brazil and Chile*. Nashville: Vanderbilt University Press.

Woodberry, Robert Dudley, and Timothy Samuel Shah. 2004. 'The pioneering Protestants'. *Journal of Democracy*. 15 (2): 47–61.

Chapter 6

FLYING UNDER SOUTH AFRICA'S RADAR: THE GROWTH AND IMPACT OF PENTECOSTALS IN A DEVELOPING COUNTRY[1]

Ann Bernstein and Stephen Rule*

Introduction

Growth in the numbers of people attending Pentecostal churches in South Africa appears to mirror similar religious trends in other parts of the world. In Latin America[2] during the twentieth century, huge numbers made the change from being nominal Catholics to active Pentecostal Protestants, most notably in Brazil, Chile and Guatemala. By the mid-1980s, the (Pentecostal) Full Gospel Central Church in Seoul, Korea was thought to be the largest in the world with 500, 000 members. Similarly, many new Pentecostal churches have been established in Nigeria[3] and elsewhere in Africa[4] in the last few decades. As many as one in six (16,6%) Africans is a member of a Pentecostal

* This paper is based on a large research project managed by the Centre for Development and Enterprise. It has been a collective effort. The research design was guided by Professor Peter Berger, Professor James Hunter and Professor Lawrence Schlemmer. The commissioned research was managed and synthesised by Dr Stephen Rule and at an earlier stage by Dr Tim Clynick. The final CDE reports on this work are part of a series edited by Ann Bernstein and written by Professor Lawrence Schlemmer and then a shorter version summarized by Dr Sandy Johnston and Ann Bernstein, and entitled *Under the Radar: Pentecostalism in South Africa and its potential social and economic role*. CDE In Depth no. 7, 2008. The original research papers were written by Prof Tony Balcomb, Prof Phil Bonner, Monica Bot, Dr Tim Clynick, Prof Steven de Gruchy, Godfrey Dlulane, Rev Prof Bill Domeris, Riaan Ingram, Rev Paul Germond, Hudson Mathebula, Lehasa Mokoena, Tshepo Moloi, Montagu Murray, Prof Lawrence Schlemmer and Dr Attie van Niekerk.

Figure 6.1. Growth of Pentecostal and Charismatic Christians in Africa, 1900–2005.

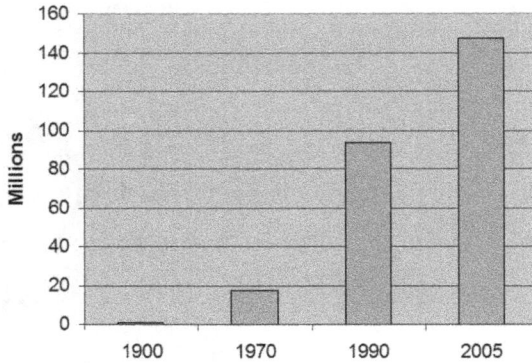

Source: World Christian Encyclopedia (2001); World Christian Database (2006) quoted in Pewforum website (2007).

or Charismatic church, representing growth from a mere 0,8% in 1900 to 4,8% in 1970 and 15,2% in 1990.

Although there are records of Pentecostal revivals from as early as the first century[5], the current phase of expansion of the movement can be traced to the Azusa Street Revival in Los Angeles in 1906[6]. Five decades later, the Holy Spirit blessing received by an Episcopalian minister led to a charismatic revival amongst tens of thousands of Anglicans and Catholics world-wide[7]. Anderson[8] sees a reflection of these developments taking place in South Africa. In his view Pentecostalism arrived in southern Africa as an agent of racial integration amongst the poor. It soon began to reflect the racial constructions of the Union of South Africa, with the development of separate black and white congregations[9]. Almost one-third (32%)[10] of Christians in South Africa belong to African Independent Churches (AICs), the largest of which are the Zionist Christian Church (ZCC) and Shembe. A study of the religious fabric of the people of Soshanguve, a Black township near Pretoria[11] found 254 different churches, many of which focused on experiences of the Holy Spirit, either individually or communally. The churches were categorised as 'Pentecostal Mission churches' (started by the missionaries), 'Independent African Pentecostal churches' (such as Grace Bible Church – independent from but closely resembling the mission churches,), and 'Spirit-type churches'[12] or Zionist (including as the most important example, the ZCC).

With the transition to a democratic South Africa eighty years later, there was a narrowing of the gap between traditional Pentecostal churches and the Charismatic wings of traditional Protestant and Catholic churches. This occurred simultaneously with a growth in concern and activism in relation to

Figure 6.2. Adherents (in Millions) of Major Religions in South Africa.

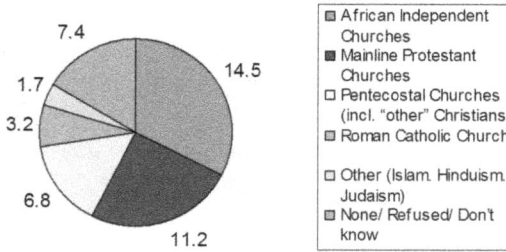

Source: Statistics South Africa, Census 2001; Rule, 2007.

poverty and HIV/AIDS. Scores of new Charismatic churches and the house church movement have grown in South Africa as well as in Asia, South America. New groupings include the Vineyard Movement, the Australian Hillsong Church and the New Zealand New Life Churches. Membership of these new churches has come from new converts as well as previous adherents of mainline Protestant churches and AICs. With the rise of a black middle class, there has been a distinctive move from township churches into previously predominantly white suburban churches[13].

An important event was the experience of pastor Ray McCauley of the Rhema Church, at the Rustenburg Conference of South African church leaders in 1990. It was here that South African Pentecostalism was catapulted into the world of social ethics and social action[14]. McCauley and Steele made an impassioned defence of Rhema's dramatic departure from traditional Pentecostal social and political quietism[15]. Unlike the 'new Rhema' which emerged with the 'new South Africa', Pentecostals, traditionally, shunned political involvement. Their historically pietistic approach made them zealous to win the lost, but unlikely to protest publicly against the indignities that apartheid imposed on millions of people. The outcome was that the Pentecostals were seen as supporters of apartheid. Frank Chikane, then General Secretary of the South African Council of Churches (subsequently Director-General in the Office of President Mbeki) and a key organiser of the conference saw it as 'Extraordinary in that it brought together a cross section of all the traditions and confessions of Churches in South Africa. The Conference brought Catholics, Anglicans, Methodists, Lutherans, and Reformed Churches including the white Dutch Reformed Church, Pentecostals, Evangelicals and African Independent Indigenous Churches together in a way that, I believe, has not happened before. For the first time, we have condemned the system of apartheid together with those who supported it in the past'[16].

Pentecostal Typologies in South Africa

As indicated, in relation to the influence of Pentecostalism, three broad categories of Christian churches are identified in the study by Anderson. These are Mission Churches, Spirit-Type Churches and Independent Pentecostal or Charismatic Churches.

Mission Churches are the traditional mainline denominations established in the country during the colonial period. These include Catholic, Anglican, Methodist and Baptist. The charismatic revival has impacted many of these churches. Consequently, the differences between one church (which espouses a charismatic orientation) and another (which espouses a more traditional view) in the same denomination may be greater than those between churches of different denominations which espouse similar charismatic views. Additionally, these churches include those which come out of the early 20th Century Pentecostal Tradition, such as the Assemblies of God and the Apostolic Faith Mission. There are clear links between such churches and the Charismatic wing of the traditional churches and in recent years the line between the two has become rather indistinct.

The distinguishing marks of Spirit-Type churches are practises such as the wearing of uniforms, baptism by immersion, dancing in the services, the casting out of demons, and healing[17]. Sometimes the veneration of ancestors and divination are core elements and often there are prohibitions on polygyny, (African) beer, smoking, and pork. The most striking form of this church is found in the ZCC which is the largest denomination in the southern part of Africa, numbering some 7 million members[18]. ZCC may be linked with Azusa Street through the Christian Catholic Apostolic Church in Zion City Illinois. One of the key doctrines was the strong emphasis on a priesthood of all believers. Each year over a million members make their way to Mount Moria (near Polokwane) for the annual Easter pilgrimage. Much of the weekend is spent in dancing, singing and in listening to the address of the Bishop. The first time the media were allowed to be present at this occasion was in 1997. Much about the ZCC remains unknown, in spite of the research already done[19], and in particular the extent to which cultural practices, like the veneration of ancestors and sacrifice, impact upon the Christian theology of the church[20].

A major area of debate, and one of considerable significance, is the question as to whether AICs can be classified as Pentecostal-type churches. Although the South African Census distinguishes between AICs and Pentecostalism, many writers include AICs under the rubric of Pentecostalism. Becken argues that even though Zionists share common roots with Pentecostals and have features in common, Zionists are to be distinguished from Pentecostalism primarily in their embrace of aspects of African traditional religion[21]. Current research indicates that at least three important issues areat stake, and require further investigation: (1) The different relationship between AICs and Pentecostalism and African culture[22] (2) The minor influence of Pentecostal prosperity theology in AICs; and (3) the fact that AICs have a very complex relationship to modernity and capitalism, whereas on the whole, Pentecostalism articulates itself within the idiom of consumer capitalism. Anecdotal evidence suggests that part of the reason for movement in the townships from AICs to independent Pentecostal churches is the issue of ancestor veneration. The latter do not support the veneration of the ancestors and view the AICs as serving the interests of Satan.

Finally, there is a multiplicity of Independent Pentecostal and Charismatic Churches in the urban townships. New congregations have been emerging frequently during the last two decades, one of the largest being the Grace Bible Church in Soweto, which has a 5000-seat hall in Pimville, Soweto[23]. The growth of churches has been partly influenced by the increasing levels of immigration from Nigeria, the Democratic Republic of the Congo and other African countries. Accompanied by their spiritual capital, the migrants have liberally planted new churches in South Africa's inner city and township areas. One of the newest is the Universal Church of the Kingdom of God (UCKG), established by Brazilians in Johannesburg in 1992 and now boasting an 8000-seat cathedral in Soweto[24].

The Protestant Ethic

Pentecostalism, which constitutes a new wave of Protestantism, has been linked to individual economic success and correspondingly, to broader social-economic development. This line of argument originates with Max Weber. The Reformation of 16th and 17th century constituted the first wave. The evolution of an alternative form of Christianity countered Roman Catholic abuses and favoured the rational pursuit of economic gain by promoting a 'Protestant ethic' characterised by 'this-worldly asceticism'[25]:

- A disciplined attitude to work.
- A disciplined and ordered family life, or 'life discipline'.
- An emphasis on savings over consumption and the delay of gratification.
- A world free of magic: the 'disenchantment of the world'.
- High value placed on education.
- A propensity to create voluntary associations of non-elite people.

The Protestant ethic declined after it had had its effect in the early stages of economic development and is thus present only in an attenuated form in mainline Protestant churches[26]. The nature of Pentecostalism – 'non-mediatory in ritual, conversant and voluntarist in religious election, populist and lay-orientated in self-organisation and activist and missionary in its orientation to the world'[27] – fits the movement neatly within Weber's description of the Protestant ethic.

Referring to Latin America, Berger notes that Pentecostalism is closely associated with a desire for education, a strong work ethic, individualism, and an affinity for democratic politics. He refers to a 'wildfire expansion of Pentecostal Protestantism' which constitutes a 'cultural revolution, sharply deviant from traditional Latin American patterns'. The new culture

> promotes personal discipline and honesty, proscribes alcohol and extra-marital sex, dismantles the compadre system (which…with its *fiestas* and other extravagant expenditures discourages savings) and teaches ordinary people to create and run their own grassroots institutions. The roles and contribution of women in society are recognised and expanded, as is the importance of education for children. It is a culture that is radically opposed to classical *machismo*…women take on leadership roles within the family, 'domesticating' their husbands…and paying attention to the education of their children[28].

Where the macro-economy offers opportunities, Berger points out that 'one can observe a positive correlation with social mobility and with it a truly novel phenomenon in Latin America – a growing Protestant middle class, economically productive and increasingly assertive politically' and possessing a 'comparative cultural advantage'. He argues that it is not necessary for entire populations to adopt a Protestant ethic for development to take place: a highly active minority or 'vanguard' can serve as the vehicle for development as exemplified by the Huguenots in Prussia, Jews in Poland, Armenians in the Middle East, Jains in India and overseas Chinese in South East Asia[29].

Harvey Cox points out the transformation brought about by Pentecostal churches in Korea: 'members learn from the absolutely dazzling organisation genius that these churches demonstrate'[30]. Paul Gifford continues:

> …hundreds of thousands of people whose parental culture, if not their own, had been rural and traditional learned the bottom-line skills of a modern, market economy. They learned to communicate a simple message; to organise promotional efforts, make lists, use telephones, to solve personality clashes in task orientated groups; to coordinate efforts both horizontally and vertically, to set goals and reach them; and to come to meetings on time, run them efficiently and then to implement decisions made there. This training constitutes a 'concentrated crash course in what

millions of others who fill the lower and middle echelons of modern corporations learn at business schools and sales institutes[31].

In Latin America, David Martin argues that the 'monopolistic' nature of Catholicism has 'inhibited differentiation and has tended to give rise to rival secular monopolies under the aegis of the state'[32]. On the contrary, Paul Gifford (citing David Martin) points out that Pentecostalism could help build strong, autonomous civil societies, as in these churches individuals

> ...learn how to function democratically; they elect their own officers, they learn to exercise leadership themselves, thus developing leadership skills. They learn to participate in, and run meetings, to conduct business, to handle money, to budget, to plan, to compromise, to formulate and 'own' a course of action, to implement it, to critique results, to change direction in the light of experience[33].

Moreover, Pentecostalism takes the form of a 'protective social capsule' by allowing marginalised people such as rural-urban migrants to acquire 'new concepts of self and new models of initiative' 'in an atmosphere of hope rather than despair'[34]. In Guatemala, Pentecostal networks

> ...provide an intensive and extensive information service and offer a kind of insurance as well as the emotional support of stable relationships. Beyond that they inculcate North American norms of behaviour and educate members in such matters as household budgeting, social comportment and table manners. To this one would add the way in which membership in Protestant groups provides a marriage and sexual discipline and along with that some break in the cycle of endemic corruption.[35]

Martin offers a nuanced conclusion:

> ...the impact of Pentecostal Protestantism varies according to the local channel most receptive to it, and this is true both economically and politically... In one situation it may console and buttress those who lose from social change; in another situation it may select precisely those that can make the most of chances that change offers to them... But the personality it nourishes will be one with a new sense of individuality and individual worth and, therefore, possessed of a potential for assessing its own proper activity, in which will be included activity in the economic realm. Experience of the way social mobility has come about elsewhere,

as well as common sense, suggest that the capacities built up and stored in the religious group may take two or three generations to come to fruition[36].

In a recent advocacy for religion more broadly, a review of 669 mainly medical studies pointed out that religious faith is related to beneficial outcomes in the areas of hypertension, longevity, depression, suicide, sexual behaviour, alcohol and drug use, youth delinquency, well-being, hope, self-esteem and educational attainment[37]. In each area, between 68 and 97 percent of the studies found a positive effect.

Demonstrable physical and psychological health and personal benefits coupled with a growth in community and nation-wide positive social, political and economic developments suggest a winning formula in the mass adoption of active Pentecostal or Charismatic Christianity, to say nothing of the long-term eternal benefits that are (presumably) the underlying motivation.

Review of Previous CDE Research

For several years, CDE has undertaken research into the growth of Pentecostal and Charismatic Christianity in South Africa[38]. In the absence of much previous academic work, the research has all been of an exploratory nature.

In 1999, Domeris conducted research for CDE into the impact that Christian churches – especially AICs – have on entrepreneurship and the world of work[39]. The study involved field research of six ZCC congregations and another four mainline or Pentecostal churches.

He found that the ZCC mainly included labourers and domestic workers, but also businesspeople and professionals. The ZCC was found to encourage business ownership amongst its members and serves as a networking basis for employers and employees. The values it encourages correspond closely with the values that they perceive employers to be looking for.

Black middle class Christians were found to have less rigid values than other groups. All interviewed subjects reported that they picked up skills from the church which were transferable to business contexts. Leadership skills, in particular, are activated in cell group activities.

Domeris recommended that:

• the church is an ideal base of encouraging and training entrepreneurs and for networking in the labour market;
• the members of churches play a major role in community projects around them;
• the church teaches a host of skills which are readily transferable to a business context; and

- there is a close correspondence between the values of the church and those sought by employers.

A study conducted in Cape Town's coastal suburb of Hout Bay investigated the dynamics of local Pentecostal congregations[40]. The responses of the 120 survey interviewees varied between the Pentecostal, Zionist, mainline churches (Catholic, Anglican, Methodist), Apostolics and others. They were asked 'What will be most important in helping the people we see in poverty around us?' and 77% selected the option 'What they can do to help themselves'. Most of the rest (19%) said 'Help and support from government or welfare', the balance (4%) saying 'both'. Contrasting with the Pentecostals, only 63% of Apostolics, 59% of Zionists and 53% of mainline church members said that the most important way of helping people in poverty was 'what they can do themselves'. The Pentecostal responses suggested a sense of capacity derived, especially amongst coloured respondents, from faith-based confidence.

In listing things that could make a difference to poverty, the spontaneous responses across all groups emphasised the role of religion, including conversion, sacrifice, prayer and trust in God. However, Pentecostals were much more likely than the mainliners or Zionists to mention that churches had a role to play in addressing poverty, or that people needed to change their mindsets on issues of discipline, hard work and self-reliance.

In Witbank[41], the vast majority of respondents to a survey were found to be 'in the process of urbanisation and acculturation' entailing adaptation to a context where:

- An African traditional worldview of spirits and powers is challenged by a modern, secular worldview.
- Traditional values and norms, previously kept relatively intact by the hierarchical social structures of traditional African society, are undermined by modern values and norms as people move into town in search of employment.
- Marginalisation, joblessness and powerlessness are common experiences.

It appeared that the Pentecostal churches in the study played an important role in providing a new hierarchical social structure, and in enforcing a new set of rules and taboos. The morality to which people from a traditional African background are accustomed is in this way substituted with an alternative, which is on the one hand compatible with the conception of morality and selfhood with which they grew up traditionally, but which is on the other hand more akin and adaptable to the new urban environment. Additionally, Pentecostal churches provided newly urbanised people with a place to feel more at home.

Colonialism, apartheid, modernisation and urbanisation have led to western domination of the public environment, including the workplace, institutes of learning and the economic sphere in general. This led to black people being marginalised. Although measures are currently being taken to rectify this situation, many black people still feel uncomfortable in 'the white man's world'. By establishing alternative assumptions, and applying them not only in church, but specifically within the public sphere, for example for healing and economic initiatives, Pentecostals are able to contribute towards black people feeling more comfortable and respected within certain spheres of public life.

A series of in-depth interviews were undertaken with some 35 residents of two townships in South Africa's East Rand, close to Johannesburg[42]. The healing powers of the Holy Spirit occupy a central role in the testimonies collected. What was striking, although probably not surprising, in many of these testimonies, is the way in which Pentecostalism is being deployed against the spread of HIV/AIDS. More surprising within the context of much government denialism (at that time) of the extent of the pandemic, was the way in which HIV/AIDS was acknowledged and named by Pentecostals, and not hidden or disguised as is the case in many parts of African society.

Several of the interview extracts presented attest to the battle being waged within African urban communities between witchcraft beliefs and Pentecostalism. It could be argued, that belief in witchcraft diminishes a sense of personal responsibility for one's own actions. Good fortune is not necessarily to be secured by personal effort. Ill fortune, conversely, is not a result of defective personal behaviour (*per se*). A central belief of these Pentecostal converts is the reverse. From this point of view the entire mindset of Pentecostalism is congruent with self and group progress and advancement.

A recurring feature of the research is the contention of respondents that conversion and church membership promoted self-discipline, self-control, self-respect and respect for others. One gets the feeling that this in and of itself almost involuntarily elevated converts above other members of their community. They were no longer grudge-bearing or vindictive. They had been endowed with huge personal social capital. Beyond that most interviewees articulate a striving for self-improvement and self-advancement and in some cases a plan or vision for the future. In all there is a conviction and a sense of will that this will happen – a self-confidence to accomplish. The church itself sometimes concretely enables this, at such times for example as when jobs are advertised in the church. In one other instance an impatience with 'the lazy' was also articulated.

Recent Empirical Research

In 2005–6, a series of papers were commissioned to provide insights into the lives of Pentecostal pastors and members of their congregations, some businesspeople, some political or social activists and others, 'ordinary' members. This research formed part of an international research project involving Professor Peter Berger (Boston University) and Professor James Hunter (University of Virginia). The purpose was to explore the role of Pentecostalism in developing societies. Berger's pioneering research on Pentecostalism on Latin America, led to the conclusion that contemporary Pentecostalism has positive consequences for modern economic development very similar to those of the 'Protestant ethic' in the context of early capitalism in Europe and North America. As Berger put it, 'Max Weber is alive and well and living in Guatemala'[43]. The South African component of the project could be described as an exploration of the hypothesis that Weber also lives in Soweto, and analysis of the data suggests that this is indeed the case. The research involved a series of studies and several workshops in Johannesburg[44].

Perspectives from Pentecostal Pastors

Interviews with Pentecostal pastors in Johannesburg and Durban[45] revealed the diversity of issues that occupy the minds of the church leadership.

A Hillbrow pastor was of the view that people did not need another church but they needed healing, comfort, reassurance, to repent of their sin, and they could not find these things in mainline churches. His church offered hope, assurance and healing, people came as though they were coming to a hospital – for therapy, counselling and healing. As a result of many testimonies, the church has grown. The church preaches repentance, forgiveness, and a belief that one can 'do it' oneself. The philosophy is – do not give me a fish, teach me how to fish. This message is especially relevant in Hillbrow, where church membership comprises immigrants from all over Africa. The pastor affirmed that 'Jesus is not just history or a theory, he is a reality. He is a real person that we can relate to'.

A pastor in Soweto indicated that the main message is that God wants us to reach our potential. He said that if a church member wants to become a politician he or she is usually afraid, however the church says this is a godly calling. He asked the researcher to imagine what good things would happen were the president and other leading people to be born again. This church also propagated the view that money in itself should not be viewed as evil. If God wants to bless you with these things then you must get them. As long as they do not possess you. You must possess them.

A pastor in Tembisa indicated that God had called him to work with the poor. His main message is one of hope. He tells the people that their opportunity will come, that the Lord will turn their situation around. He indicated that there is no other message for people in that township. Hope for those who are jobless, hope for those who are homeless, hope for those who are sick, hope for those who aspire to better their situation in life. He said that he did not know when or how it would happen but simply that it would happen.

A pastor in Mohlakeng, west of Johannesburg, said that the essence of his message is freedom from mental slavery. The church is situated in an informal (squatter) settlement where people feel that they are third class citizens. He indicated that youth needed to be taught to 'go beyond perpetual dependency' and freed of the idea that they should be employed by white men. Another Soweto pastor felt that the message of the church is to take the teachings of Jesus as seriously as those of Marx, Slovo and Mandela. In practice this meant taking care of the poor. His church contributes to the school or university fees of its members, care of HIV/AIDS patients and food for poor people in the community. He said 'We are here because we love Jesus and this means that we must love the poor'.

A pastor in Durban interpreted his mission as being to take the message that Nicholas Bhengu preached to the 'Red people' of the Eastern Cape forty years ago – to be proud of being an African and to empower yourself. A white pastor in Hillcrest, west of Durban said that the essence of the message is 'Christ in me the hope of glory' (Colossians 1:27), emphasising the potential of a human life with Christ in that life. He saw a human being as comprising spirit, soul and body. The spirit is completely Christ's work but the soul entails collaboration with God to transform our lives. The implication is to 'do business differently', 'do marriage differently' and 'do kids differently'. The pastor indicated the need for lives to transform in order for fruit to be seen. Christians must be able to say 'Don't do what I tell you to do, do what I am doing. Look at my life and see how God is transforming me'.

Among the pastors interviewed, there was a strong emphasis on family values, which impacts quite strongly on other aspects of social intervention, resulting in intolerance of departures from a conservative norm. Although Pentecostals were generally politically inactive before the first democratic elections in April 1994, since then there has been opposition to the liberal constitution where it contradicts basic Pentecostal values. For most Pentecostals freedom of expression is seen to result in pornography; freedom of choice promotes abortion; freedom of religion encourages idolatry; and non-discrimination on the basis of sexual orientation results in sodomy. All of the informants had strong views concerning the political situation in South Africa, but many struggle to understand how their theological convictions can be translated into practical social intervention. Social interventions seldom take them too far out of their comfort zones, though there are some exceptions.

Entrepreneurship is a central feature of these churches. This is noticeable in three areas – the churches themselves have usually come about through a considerable amount of entrepreneurship; there are many entrepreneurs in their membership; and entrepreneurship skills training features as the highest single kind of intervention after addressing issues relating to HIV/AIDS.

The message of these churches is very positive and affirming. It takes on a variety of forms and permutations, depending on the context in which it is being expressed, around the theme of self-worth and positive engagement with life. The protagonists of this message believe that it is essentially new and that God wants to do new and fresh things in their lives every day. Their worship is designed to attract and entertain and their ethos is highly voluntarist. They make conscious attempts not to be 'religious' in the conventional sense, modelling themselves rather along the line of a family, community, business, or all three. Church is seen as a lively and self-affirming continuation of every day life where one should be subjected to as little discomfort as possible and where one can be encouraged, instructed and affirmed in one's ambitions and worldly pursuits. Continued growth of Pentecostalism in the country is likely to impact significantly on the society, its economy and politics.

The Experience of Grassroots Members of Pentecostal Churches

In-depth interviews were conducted with 75 members of Pentecostal or Charismatic churches in Johannesburg, Pretoria and Durban[46]. The interviews used a narrative approach, because telling stories is the most natural way in which people make sense of themselves, and 'giving testimony' is familiar to the Pentecostal experience. This approach especially proved to be effective in the case of uneducated and shy people. An important caveat was that the interviewees were recommended to the researchers by the pastors of each church. As such, they are likely to be among the more exemplary members of the congregation. Many of the interviewees would have seen the research as an opportunity to 'bear witness' or 'testify' about the power of the Holy Spirit and would have accentuated the more positive aspects of their personal transformation and underplayed still-existing problems in their lives.

Several themes emerged repeatedly in the interviews. Many of the interviewees revealed how their conversion boosted their self-esteem and gave them confidence. It allowed many to overcome the effects of abusive relationships with siblings, spouses or other family members. Most pointed out that being 'born again' led to conflict with their parents over the rejection of traditional customs such as ancestor worship and the use of *umuthi* (traditional medicine) for healing. Aside from the more common emphasis on faith healing, a few interviewees exhibited a worldview which included magical and supernatural forces. There were a few cases where parents or husbands who belonged to a mainline church did not like their children or wives attending a different church.

Another common claim was that being reborn had led to an improvement in health and even spontaneous and dramatic healing. Many reported that their relationships improved after being born again. Some of the male interviewees spoke about how they stopped mistreating their wives and started providing and caring for their children. Others mentioned how their negative attitudes to other people changed for the better.

Many of the interviewees said that they became better at managing their income and expenses, with most pointing out that they set aside ten percent of their income as a tithe. A few said that they now invest some of their income. Other frequent impacts had been that people had stopped drinking, using drugs, or participating in extra-marital sexual relations.

A number of the black respondents mentioned how their faith had helped them to overcome racial hatred and to forgive white South Africans for the political past. Several described how their conversion helped them overcome the crippling sense of racial inferiority, with which apartheid burdened them because they were black. White respondents expressed more ambiguous views. On the one hand, some mentioned how interacting with black people enlightened their perceptions, while others seemed to suggest that not much had changed in their church.

It also emerged that people's faith gave them a sense of agency and a feeling of purpose. In some cases they emphasised a *quid pro quo* relationship where God rewards proactive behaviour. Many described how their financial situations had improved after their conversion. Although there were some cases of great financial success, most simply reported that they no longer worried about money. Some said that they began doing volunteer work with their communities after their conversion. This involved activities such as assisting poor people with food and prayer or coaching children in soccer or karate.

Many held strong views on HIV/AIDS. Abstinence is regarded as the only way to prevent AIDS, while some felt that God could cure it. A number regarded AIDS as a divine punishment for immoral behaviour[47]. Some noted how they had made sacrifices in order to educate themselves. Others emphasised how important it is for their children to receive a good education. Some reported that they used to be involved in illegal activities which they stopped after their conversion. One mentioned his experience of ongoing harassment by former associates from his criminal days. Two of the interviewees mentioned how their conversion led to them stopping corrupt activities. Some congregants showed a disciplined attitude to work. One person said 'When God meets us, He meets us on what we have done. ... God does expect us to do things. God expects us to use the mind He has given us, so that when we do things, He will provide us with the wisdom to do it'.

A number of the interviewees likened Jesus to a communist or drew out communist themes from the Christian message. Some expressed disquiet at state-sanctioned abortions, human rights and AIDS policy, which translated into an ambivalent attitude to democracy.

The common themes of the interviews can be reduced to two characteristics[48]: a growth in self-confidence and Weberian 'this-worldly asceticism'. Self-esteem, feelings of independence and personal agency had increased through their faith. For many this related to overcoming self perceptions of inferiority stemming from the racial classification of apartheid. Values emphasising personal and financial responsibility, education, work and an eschewal of extra-marital sex, drugs, alcohol, crime and corruption mark Weber's 'this-worldly asceticism'.

The competing forces of tradition and modernity are challenging people's identities, and the hopes and fears of urban life – crime, social mobility and value change – are creating uncertainty. In this confusing world of promises and threats, Pentecostalism offers a 'protective social capsule' that enables the individual to mitigate the negative forces in their lives while spurring on the positive. As Peter Berger describes it,

> As long as the individual can indeed find meaning and identity in his private life, he can manage to put up with the meaningless and dis-identifying world of the mega structures. … The situation becomes intolerable if 'home', that refuge of stability and value in an alien world, ceases to be such a refuge – when, say, my wife leaves me, my children take on life styles that are strange and unacceptable to me, my church becomes incomprehensible, my neighbourhood becomes a place of danger, and so on.

Pentecostalism also provides some material conditions for individual success. The support and referral network offered by the congregation adds to people's opportunities and career prospects and provides a safety net for those going through a crisis. These churches often have many organisational units for youth and outreach, for example, as well as 'home cells' where small numbers of congregants gather together outside of normal church hours. These organisational structures offer ample opportunity for people to get involved in leadership and administration. Many of the interviewees spoke about setting up their own home cells and being involved in church administration or community outreach projects. People who may have come from a rural, traditional background learn telephone skills, financial planning and how to organise small functions, hold meetings and deal with workplace conflict. It is important to note though, that since this sample was built up through references from the pastors, the most exemplary and 'involved' congregants were likely to have been selected. It nevertheless seems likely that a member of a Pentecostal church has more access to skill-endowing opportunities and positions than an average South African.

Tithing presents a similar phenomenon. The interviews revealed how the requirement to tithe ten percent of one's income every month forced people to start thinking about how they allocate their income and about ways to manage their money. Some pointed out that tithing compelled them to start using stop orders – a simple financial tool that can also be used for savings and investments.

The most powerful social-level effects of Pentecostalism may be on the fabric of society. Domestic violence, child abuse, teenage pregnancy and child-headed households are all common in South Africa. The interviews showed that the proscription of alcohol, drugs, extra-marital sex, domestic violence and crime are the most clearly articulated views from the Pentecostal quarter. If these result in behavioural changes, as the interviews suggest, then together with the reported improvement in personal relationships, Pentecostalism may be able to 'knit up the ravelled sleeve' of the social fabric.

The social fabric is not just important in itself: it also underpins economic growth and development. Confidence, trust in the system and in others, willingness to take risks and entrepreneurship are all crucial 'soft' factors that complement the 'hard' policy-driven factors of growth. Entrepreneurship is especially important. The creation of small businesses is the best means to spur on economic development and job creation in South Africa, and the Pentecostal ethic of hope, personal agency and responsibility could be the breeding ground for such start-ups. Pentecostalism's moral codes and propensity to create stronger families would also aid the development of small enterprises, which are often family-run in the developing world.

The strongest effect is most likely to be the mending of the social fabric. The improvement in family life and cessation of drugs and crime was a clear tendency in the interviews. Growth in entrepreneurship, the consolidation of democracy, political reconciliation, education and skills development and improved health are all likely to be beneficial outcomes, albeit with weaker effects than for the social fabric. Entrepreneurship and democratic consolidation are both possible consequences of typical Pentecostal behavioural patterns, but are mediated by other processes that make their outcomes more uncertain. Political reconciliation, education and skills development and health improvements could also all be possible results of the spread of Pentecostalism, but were less strongly observed in the interviews than were social fabric factors. Finally, the effects of Pentecostalism on the HIV pandemic are ambiguous and possible slightly negative given the countervailing forces described in the previous section.

Charismatic and Pentecostal Politicians and Activists

Interviews were conducted with 25 politicians or other social activists who are Pentecostal or Charismatic Christians[49]. The smooth transition to a 'New South Africa' without bloodshed was ascribed to God's working in the lives of politicians and white and black South Africans and the transition to a non-racist society was a direct answer of God to the prayers of Christian believers. However, it was felt that God is still waiting for mankind to repent given that there are still many wrongs in the country.

It was also felt that God uses political leaders and activists, even non-believers, to achieve His goals. The community in general and the Christian community are often seen as being almost the same. This is mostly seen as a good thing, because the church played an active part in the liberation struggle against Apartheid, but one respondent pointed out that, in Zimbabwe, church leaders took part in the so-called land grab. Respondents felt that the church should help to develop the nation by giving it purpose and values.

Several expressed the view that Christians should not try to establish a Christian state, but rather support general fairness and respect for human rights in which they can freely exercise their own religion and values. Jesus' life on earth was viewed as a model for political involvement and the church, as servant of God, should be setting the standard for the government and not the other way round.

Apart from their views about the broader context, participants in the research felt callings in respect of very specific issues such as ministry in prisons, or fighting crime or alcohol abuse. They were generally comfortable referring to their own political involvement as proof that it is possible for Christians to engage in political activities without becoming corrupted and their willingness to continue playing a role in the future. Some commented on the way that conversion to Christianity changed oppressed personalities or made it possible to abandon violence and bloodshed as means to gain political emancipation.

It was felt that God's blessing for South Africa is not unconditional and that the church could play a unifying role in the South African 'rainbow context', a society with enormous cultural, racial and economic diversity. Dealing with critical political issues such as the crisis in Zimbabwe and the ongoing need for reconciliation were essential.

There was a feeling that the South Africa Government's 'entrepreneurial drive' only benefits a selected few. The government should do more to understand and explain what entrepreneurship is all about at grassroots level. A number of respondents indicated that they engage in entrepreneurial activities themselves. It was felt that everyone has a God given right to work but some said that the current government policy that embraces the free market economy is to be blamed for the lack of jobs and the high levels of crime in South Africa. Another perspective was that a market economy should generate money that can be used to help those in need. The new elite run the danger of repeating the wrongs of the past and because the church has played an important role in the nurturing and training of leaders in South Africa, it should continue to do so.

God could help South Africans to conquer the HIV and AIDS pandemic, but neither the government nor the church is doing enough in the struggle against HIV/AIDS. The misconception that political freedom is a license to sexual freedom worsens the HIV and AIDS pandemic and sound morals were seen to be preferable to 'condomising'. The respondents felt that one should be careful when ascribing HIV and AIDS to a punishment from God.

It is evident that the activists take seriously God's command to care for the poor. To their fellow congregants that have lived in low-income conditions it is self-evident that the church should play a role in the alleviation of poverty, but all churches do not see that. It was also felt that strong moral values involving refraining from drinking alcohol and staying clean of corruption can contribute to the alleviation of poverty. Social grants (monthly monetary allocations by government to targeted disadvantaged categories of individual) are seen as a blessing that should be encouraged, although it is admitted that these grants sometimes end up in the wrong hands and have unintended results. Some expressed the opinion that the church could implement solutions that provide better value for money than social grants.

Traditional African culture remains an important factor; to return to the old ways might mean backwardness for one respondent and progressiveness for another. The Bible offers a better and more practical way forward, however, magic and myths are a reality.

The Views of Pentecostal Businesspeople

Interviews were conducted with 25 businesspeople with Pentecostal or Charismatic church links in the Johannesburg and Ekurhuleni metropolitan areas[50]. 'Classic' marketplace Christians can be defined as those individuals who believe that they have been anointed to minister in the workplace. This means that they have been chosen and empowered by the Holy Spirit for a divinely sanctioned assignment. 'Ministry' means that they do more than witness; they bring transformation to their jobs and then to the marketplace as a whole. 'Transformation' implies that both ministry and occupation are dedicated to divine service to 'bring the Kingdom of God to the heart of the city'.

In defining 'classic' marketplace Christianity in this way, Clynick[51] suggests that such individuals would effectively emulate the apostles and new disciples of the first century. Very few individuals in South Africa today can be realistically described as classic 'disciples' in the marketplace. Most play lesser roles or they simply maintain a marketplace presence necessary to making a living. This spread of involvement or roles may apply to all Christians – whether Born Again or not. Clynick defines four different roles that Born Again Christians play in the marketplace:

1. Christians on level one believe that the marketplace is an evil place. Their role is to survive and hold their ground as Christians. In essence, they believe that they are prisoners from Monday to Saturday. Every Sunday they are granted furlough. Their overriding objective is to survive with their dignity as Christians intact. Their faith accordingly is in need of regular 'maintenance' and 'strengthening' since the marketplace is a place of sin and temptation (this often necessitates 'short term' spiritual tending during the week). The church community, pastor and/or family are therefore the most important elements in their spiritual life enclosing the individual in close embrace or sphere.
2. The second level represents those who apply Christian principles or beliefs in the marketplace. Those principles allow individuals to overcome temptations to some degree on their own and to keep their reputations intact. They will not change the marketplace and the marketplace will not change them: they basically will settle for a draw. The church and the pastor are still vitally important to their spiritual life: however they sometimes operate independently as individuals beyond the encircling embrace of their pastor and the church. They demonstrate growing individual spiritual maturity in respect of their day-to-day marketplace interactions.
3. Level three Christians wholeheartedly believe that they can work in the fullness of the power of the Holy Spirit: 'They seek God every day, they hear from Him, and they implement what he tells them'. As a result they don't fear the marketplace; on the contrary they view their work as an opportunity to witness to the love of Christ. Their need for spiritual growth often leads them to seek out likeminded believers. They play an active intercessory role in respect of their marketplace colleagues.
4. The fourth level represents those who, after they have experienced God's transforming power in their businesses, actively see themselves on a mission to transform the marketplace and change the world ('classic marketplace Christians'). They 'seek the Kingdom' and bring their ministry and their work into complete alignment. Level Four Christians are very rare indeed though not entirely absent or inactive in the country as we shall see.

This model suggests that, when applied to Christian businesspeople, all four types of broad personal faith orientations can be found. Relative differences across all Christian forms should become evident if and when applied to a similar control sample of business people from say 'mainstream' Protestant churches. Respondents categorised as level 1 exercise their faith more privately, using biblical principles to run their businesses, those in category 4 tend to employ only 'Born Again' Christians, pray during business meetings and openly discuss their Christian testimonies.

'Born Again' Pentecostal business people's primary identity is as members of particular faith communities or churches. Any wider effort to mobilise this constituency successfully will have to begin with an acknowledgement thereof. There are already many examples of local church/faith led initiatives by church members amongst congregations and within particular communities which have had significant effects/impacts. There is little evidence of sustained success in establishing work-based support networks: faith networks should thus in principle be church-based and local.

Born Again business people are a subset of the wider group of believers and share with them values and behaviour which are derived from their identities as believers, not as business people. It follows that the kinds of initiatives which would garner support amongst business people are faith or value based: identifying such elements would be crucial. The research showed that Born Agains don't lend to each other or invest in other Christian businesses simply because they are run by 'Born Agains' or Christians in general. An element critical to the success of any public and private initiatives in support of believers is trust. State interventions should be made to support local faith-based organisations in providing faith-based 'market friendly' services and support to individuals and families who are local members of churches. Such interventions might include providing local churches with funds contributed by the private sector to a foundation that would oversee applications from individual churches to appoint or train suitably qualified church members to deliver a set of distinct services consisting of the following tasks:

- Identify opportunities to promote individual self-help and self improvement amongst church members.
- Support and strengthen families and family resources, and identify mechanisms and vehicles that promote Christian based family values, amongst church members and within wider communities.
- Identify and provide church based business mentoring and coaching to church members who are business owners.
- Church advice and support for individuals to access government grants and subsidies. Provide wider support to enable church members to access business support services, training providers and local procurement agencies.
- Help create and build local business networks based on inter-denominational and wider community structures to allow sharing of knowledge and experience between established local business people, providing opportunities for local

medium to large companies to address such networks on employment prospects, skills development plans, employment equity programmes and procurement policies.

Targeted Survey of Charismatic and Pentecostal Christians

A sample survey of 350 Pentecostal and other Christians[52] revealed some differences, although no major ones, in attitude and perception between members of the Old (classical) Pentecostal churches, the New Pentecostals, the mainline churches and the non-religious control group, as well as between respondents living in predominantly black African townships and the mixed race populations of the middle class suburbs. The tables illustrate some divergence in levels of dissatisfaction with the various aspects of life in South Africa. Overall, in the black African township areas, dissatisfaction amongst Old Pentecostals is lower than that amongst New Pentecostals in respect of the economy, education, morality, crime, health policy, the acceptance of homosexuality and reduced censorship.

In the suburban areas, it emerged that New Pentecostals are more satisfied (i.e. less dissatisfied) than most others with the economy and standard of living,

Table 5.1. **Township Levels of Dissatisfaction with Different Domains by Religious Group**

Domains	Old Pent.	New Pent.	Mainline Churchgoers	Separatists	Non-Churchgoers
Economy & Standard of living	2,1	2,3	2,5	2,2	2,4
Education	1,5	1,8	2,1	1,9	2,4
Attitudes to work	2,3	2,5	2,6	2,7	2,3
Morality/honesty	2,6	2,9	3,1	2,8	3,0
Crime and safety	2,7	3,2	3,3	2,6	3,1
Religion and Spiritual life	1,8	1,8	1,7	1,9	2,4
Race relations	2,3	2,0	2,2	2,2	2,2
Govt. Political Leaders	2,9	2,9	2,9	2,6	3,3
Health policy	2,3	2,6	3,0	2,6	2,9
Govt. delivery, Performance	3,0	3,1	3,2	2,9	3,4
Changes in Gender rights/Roles	1,7	1,5	1,7	1,6	2,3
More Sexual Openness	1,9	1,8	2,0	2,0	2,1
Willingness to question govt. authority	1,9	2,1	2,2	2,0	2,2
Acceptance of homosexuality	3,0	3,2	2,9	2,8	3,0
Racial equity laws	1,8	1,8	2,0	2,0	1,9
Less censorship	1,9	2,1	2,1	2,0	2,3
Promotion of condoms, teenage birth control	2,0	1,8	1,9	1,9	1,9
Global influences	1,9	2,1	2,0	1,9	2,3

Note: Dissatisfaction maximum=4; minimum=0.

Table 6.2. **Suburban Levels of Dissatisfaction with Different Domains by Religious Group**

Domains	Old Pent.	New Pent.	Mainline Churchgoers	Non-Churchgoers	All Charismatics
Overall	3,5	2,9	3,2	2,9	3,0
Economy, Standard of living	2,7	2,1	2,4	2,1	2,3
Education	2,9	2,5	2,7	2,5	2,5
Attitudes to work	2,7	2,7	2,7	2,4	2,6
Morality/honesty	3,2	3,1	3,2	2,9	3,1
Crime and safety	3,8	3,3	3,5	3,3	3,6
Religion and Spiritual life	2,2	2,6	2,4	2,2	2,4
Race relations	2,6	2,6	2,6	2,4	2,6
Govt. Political Leaders	3,5	2,8	3,1	2,8	3,0
Health policy	3,5	3,1	3,1	3,1	3,2
Govt. delivery, Performance	3,6	3,2	3,2	3,3	3,3
Changes in Gender rights/Roles	1,8	1,9	1,9	1,6	1,8
Sexual Openness	2,3	2,5	2,2	2,0	2,4
Questioning govt. authority	2,3	2,1	2,2	1,9	2,0
Acceptance of homosexuality	2,9	3,1	2,6	2,2	3,0
Racial equity laws, etc.	2,4	2,1	2,2	2,0	2,1
Less censorship	2,7	3,0	2,6	2,1	2,8
Promotion of condoms, teenage birth control	2,5	2,5	2,2	1,6	2,5
Global influences	2,6	2,2	2,0	2,1	2,2

Note: Dissatisfaction maximum=4; minimum=0.

education, political leaders. Conversely, their level of dissatisfaction is higher than that of others in respect of the state of religious and spiritual life in South Africa and the recent changes with regard to sexual openness, homosexuality, censorship and the promotion of condoms for birth control amongst teenagers.

Drawing on a wide range of other statistics in the survey, a preliminary conclusion was that 'Religion trounces politics in the search for the better life'. Findings, both in the townships and in the suburbs, suggested that religion has achieved far more in improving lives and morale than have political programmes and promises in the past few years. Among both black Africans and minorities, but particularly in the black communities, religion has imparted a buoyant mood among the faithful that contrasts significantly with a relatively hesitant mood among non-churchgoers. Both the suburbs and the black areas feel oppressed by crime, the opportunism of politicians and leaders, unemployment and the lack of delivery by government. Nevertheless, personal spheres of life seem to be insulated from these harsher realities. The insulation offered by faith is thinner in the black areas than in the suburbs but it is effective in ensuring overall well being nevertheless. The author perceives that South Africa's over-politicised and quite myopically rationalist media miss this point almost completely.

Religion often stands accused of being 'other worldly' and somehow less than relevant in assessing the state of society. This study shows once again, however, that religious commitment and engagement generates a resource that is highly relevant to coping with the stresses and strains of life. Various aspects of the results show that, if nothing else, the solidarity and support of religious congregations and the emotional resilience and confidence in the future that faith seems to impart are in themselves empowering for people. Furthermore, for significant minorities in all the religious categories, this mindset is at least associated with greater determination, financial savings and better human relations in the workplace or businesses.

The main point being made here is that while the focus on the Pentecostal movement has yielded valuable insights, the more general evidence is that any committed form of faith and collective worship is the key variable. The largest contrasts in the findings reviewed are between people who are religiously active and those who are not, implying that religion is an under-exploited resource.

In the black areas, the most promising findings emerged not among new Pentecostals but among the long-established classical churches. These old Pentecostals, despite material and occupational setbacks in their own lives, show above average or meaningful tendencies like the following:

- A propensity to save money, despite being among the poorest respondents
- An above average commitment to children's education
- Large numbers of close friends within the church community
- A relaxed, trusting and positive attitude to new acquaintances
- A determination to shape their own lives
- A balanced conception of what business success requires
- Despite deep faith, no over-reliance on divine guidance but a clear concept that God helps those who help themselves
- An above average tendency to translate faith into discipline and hard work
- An above average interest in studying and improving themselves.
- An understanding that education is not only about hard skills, but also wisdom and judgement

In many respects they are old-fashioned, have a tendency to integrate ancestors into their religious commitments, and believe in discipline for children. They have intense family commitments. They are not 'progressives' probably because their standards of education are slightly lower than average. They are slightly poorer than the other religious categories, but they have the lowest rate of unemployment of all the categories in the black sample.

They are among the happiest respondents, have the most optimistic beliefs that life will get better. From rather humble stations in life – this category has most poor people, they believe in economic growth, science and technology and self-reliance as routes to success for South Africa. They tend rather less than others to endorse affirmative action and engineered progress for blacks. They also have a keen interest in politics and are a benign – if still reticent – direct influence in shaping national political values.

The new Pentecostals are highest in spiritual capital. Their religious experience is the most intense of all. They are also more altruistic than average and most inclined to believe in good works. They are generally more encapsulated within their religious activity than old Pentecostals and do not have the same level of commitment to shaping their own lives. They tend to hand over to a spiritual agency more than the old Pentecostals, and also emphasise spirituality most in the upbringing of children. Almost inadvertently, their faith gives them self-confidence.

Their social capital and networks are rather weak, however, having less close personal friends than, but similar low levels of involvement in voluntary organisations to, Old Pentecostals. Although they are most dissatisfied with policies and politicians they are also very patient and accepting in their work and lives generally. They enjoy high levels of personal happiness. They do not seem to have the same level of challenge as old Pentecostals, and may tend to be rather too 'other worldly', sheltered by their faith.

The Separatists-Zionists have many of the orientations of the old Pentecostals but have a handicap in that the attraction of their religion is its promise of working miracles and curing illness. Their background in African traditional values and rituals takes them a little too much out of the mainstream of development. What their faith does give them is confidence that they can succeed – in other words abundant spiritual capital. On the other hand, their faith comes a little too close to being a crutch in life.

Analysing the suburban (in contrast to the township) congregations requires a change of gear. Although some 50% of their households have incomes of less than R17 000 a month and are therefore fairly financially constrained, they are worlds apart from the material conditions in the black areas. Hence the issue of socio-economic development is much less pressing. The new Pentecostals are positioned midway between the old Pentecostals and the mainline denominations as regards socio-economic level. They do have more university degrees, however – although not at the rate of the upper middle classes among non-churchgoers.

New Pentecostals are more interested in politics than any other denomination, although they have a tendency not to vote. The new Pentecostals would vote if religiously oriented candidates were to stand. They are however the group most satisfied with trends in the country. This is despite high levels of dissatisfaction with crime, health policies, public morality and government performance generally. Hence their satisfactions tend to derive largely from the economy. This suggests that they are much more materialistic than their overt commitments would suggest. They are also happier than the mainline church members in their personal situations.

As regards the criteria they would adopt in judging progress and a better life for all in South Africa, the new Pentecostals are progressive in that they endorse better education, more generous welfare provision, anti-poverty strategies and affirmative action for previously disadvantaged people. They are inclined to support charity and are cautious about state involvement in social affairs.

They have many friends in their congregations and luxuriate in the warmth of the religious community, but tend to be less trusting of people and cautious with strangers than are the old Pentecostals. Although they value education and express an interest in further education for themselves, they are not exactly burning with ambition to make personal progress. This is because they are so thoroughly captivated by their spiritual rewards. Of all categories in the sample the new Pentecostals are most enmeshed in their relationship to God, which to them is immediate and joyous. Nearly 90% of them have been saved and reborn. The spiritual rewards of their faith tend to dominate their answers to how their lives have been changed by the church. They seem to live in a constant state of spiritual arousal. At the same time, this immersion in the experience of the Spirit seems to impart a confidence and even a determination in their working lives. Similarly to the Hout Bay study[53], 'it is almost as if their spiritual lives release their energy and performance in material things because these things mean so little'. The new Pentecostals have experienced material progress, which they attribute to their faith. Hence in their choices about spending money they include quite a lot of consumer durables and adult 'toys'. They are not ascetics by any stretch of the imagination.

But there are some fairly large contradictions in their lives. Amidst all the warmth, the solidarity within the religious community and their concerns about poverty, inequality and with racial reconciliation, they erect some very hard barriers. Some 70% of them regard inter-race marriage as a form of sin, their relative caution with strangers is another barrier. The moral fortress that they build is the most impregnable barrier of all, and this is a dubious side of the dynamic of intense religious experience among all the religious categories. The new Pentecostals are significantly more puritanical on moral questions than any other denomination, however. Although South Africa desperately needs more moral sanctions on a whole range of behaviours, the new Pentecostals are reminiscent of the morally and socially conservative 'blourokkies' of several decades ago. It is possible that the 'progressive veneer and the expressions of concern about poverty and race relations' amongst New Pentecostals is 'a front to disguise some very hard and judgmental people'.

The research concludes that direct Pentecostal influence in public affairs is likely to remain limited. The likely influence will be indirect and will be associated with the growth of the movement and the interpersonal influence of Pentecostals in everyday community life. In this respect the Pentecostals have 'social capital' in their side. Their friendship and religious networks are dense, and this would make for influence beyond the scope of their numbers. Their self-confidence will also assist in spreading their influence. It may just be realistic to assume that as the influence of liberation politics and the politics of transformation subsides in South Africa, the currently overshadowed influence of the attitudes and values of rank and file Christians and other religious people in South Africa will come to the fore, but from the bottom-up as it were. South African democracy and strategies for development will benefit greatly when this occurs, for example in education, with school governing bodies leading the way. The pronounced interest of new Pentecostals in education suggests that their involvement in this sphere may happen sooner rather than later.

A possible counter-productive tendency might be that religious solidarity becomes the basis for social enclaves, sealed off from the wider society, and with social support within congregations 'deteriorating' into a social crutch, a retreat from the unseemly behaviour of society at large.

Schlemmer expresses the view that religion often stands accused of being 'other worldly' and somehow less than relevant in assessing the state of society. There is always an understandable fear among many intellectuals and decision makers that everyday religion is not sufficiently analytic and strategic to be effective in public life and development in society. This is probably true. This survey provides scant evidence of tough strategic involvement by Pentecostals in their wider communities. What is does show, however, is that religious commitment and engagement generates a resource that is probably more relevant than anything else to coping with the considerable stresses and strains of life in South Africa today. Numerous aspects of the results show that, if nothing else, the solidarity and support within religious congregations and the emotional resilience and confidence in the future that faith seems to impart, are in themselves empowering for people. Furthermore, for significant minorities in all the religious categories, this mindset is at least associated with greater determination, financial savings and better human relations in the workplace or businesses. A cohesive religious movement, therefore, must surely rise in influence, albeit slowly and imperceptibly.

Finally, we conclude that the more general evidence is that any committed form of faith and collective worship is the key variable. The largest contrasts in the findings reviewed were between people who are religiously active and those who are not. Religion is an under-exploited resource in South Africa as it doubtless is in many other countries of the world. Members of the Pentecostal churches specifically may not be the only category relevant to the questions posed in the research programme. Nevertheless, Pentecostals can contribute a great deal. A strengthened form of non-ideological ecumenical association in South Africa and inclusive of mainline, Pentecostal and other denominations can only be good for democracy and development.

Church Visits in Johannesburg

On completion of the formal research interventions in August 2006, four Pentecostal churches were visited in the Johannesburg region. The first visit was to the mega church called Rhema, mentioned earlier. This is a well-known phenomenon operating in the middle class suburbs of the city. Attendance at the 10:00 service on a Sunday entailed walking into a large auditorium which could seat some 3000 to 4000 people, and set amidst other impressive buildings. It is a state of the art auditorium with comfortable seats, carpeted floor, and excellent audiovisual equipment including two very large screens. The auditorium that day was packed with not a seat to spare, and many people

Figure 6.3. Congregants Stream into the 10:15 Sunday Service at Rhema Bible Church.

standing in the doorways. Congregants were overwhelmingly black Africans of all ages, especially parents and their children, somewhat unexpected in the middle of the formerly white northern suburbs of Johannesburg. The attendees were particularly well dressed and many people arrived in expensive motorcars including BMWs, 4x4s and Jaguars. A number of buses had clearly brought people from the poorer formerly black townships some 20 km away.

The service began with about 30 minutes of singing led by two choirs. There were two lead singers – the woman resembled a 'country and western' diva and the man less colourful, with guitar players and other singers on the stage. The first short song was in an African language and the rest of the songs were all in English. Many of the songs were the same as those sung in other Johannesburg churches and in equivalent mega-churches in the United States. The experience for a newcomer was rather like a 'rock concert lite'. After the singing, announcements were made of various initiatives and self-help/ learning groups and activities taking place within the Rhema community over the next week. These ranged from charitable giving and assistance, to membership of an entrepreneurs network to bible study and home cell meetings during the week in member's homes to study and get to know one another. Inspirational messages could be accessed by texting a request by cell phone at a cost of R10 ($1.40). Part of the proceeds of this was to be directed to charitable initiatives. The sermon, given by the founder of the church, Pastor Ray McCauley was the highlight of the service punctuated by a lot of participatory exclamations from members. The essence of his message concerned the need for people to have confidence and to overcome the obstacles they perceive to exist in their life however large. He received the loudest reaction when he identified one of these obstacles as getting out of debt. He said that people should not look back, they had already gone a long way 'out of slavery' and better things were to come. He indicated that with their belief in God and with his help, they could overcome all in their way and that a better future was available to everyone.

The second church visited is one of many located in Hillbrow, a densely populated high-rise inner-city suburb. Until the 1980s the area was home to large numbers of European immigrants and had a continental flair, hosting the city's best bookshop, music store and first all night eatery. Since the late 1980s and as a result of desegregation and other factors affecting the city and its growth, the area now struggles to cope with an influx of much poorer residents, especially from Nigeria and the Francophone countries of central and west Africa, who often live in overcrowded apartments. The streets are not clean and the middle class shops have been replaced by many much smaller establishments catering for a different clientele. The pastor of this church, called the Harvest Bible Church, has the title 'Bishop'. He is an immigrant from Malawi who had 'planted' the church seven years previously

Figure 6.4. One of the Dozens of Inner-City Pentecostal Churches in Johannesburg.

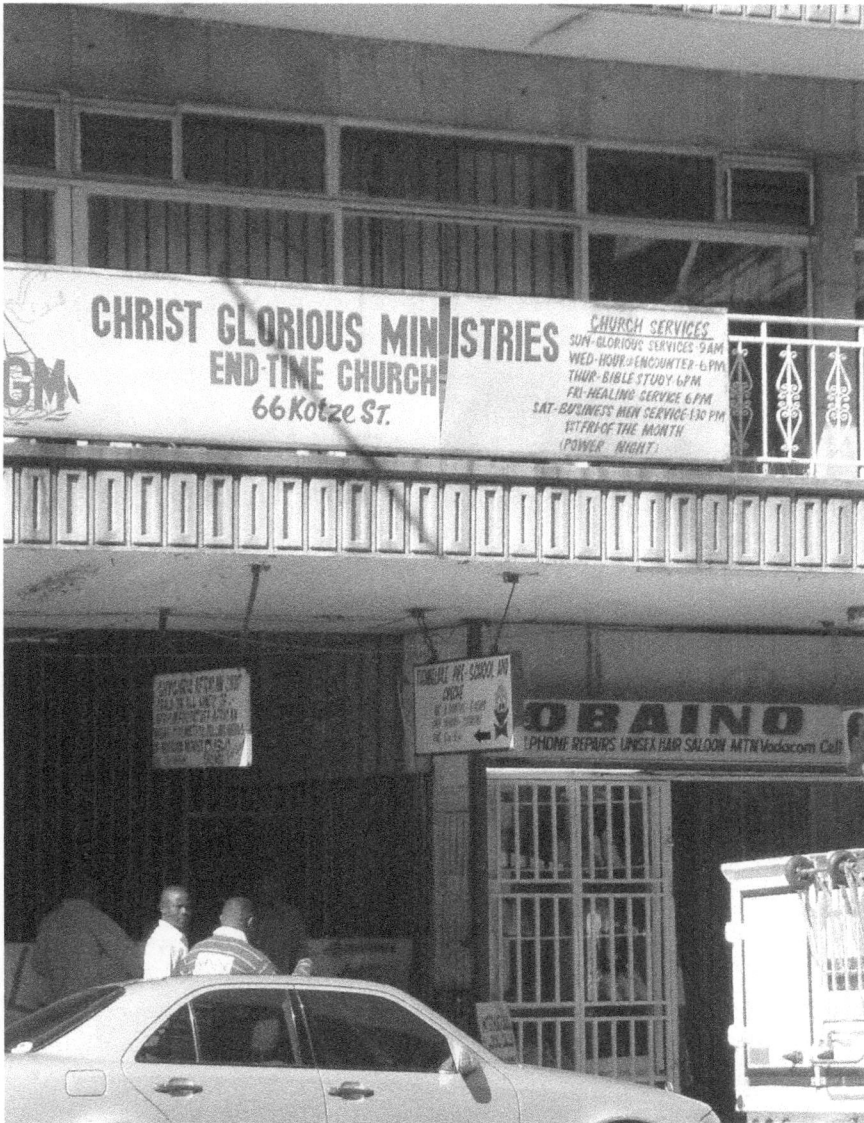

in response to the request of a woman whom he had helped. The congregation had grown sufficiently so to effect fundamental change in his life. Initially he had shared a small apartment across the road from the church but now he lived in a middle class suburb located 10–15 minutes drive from the church. His children attend a private school located close to the church and run by a Pentecostal Christian. His church meets in a formal building, next to a grand Lutheran church, and he claimed to have a growing congregation. His services are in English and his pastoral work covers many areas including: finding jobs for congregants in an area where unemployment exceeds 30%; talking about HIV/AIDS and sending people to the city clinic across the road for anti-retroviral treatment. Asked about the issues of abortion and gay relationships, he said that these were not sermon topics but points of private discussion with people who had problems in these areas. He further indicated that the previously rampant crime in the area had declined noticeably since the establishment of the church.

The third field trip consisted of a visit to Soweto, the sprawling Johannesburg township of well over 1 million people. The pastor lives in a new area on the western periphery. He and his wife (a fellow pastor in the church) live in a brick-walled and modestly furnished four-roomed house. A large poster of Martin Luther King making his *I have a Dream* speech adorns his lounge wall. His congregation of 200 has purchased land for a new church building and auditorium to hold 20,000 people. The optimism involved in this purchase was especially striking in view of the fact that his church had recently suffered a break away from one of its members deciding to lead a large number of congregants out and start a new church. As with the other pastors visited, the message conveyed is that the Lord and the church empowers individuals with the capacity to take control of their own lives. A particular feature of this church was that a Bishop in the USA had laid hands on the local Bishop at his consecration. The pastor suggested that this had established a link with the 'apostolic succession' claimed by Catholics and Anglicans. Unlike most Pentecostal churches, this one makes use of clerical vestments similar to those used by the mainline sacramental churches.

The fourth church visited, Global Harvest Church, is located in Tembisa, a township located east of Johannesburg. The pastor had grown up in a family that belonged to the Methodist church[54]. In the late 1980s he was born again and studied to become a Pentecostal pastor. He resigned from his job in 1994 and began working as a pastor of eight people in a fulltime capacity. He used his retirement package to buy the church currently used, and although the area was considered unsafe, he believed it was the right place. Prior to purchasing the building he preached from an office building, neighbouring other churches that continue to preach from there. He purchased the building and land for R100,000 ($14,000) and the church moved to the new location in 2001. The congregation now comprises over 350 people, mainly Tembisa residents in the 17–35 year age group. Unemployment is very high in the area (approximately 80%) but according to the pastor, it is lower among church members (60–70%). Employment is promoted but, given limited job opportunities, many members may only be given contract/temporary work and members are encouraged to tithe and to live within their means. Music appears to be central to the church with two organs, drums and guitars available for playing at services. Home visits appeared to be utilised initially to expand the membership base and members are encouraged to share their experiences of being reborn with the community. The pastor works closely with the local police force and visits prisoners on a weekly basis. He is involved with TEASA (The Evangelical Alliance of South Africa), and attends weekly meetings with approximately 30 pastors to discuss issues of relevance and challenges facing the churches.

Prior to accepting membership at the church, potential members are given an opportunity to meet with the pastor, who explains membership requirements and presents each new member with a membership booklet. A key requirement for membership is that members denounce ancestral beliefs and commit themselves to refrain from participation in related practices. The pastor explained that certain traditional rituals require full family participation and when he had moved to the Pentecostal movement, this proved to be a source of conflict between him and his family because of his refusal to engage in these practices.

The church's opposition to the practices of promiscuity, homosexuality and abortion are clearly explained to potential members. With regard to HIV/AIDS, the church opposes government's view on condoms and instead promotes abstinence (shifting focus on government's national anti- AIDS campaign, A (abstinence) B (be faithful) C represents Christ rather than condoms). The area in which he works is plagued by a high crime rate but he has not been affected by this. He stated that pastors should visit the prisons to determine which of their congregation members are involved in crime and to take an active role in their rehabilitation.

The pastor indicated that he is prepared to 'lay hands' on members to pray for healing from HIV/AIDS but he is aware of the limitations in this respect. He said that counselling is provided and that they offer services at clinics that provide counselling and encourage a move towards religion for HIV/AIDS patients. He actively promotes the church's views on monogamy and abstinence prior to marriage in the hope that it will play a role in prevention, however, counselling is provided given the extent of the pandemic. He chooses to avoid public discussions on AIDS so as not to make HIV positive members feel uncomfortable. At a subsequent workshop with CDE researchers, the pastor responded to a question on how he dealt with sin by saying that he left it to visiting preachers, effectively sub-contracting that part of the 'business' to others. His aspiration is to grow the church and encourage suitable members to assume careers in the field. Once they are educated he hopes to erect tents throughout the township that will act as satellite churches, once again building a membership base as he did through home visits. He is optimistic about the future of his church and of the Pentecostal movement in the area.

Conclusions

The emerging picture is that growth in the numbers of Pentecostal and Charismatic Christians is indeed having an impact in the social, political and economic spheres. The movement away from a degree of marginalisation in the African Independent churches and an element of 'nominalism' in the mainline churches appears to result in higher levels of self-confidence and less fatalism. However, the extent and depth of the impact on the wider society is not clear. Further analysis of the data will have to be cautious in drawing conclusions on the basis of interviews with respondents who would generally have been disposed towards exaggerating the positive elements of their faith and religious experiences.

Nevertheless, significant impact has been discerned in respect of at the very minimum, a theoretical commitment to honesty, reliability and moral responsibility in relation to sex, money and politics. This emerges even through the lenses of researchers who appear already to have applied a healthy dose of cynicism to their findings. Admittedly, pro-active engagement with critical challenges in the country does not feature strongly in the findings. Nevertheless, there is evidence of social capital upon which the religious faithful can draw as a means of dealing with the pervasive pathologies in South African society to the extent that these affect their personal lives. Such social capital is not something that can easily be generated by state intervention and the state would therefore be well advised to promote and encourage the growth of the Pentecostal movement and the religious sector in general.

In February 2006 the then South African president and his Finance Minister declared that the country had now entered 'the age of hope'[55]. They were referring to the economic situation and the prospects for increased growth and development of South Africa's society and population. It is striking that one of the strongest themes coming through from this research is the message of hope that is being preached by Pentecostal pastors and reported back by the many congregants. Many African Pentecostals live in communities that are wrestling with very violent crime; extraordinarily high levels of unemployment; and a wide range of social challenges from dysfunctional families to teenage pregnancy and abuse of women. In this context the message of hope and the all-embracing nature of Pentecostal beliefs and approach are all the more remarkable and potentially interesting in terms of their unintended consequences for the individual and communities involved. Preliminary analysis of the data raises several important questions.

Is South Africa experiencing a dramatic growth in the numbers of Pentecostals? Will this be sustained into the future? Can their influence – direct and indirect, intended and unintended – be distinguished from that of other religious groups in what is a deeply Christian country? If they are starting to have a profound impact why is South Africa still such a violent country?

According to a number of different surveys South Africa scores way behind many other developed and developing countries with respect to the levels of entrepreneurship in the population. Apartheid was a system that prevented Africans (and other minority black groups) from developing their entrepreneurial skills and exploiting opportunities for business. A notable feature of the growth of the Pentecostal churches is their entrepreneurial character. Is this one of the outlets for entrepreneurial energy in the country? Why is it taking this form and what does it mean? As more opportunities open up for black South Africans will these Pentecostal entrepreneurs find other outlets for their talents? Will this entrepreneurial approach lead their congregants into more effective participation in the economy – through creating enterprises themselves, or finding jobs more readily?

There seems to be evidence that as African South Africans move to the cities, they start to move away from the AIC type churches and into Pentecostal churches. Will Pentecostal type churches hold large numbers of Africans as they in turn start to become more settled urban dwellers and their prospects improve? Perhaps that is where the mega-churches come in. That as some black South Africans move from the townships to the better off suburbs there is an increasing inclination to attend a church like Rhema and associate with a lot of people who are better off. And even if you can't yet move into the more peaceful, settled formerly white world of suburbia however modest, you can at least go to church in those areas and associate with people from the materially more secure world to which you aspire.

Pentecostal religious belief appears to encourage a sense of agency in its participants. The message in different ways is – you can do it; you can change your own life, you can improve your life. This is a different message from that conveyed in other sectors since South Africa's democratic transition. The ruling party and government has emphasised 'delivery' by government, what the state must do for citizens. Even they are now getting worried about a growing sense of entitlement among citizens and communities. Too many South Africans seem to perceive their role as that of waiting for government to deliver with far less emphasis on what it is that citizens should be doing for themselves. Are the Pentecostals a force promoting a different set of attitudes that encourage poor people to take charge of their own lives and not wait for every aspect of 'delivery' from an overstretched state?

One of the intriguing possibilities emerging from the research is that participants in Pentecostal churches are gaining new skills, such as in starting churches and running and participating in the different activities – from the most basic administrative skills to people management skills. In addition many of the churches talk of offering processes or workshops where the intention is to impart basic skills such as where to look for a job and how to respond in a job interview. Similar findings emerged in the Latin American research. This is an area of potential in a developing country whose education system is struggling to deliver for the poor and where the formal economy is not generating enough jobs for low skilled people. Many poor people live in households whose members have never had a formal job other than manual labour.

One of the signal achievements of the democratic government in South Africa has been its macro-economic policy and the strict fiscal discipline that has been in place now for over ten years. In this context it is interesting to reflect on the research where it is being suggested that the process of tithing by church members leads to a greater discipline with respect to the rest of their money. The extent to which fiscal discipline occurs amongst congregants of different sorts of churches or is peculiar to Pentecostals will need further examination.

The ruling African National Congress (ANC) has a worldview that has been shaped by its years in exile, alliance with the communist party, funding from the USSR when it still existed and a generally Marxist leftist approach. From this base there is growing and legitimate concern, within the ruling alliance on the need for 'better' values among South Africa's population. Their response to exposure of corruption or unbelievably violent crime is to exhort people to behave differently – comrades in the struggle shouldn't behave like this. In this context it is of real interest to see the strong emphasis of the Pentecostals on traditional family values, abstinence from alcohol and extra or pre-marital sex, better relations with relatives, and talking rather than violence as a means of dispute resolution. Similar observations were previously made in respect of the independent Zionist Christian Church[56] such that the personal moral discipline of members and their resistance to being side tracked by energy sapping social habits make them ideal employees. Whether from black or suburban areas, they are bound to make more progress in their jobs than employees at large. Could it be that the most active promoters of 'the new South African man' are to be found in neighbourhood Pentecostal churches rather than within the ANC branches?

South Africa has one of the most liberal constitutions in the world and is very proud of its new freedoms. There are intriguing questions about the extent to which the tremendous diversity within the world of Pentecostal churches encourages and reflects commitment to freedom of speech and freedom of religious activity and how Pentecostal pastors might react were the country's democratic rights ever to be threatened in a way that affected religious pluralism.

South Africa is a rapidly urbanising society with many African South Africans still caught up in the process of rural to urban migration, often landing up in informal settlements and little chance of a job. Within this context of change and uncertainty the role of Pentecostal churches in promoting the break with traditional African values and traditions as they relate to the ancestors and beliefs in spirits is potentially important. Are these churches facilitating agencies in the transition to modern life? What does this mean for the prospects of these individuals and their families? If joining Pentecostal churches involves a break with the rest of an extended family, does this help Pentecostal members to get ahead without less conscientious family members continually draining their resources. It may be that encapsulation in a Pentecostal worldview is a means of encouraging accumulation for nuclear families or individuals, often weighed down by the enormous demands of large extended family or even village or regional ties?

Pentecostal churches are often 'bottom up' phenomena. An individual decides to 'plant' a church and then has to attract congregants to his church. The pastor is frequently accountable to that local community and should they disapprove of his words or activities or the church's use of tithes and offerings, they are free to leave at any time. The entrepreneurial nature of the 'movement' means that at any time, a particular pastor could suffer a schism in his local community where a future pastor and his followers leave a church and start another one. This is a very direct form of local accountability which raises interesting questions about the consequences of this experience for the communities and individuals involved. Does this translate into the political sphere? Could it? Can these local level churches start to form – in David Martin's phrase – the 'little platoons of democracy'[57] where they start to apply principles of local accountability to local politicians or MPs for example?

There is much talk in South Africa of what communities and individuals can do to combat crime. In this context it was striking to find that many of the pastors interviewed want to be involved in crime prevention and see the church as having an active role to play. This may take the form of talking to the local police captain every week or asking the police to come and talk to members of the congregation or finding out to which church offenders belong, there are a range of strategies being discussed and applied. However, public officials and business leader in South Africa seldom mention these communities or the group of pastors as possible resources in combating crime.

In sum then, South Africa's public debates appear to be influenced by secular concerns, often surprisingly directly shaped by the concerns and priorities of politically correct elites living in America or Europe. The front page headlines are moulded by immediate issues that range from political succession battles within the ANC to crime and violence or government policy.

This research project has opened up a world of activity and energy and entrepreneurship of an unusual kind to an otherwise well informed South African think tank. Flying under the radar screens of the political, intellectual, academic and media classes are a large number of individuals and institutions that are actively concerned about and working on questions of values, personal behaviour, family life, personal responsibility and freedom to act, unemployment, skills creation and a range of other national concerns. For a very religious country[58] public exposure to or engagement with religious issues is remarkably underplayed. The country might have considerably more social capital in existence and in formation than any politician or intellectual can imagine.

Political leaders often talk about an African Renaissance. Is it possible that this renaissance will be driven by the entrepreneurial and moral energies of a burgeoning Pentecostal 'movement' with greater effect than by the politicians? Or to put it another way, can the efforts of the politicians to create sustainable democratic politics and more effective enabling environments for business activity be considerably bolstered by the little platoons or enclaves of local civic religious and other activities encouraged by the Pentecostals?

Two questions arise: should the state be interested in Pentecostalism and, if so, what should it do? Given the possibility of positive behavioural and social change, the state should be interested in the Pentecostal movement. But its role should be to tread lightly. The main attraction for the government's development agenda is Pentecostalism's powerful effect in stopping deleterious individual behaviour and reconstituting the family unit. Not only is this aligned with the state's interests in development and social well-being but Pentecostalism is more successful at mending the social fabric than any state intervention.

The state cannot create sustainable economic growth. The best it can do is to manage the market to allow its citizens the opportunity to buy, sell, save, open businesses, innovate and prosper, but a country's people need enough personal responsibility, individual agency, and optimism to engage in this economic behaviour. However, traditional hierarchical social networks, as well as the disempowering effects of the psychology of apartheid, mean that many South Africans have passive attitudes to their own personal success. Pentecostalism seems to be able to reach where the state cannot by teaching people to adopt a sense of ownership and agency in their lives. Pentecostalism also complements the state's goals for economic development.

The Pentecostal movement can support the government's macro-level development programme by providing micro-level interventions in people's attitudes and family life. Not only are these interventions more successful than state attempts, but Pentecostalism seems to be able to reach deeper into shaping human motivations and ambitions than the secular non-totalitarian state is able to do. This does not, of course, mean that the state should incorporate

Pentecostal interventions into its own programme of action, but neither should Pentecostal churches be showered with money to facilitate their work. State aid to Pentecostal churches will upset the delicate ecosystem in which these institutions have evolved. It is surely not coincidental that they are both the most 'market-orientated' of religions, in that they see themselves as providing a service for which there is great need, and that they have such a profound ability to shape people's attitudes and behaviours. The strong norms around tithing show how the relationship between church and congregant is not that of a public service, but takes the form of a principal-agent relationship: Pentecostal churches provide the kind of salvation that people want precisely because religious 'consumers' can choose between hundreds of suppliers and without customers they will perish. State aid to churches could result in their 'capture' as they become more concerned with serving their paymaster, the state. This will remove the churches' incentives to produce the beneficial social outcomes that may have encouraged the state to get involved in the first place.

Notes

1 This paper is based primarily on a series of workshops and research papers commissioned and edited by the Centre for Development and Enterprise. The contributors were Stephen Rule, Tim Clynick, Lawrence Schlemmer, Tony Balcomb, Riaan Ingram, Attie van Niekerk, Bill Domeris and Paul Germond.

2 Martin, 1990.

3 Gaiya, 2002.

4 http://www.pewforum/surveys/pentecostal/africa

5 See http://encyclopedia.thefreedictionary.com 4th January 2006 and http://www.victorious.org/sprgifts.htm 2nd January 2006. Dale A. Robbins traces the writing of the early church father Irenaeus (ca. 130–202): '...we hear many of the brethren in the church who have prophetic gifts, and who speak in tongues through the spirit, and who also bring to light the secret things of men for their benefit [word of knowledge]' he continues 'When God saw it necessary, and the church prayed and fasted much, they did miraculous things, even of bringing back the spirit to a dead man' and of similar incidents recorded by Tertullian (ca. 155–230), Origen (ca. 182–251), Eusebius (ca. 275–339), and Chrysostom (ca. 347–407)

6 http://encyclopedia.thefreedictionary.com. 6 January 2006. The revival commenced in the home of Edward Lee (312 Azusa Street, Los Angeles), who experienced what he felt to be an infilling of the Holy Spirit in a new way during a prayer meeting. The attending pastor, William J. Seymour, also claimed that he was overcome with the Holy Spirit on three days later. The Los Angeles Times (April 18, 1906) ran a front page story on the movement.

7 http://encyclopedia.thefreedictionary.com. 23 December 2005. The Rev. Dennis Bennett, an American Episcopalian (Rector of St Marks, Van Nuys California) received the blessing of the Holy Spirit in 1960, leading to numerous seminars and workshops on the Holy Spirit in Vancouver and elsewhere. A key figure in the Catholic Church was Fr Kevin Ranaghan from Indiana. The movement was soon firmly established throughout the English-peaking world causing a major revival in the UK, Australia and South Africa.

8 Anderson, 2000.
9 LaPoorta, 1996.
10 Republic of South Africa, Census 2001.
11 A Anderson, 1992.
12 Following the nomenclature of Daneel, 1971, p. 285.
13 Domeris, 1999, cf. pp 42–57.
14 Alberts & Chikane, (eds), 1991.
15 McCauley in Steele, 1996.
16 Chikane, Foreword, in Alberts & Chikane (eds), 1991, p. 10.
17 Anderson, 1992, pp 129–158.
18 Sunday Times, March 30th, 1997.
19 See the work of Pretorius & Jafta, 1997, pp 21–226; also Anderson, 1992, pp 129–133.
20 For a review of the literature and an argument for distinguishing Zionists from Pentecostals see Frahm-Arp, 2001, pp 43–60.
21 Becken, 1993.
22 Garner, 2000.
23 http://www.gbcsoweto.org.za
24 http://www.universalark.com
25 Berger, 2004.
26 Berger, op. cit.
27 Shah, 2003.
28 Berger, op cit.
29 Berger, op cit.
30 Harvey Cox quoted in Gifford, 2004.
31 Gifford, op. cit.
32 Martin, 1990, p. 278.
33 Gifford, op. cit.
34 Martin, p. 284.
35 Martin, p. 218.
36 Martin, pp 231–232.
37 Johnson et al, 2002.
38 The first phase of the research resulted in papers by Domeris; Germond & de Gruchy; Bonner, Moloi & Dlulane; Ingram, Mathebula, Mokoena & van Niekerk; and Schlemmer & Bot.
39 Domeris, 1999.
40 Schlemmer & Bot, 2004.
41 Ingram et al, 2004.
42 Bonner et al, 2004.
43 Berger, 2004. Guatemala has the highest percentage of new Protestants, most of them Pentecostals, in Latin America – between a quarter and a third of the population.
44 The papers were written by Balcomb; Clynick & Moloi; Domeris & Germond; Ingram; Schlemmer; van Niekerk, Murray & Mokoena. The findings are summarised in CDE's March 2008 publication *Under the Radar: Pentecostalism in South Africa and its potential social and economic role*. Other resulting publications are *Faith and development: a global perspective* (summary of a lecture presented by Professor Peter Berger at the launch of Under the Radar) and *Faith on the Move: Pentecostalism and its potential contribution to development* (proceedings of a CDE workshop held on the topic in March 2008).
45 Balcomb, 2005.
46 Ingram, 2006.

47 AIDS was discussed in most, but not all, interviews. As the interviewers used an ad hoc, unstructured approach to elicit cooperation and honesty, there were no specific questions on AIDS or any other issue that were asked in all interviews.
48 Analysis by Christopher Claassen, CDE researcher, 2006.
49 van Niekerk et al, 2006.
50 Clynick, 2006.
51 Clynick, op. cit.
52 Schlemmer, 2006.
53 Schlemmer, 2004.
54 Analysis by Nicky Trope, CDE researcher, 2006.
55 ANC Today, http://www.anc.org.za/ancdocs/anctoday/2006/at06.htm, vol. 6, no. 6, 17th February 2006. Online voice of the African National Congress.
56 Schlemmer, 2006.
57 Martin, op. cit.
58 More than half of South African adults claim to attend church once a week or more.

References

Allan Anderson, 1992. *Bazalwane: African Pentecostals in South Africa*, UNISA: Pretoria.
Allan Anderson, 2000. *Zion and Pentecost: the spirituality and experience of Pentecostal and Zionist/Apostolic churches in South Africa*, Pretoria: University of Pretoria Press.
Attie van Niekerk, Montagu Murray & Lehasa Mokoena, 2006. *Views of Politicians and Social Activists from a Charismatic and Pentecostal background*. CDE Commissioned Paper.
Byron Johnson, Ralph Brett Tompkins and Derek Webb, 2002. *Objective hope: Assessing the effectiveness of faith-based organisations: A review of the literature*, University of Pennsylvania: Center for Research on Religion and Urban Civil Society.
Centre for Development and Enterprise, 2008a. *Under the Radar: Pentecostalism in South Africa and its potential social and economic role*. CDE In Depth no. 7.
Centre for Development and Enterprise, 2008b. *Faith and development: a global perspective*, Lecture presented by Peter Berger, Johannesburg, March 2008.
Centre for Development and Enterprise, 2008c. *Faith on the move: Pentecostalism and its potential contribution to development*, proceedings of CDE workshop, March 2008.
David Martin, 1990. *Tongues of Fire: the explosion of Protestantism in Latin America*. Oxford: Basil Blackwell.
Frank Chikane, Foreword, in L Alberts & F Chikane (eds), *The Road to Rustenburg: The Church looking forward to a new South Africa*. Cape Town: Struik Christian Books, 1991.
H Pretorius & L Jafta, 1997. 'A Branch springs out': African Initiated Churches in R Elphick & R Davenport (eds), *Christianity in South Africa; A political, social and cultural history*. Oxford: James Currey, 21–226.
Hans-Jürgen Becken, 1993. *Beware of the Ancestor Cult! A challenge to missiological research in South Africa*, Missionalia (2), 333–339.
Japie J LaPoorta, 1996. *Unity or division? The unity struggles of the Black churches within the Apostolic Faith Mission of South Africa*. Kuils River: Japie LaPoorta.
Jonathan Crush, Wade Pendleton & Daniel Tevera, 2005. *Degrees of uncertainty: Students and the brain drain in Southern Africa*, Southern African migration project.
K M Frahm-Arp, 2001. *Problematising Pentecostalism: towards understanding a modern religious movement in South Africa*, MA Thesis, Johannesburg: University the Witwatersrand, pp 43–60.

Lawrence Schlemmer & Monica Bot, 2004. *Faith, Social Consciousness and progress: a case study of members of the Pentecostal, African Zionist and other churches in Hout Bay, South Africa*. CDE Commissioned Paper.

Lawrence Schlemmer, 2004. *Memorandum: Religion and Development in South Africa*, CDE.

Lawrence Schlemmer, 2006. *The wider impact of Faith: An investigation among members of Pentecostal and other denominations in Gauteng*. CDE Commissioned Paper.

Louw Alberts and Frank Chikane, (eds), *The road to Rustenburg: The Church looking forward to a new South Africa*, Cape Town: Struik, 1991.

M L Daneel, 1971. *Old and new in Southern Shona Independent Churches* Volume 1, Mouton: The Hague.

Musa A.B. Gaiya, July 2002. *The Pentecostal revolution in Nigeria*. Occasional Paper, Centre of African Studies, University of Copenhagen.

Paul Germond & Steven de Gruchy, 2001. *Review of the literature on the social contribution of African-initiated churches (AICs) in South Africa*. CDE Commissioned Paper.

Paul Gifford, 2004. *Pentecostalism and public life*, Keynote presentation: Pentecostal-civil society dialogue, October 18 2004, Lagos, Nigeria.

Peter Berger, 2004. 'Max Weber is alive and well and living in Guatemala: The Protestant ethic today', Paper prepared for conference, *The norms, beliefs, and institutions of 21st-century capitalism: Celebrating Max Weber's the Protestant ethic and the spirit of capitalism*, Ithaca, NY, 8 October 2004.

Phil Bonner, Tshepo Moloi & Godfrey Dlulane, 2004. *Faith for Development: Provisional report on Pentecostal churches in Tembisa and Katlehong*. CDE Commissioned Paper.

Ray McCauley in Ron Steele, *Power and Passion: Fulfilling God's Destiny for the Nation*, Cape Town: Struik Christian Books, 1996.

Republic of South Africa, Census 2001.

Riaan Ingram, 2006. *The Social, Economic, Political and Personal Potential of Pentecostalism*. CDE Commissioned Paper.

Riaan Ingram, Hudson Mathebula, Lehasa Mokoena & Attie van Niekerk, 2004. *The impact of Pentecostalism on society, with special reference to their impact on black economic empowerment, Witbank, a case study*. CDE Commissioned Paper.

Robert C.Garner, 2000. 'Religion as a source of social change in the new South Africa', *Journal of Religion in Africa* 30 (3), 310–343.

Stephen Rule, 2007. Religiosity and quality of life in South Africa. *Social Indicators Research* 81 (2), 417–434.

Sunday Times, March 30th, 1997.

Timothy Clynick & Tshepo Moloi, 2006. *Anointed for business: South African 'new' Pentecostals in the marketplace*. CDE Commissioned Paper.

Timothy Samuel Shah, Evangelical politics in the third world: What's next for the 'next Christendom'?, *The Brandywine review of faith and international affairs*, Fall 2003, 21–30.

Tony Balcomb, 2005. *Interviews with South African Pentecostal pastors and leaders – Analysis and Impressions*. CDE Commissioned Paper.

William Domeris, 1999. *The church and the spirit of entrepreneurism: A study of selected Christian communities in South Africa*. CDE Commissioned Paper.

William R Domeris & Paul Germond, 2006. *Pentecostal/Charismatic Christianity – A South African Survey*. CDE Commissioned Paper.

Websites

http://encyclopedia.thefreedictionary.com

http://www.anc.org.za/ancdocs/anctoday/2006/at06.htm, ANC Today, vol. 6, no. 6, 17th February 2006, online voice of the African National Congress.

http://www.gbcsoweto.org.za

http://www.pewforum.org/surveys/pentecostal/africa, Overview: Pentecostalism in Africa.

http://www.universalark.com

http://www.victorious.org/sprgifts.htm

Chapter 7

IMPORTING SPIRITUAL CAPITAL: EAST–WEST ENCOUNTERS AND CAPITALIST CULTURES IN EASTERN EUROPE AFTER 1989

János Mátyás Kovács

...of the last stage of this cultural development, it might well be truly said: 'Specialists without spirit, sensualists without heart; this nullity imagines that it has attained a level of civilization never before achieved'. (Max Weber)

This paper is my latest attempt in a series at comprehending the spirit of new capitalism in Eastern Europe. In contrast to a widespread view according to which this spirit is extremely weak, I will suggest that its real strength cannot be discovered if one a.) looks for it only in the delicate and airy forms of economic culture; b.) focuses exclusively on the anti-capitalist legacy of communist economic culture, ignoring its pro-capitalist heritage; c.) disregards a large-scale borrowing of economic cultures from the West during the past two decades.

First the thesis of 'spiritless capitalism' will be discussed. Then, I will introduce the concepts of 'soft culture' and 'implicit spirituality', as well as sketching up the road that led me to a research project on transnational cultural encounters in the economies of Eastern Europe. In the second half of the paper, one of the project's core empirical studies, which has been made in the heart of the 'emerging markets', banking, will be revisited to test the applicability of the notion of spiritual capital in secular societies of the region. In contrast to the assumption of a lack of capitalist spirit, one witnesses a veritable pro-capitalist cultural revolution unfolding in a major field of the post-communist economies, even if its results seem rather fragile for the time being.

1. Spiritless Capitalism?

Let us imagine for a moment a continent with a short supply of spirituality. Religion is almost lacking, philosophy, ethics and aesthetics have declined, and the inhabitants cultivate only a few popular myths, primitive historical legends and ancient superstitions. Their worldview and everyday choices are instinctive and capricious, reflecting a fundamentally instrumentalist/secular attitude to life. Spontaneous relativism and social anomie prevail. The inhabitants speak the language of a kind of deserted, hollow post-modernity – and they speak it with a post-communist accent.

In fact, the self-appointed guardians of civilization in Eastern Europe have always liked to use the metaphor of a continent that, following a desperate struggle for protecting *the* European values against both communist barbarism and American-style capitalism, may sink in a cultural vacuum. Prior to that, it will inevitably lose its traditional spirituality and suffer from a decay of civilization for a long time. This *Untergang der Morgenlandes* will reveal a chaos of languishing values, habits and sentiments until culture as such disappears. Frequently, this prediction is accompanied by a whole series of jeremiads, nostalgic references to the 'good old days' or a demonization of the current state of humankind hit by globalization, misled by old-fashioned nationalists or neoliberal zealots, and inundated by junk culture[1]. Accordingly, under post-communism culture has been reduced to economic culture, the poorest form of culture in terms of spirituality, unless one considers a desperate pursuit of a rough and merciless version of economic rationality as a spiritual exercise.

Eastern Europe has no comfortable place in current history-writing if it comes to cultural/spiritual issues. Originally, the above master narrative was based on the proverbial dichotomy of the *Homo Sovieticus* reflecting the quintessence of communist culture on the one hand, and the non-communist, 'European-oriented' dissenter on the other. After 1989, this narrative could be harmonized less and less with the fact of a rapid and successful economic transformation in many countries of the region unless one referred to the revival of pre-communist capitalist cultures, and a kind of neoliberal conspiracy. The two together were supposed to suppress (not eradicate) Soviet-type culture, and – as collateral damage – also that part of 'European' culture, represented by the dissenters, which challenged 'worshipping the market' and had something to do with the spirit of equality and fraternity as well as other beauties of civic culture.

In the light of these new arguments, the most successful among the 'transforming countries' of Eastern Europe at the turn of the millennium had also been the most advanced before World War II. In a way, the frontrunners in the 1940s managed to keep their advantages under communism, and raised a minor neoliberal-minded elite in the last minutes of Soviet rule which, with strong help from their Western allies, introduced capitalism following the 1989 revolutions. Because the people at large and the anti-communist dissenters had mixed feelings about the neoliberal scenario of the transformation, this elite implemented the change in the framework of a 'reform dictatorship' that overpowered the traditionally 'European-oriented' dissenters by 'American-style' strategies of development (cf. the conflict between Václav Klaus and Václav Havel in the Czech Republic).

As regards the countries that had been less advanced prior to the communist takeover in the last century, they allegedly conserved their backwardness for many decades under communism, and follow the historical path of economic stagnation, state intervention, *democradura*, ethno-nationalism and the like after the collapse of the Soviet empire. By and large, goes the argument, the current fault line between the fast and slow (liberal and illiberal) transformers corresponds to the secular cleavage between Western and Eastern Christianity. Both alternatives of post-communist change have neuralgic points. To put it simply, fast liberalization leads to social crisis while the lack of it results in neo-authoritarian regimes. The former leads to the revival while the latter contributes to the survival of *Homo Sovieticus*. The former has happened in East-Central Europe, i.e., on the Western side of the civilizational cleavage, and the latter in 'real' Eastern as well as South-Eastern Europe, i.e., on the Eastern side of it[2].

This extension of the original narrative of spiritless capitalism has a number of weak points that arise from the strict assumptions concerning historical continuity between pre- and post-communism, and the geographical pattern of the postulated civilizational cleavage. There are too many exceptions to the rule. In addition, the dubious stereotype of *Homo Sovieticus* still looms large in the argument, and the impact of the West upon Eastern European economic cultures is specified in a horrendously simplistic way. It is suggested, especially by the Cultural Studies literature, that in the encounter between the East and the West, the worst features of the two worlds tend to combine with each other, leading to what is widely called 'Wild-Eastern capitalism'[3].

Many of those analysts who, right after 1989, celebrated the return of Eastern Europe as a whole to the West and the emergence of certain models of capitalism, in particular, the small-scale and/or welfare-oriented ones, in the region, lament the roughness of post-communist capitalism today. In their view, the region is just another victim of a global (post-colonial) decay of culture, the only difference being that the previous colonizer, the Soviet empire had also left its traces on the cultural universe of the region.

Allegedly, in that universe the Soviet legacy of mistrust, lack of solidarity, rule-bending, illegal business-making, corruption and the like paves the way for a direct transition to reckless rivalry, social polarization and lawlessness under global (American) capitalism today. Many of the former communist apparatchiks have become business tycoons, converting political domination under communism into economic power under new capitalism. From the Schumpeterian words 'creative destruction' they opt for the latter, showing no compassion with the losers of the post-communist transformation and preferring short-term enrichment to social cohesion, industrial democracy, corporate social responsibility and the like. While some of the small entrepreneurs in the informal sector of the planned economy have also turned into capitalists, at the other pole of society there remained large masses of helpless, passive, lazy – 'Oriental' – subordinates who have not had a chance to become Western-type citizens, i.e., members of the civil society.

A Counter-Narrative?

One would presume that the economists could not remain silent upon hearing such apocalyptic warnings from a large array of intellectuals including not only artists, historians and human scientists but also representatives of harder social sciences, many of whom find powerful allies in the new political parties. Interestingly enough, the above stylized narrative has not been confronted yet by a similarly compact counter-narrative based on the economic success story of post-communist transformation. In principle, that narrative might emphasize the spiritual aspects of rational economic behavior and the 'beauties' of the market[4] in order to counterbalance the thesis of spiritless capitalism. Instead, some economists take a determinist approach, and expect the new economic cultures to emerge from the success almost automatically. They put their faith in a simple feedback mechanism, contending that the takeover of Western institutions will unavoidably modify the norms, habits, values, etc. of the economic actors, and produce development that will justify, in retrospect, the change of institutions. Most economists, however, tend to ignore the horror scenario of inevitable spiritual decay by saying in an indifferent and irreverent mood: 'perhaps, it is not too bad to revitalize the distant past, emulate the West, and sink in a cultural vacuum if those give birth to our Eastern European 'small tigers'[5] with brilliant growth rates, marvelous market indicators and comprehensive institutional change'.

It is rather difficult to enchant the economists by historical/cultural explanations because they see that the post-communist success stories in the economy tend to intersect those (primarily ethnic/national and religious) boundaries which served for a long time as important explanatory variables in making distinctions between 'modern' and 'backward', 'liberal' and 'conservative' as well as 'Western-style' and 'Eastern-style' societal regimes (pre-communist, communist and post-communist alike) in the region. No matter if a given country of Eastern Europe belongs to the sphere of Western or Eastern Christianity, lies closer to or farther from the West, had a more or less advanced capitalist society before, and more or less radical market reforms under communism, was more or less deeply imbued with the spirit of liberalism, it is sharing a general capitalist take-off with its neighbors today. Thus, it would be rather difficult to explain the upsurge of new capitalism in the region (especially in its Western borderlands that have already joined the European Union) by referring to certain ethnic groups, national ideologies, religious denominations, or paths of communist prehistory. At the same time, economic determinism, I believe, would contribute as little to the explanation as historical essentialism does.

In Search of the Spiritus Loci

As a matter of fact, Eastern Europe has gone through a stage of breath-taking economic development during the past one or two decades, following the period of 'transformational recession' in the first half of the 1990s. In the wake of a deep-going liberalization (privatization and deregulation) of the planned economy, nascent capitalism seems to be robust, despite the current crisis of the world economy. Its catching-up trajectory was recently acknowledged by the geopolitical enfranchisement (NATO) and economic integration (EU) of a large part of the region by the West, which enhanced the stability of the post-communist economies. Can this capitalist turn implying complex institutional change be primarily regarded as a result of tradition-based response to current challenges, of sheer imitation, and/or of capricious choices made by economic and political actors representing an increasingly empty and spiritually poor culture?

In any event, does Eastern European new capitalism really need as solid and coherent spiritual foundations (religions, ethical norms, intellectual convictions, passions, etc.) as some other 'Great Transformations' in the past? Should one necessarily interpret the certainly turbulent cultural conditions under post-communism as a chaotic precursor of a final decay of civilization? Is spirituality evaporating or changing its configuration and fervor?

Apparently, one *can* become a capitalist entrepreneur (or a hard-working, rationally calculating, etc. employee) in an ex-communist country of the region at the turn of the millennium without going to a Protestant church every Sunday, repeating Confucian truisms when falling asleep or studying Adam Smith's teachings on the virtues of the market in a business course. He/she may just continue to follow certain quasi-capitalist routines acquired in the course of communism and refine them under the new conditions. He/she may also import capitalist culture (more exactly, various capitalist cultures) but not primarily in their airy and elevated forms as e.g., Protestant ethics mediated by an evangelical community but in those of down-to-earth cultural practices (norms, habits, modes of behavior, etc.) embedded in economic and political institutions. Can't 'worldly philosophy', to use a forgotten expression, complement (or even substitute for) philosophy, especially if the former permeates everyday economic behavior? What is the driving force of the current capitalist take-off if not – at least to a certain extent – spiritual factors? If spirituality matters, how could we grasp the new 'spirit of capitalism' with the help of social sciences? What is the *spiritus loci* of the Eastern European economies today? Too many questions, too many white spots …

'Soft Culture', 'Implicit Spirituality' and 'Surrogate Religion': A Few Words on Terminology

Although faith, transcendence, sense of belonging, revelation, giving meaning to life, emotional bonds, interiorization and the like are crucial attributes of spirituality, this paper will not identify spirituality exclusively with religious thought and sentiment[6]. Moreover, the spirit of capitalism will not be sought only in refined, ethereal, that is, 'soft' components of culture, pertaining to the world of ideas, values, beliefs, emotions, myths, magic, etc. Its 'harder', 'more tangible' components such as rules, norms, habits, routines, modes of behavior, ways of life, etc. will also be put under scrutiny[7]. Thus, one can speak of important spiritual developments in the new capitalist societies of Eastern Europe even in the absence of strong religions like Protestantism, social theories like liberalism or political ideologies like nationalism, if some harder constituents of culture incorporating a degree of spirituality become more (or less) prominent. What at a first glance seems to be a spiritual misery may be, if seen from another perspective, an enrichment of some of the harder components of culture, which carry softer ones or embody the spirit of capitalism directly. In discussing the takeover of spiritual capital from the West, I will pay special attention to this kind of 'implicit spirituality' of economic cultures. For instance, transplanting a bundle of rules governing a business organization (as we will see in our case study below) may in turn create a specific 'faith community' by transcending the world of daily, embedded, rational practices without any kind of strong religious support. In other words, a 'surrogate religion' may grow out from these practices; a kind of quasi-religion that gives its believers a new meaning of life, sense of belonging, moral cohesion, etc. without postulating a God or promising an Otherworld.

Accordingly, spiritual capital is, in my interpretation, not equivalent with religious capital (the latter is a subset of the former). From another angle, spiritual capital will be regarded as a form of cultural and social capital; a form that has something to do with faith, transcendence, sense of belonging, etc[8]. The metaphor of capital, however, will be used in a conventional way: I will regard spiritual capital as a set of resources that can be acquired, invested, accumulated, wasted, used with profit, exchanged, etc.

Antecendents

Why focus on transnational cultural encounters? Would it not make sense to accept the widespread view of an ample domestic supply of capitalist spirit in the region as a result of a dramatic revival of national(ist) and/or religious passions? That revival, I believe, must not be mistaken for a capitalist revival. Nationalism under post-communism follows statist (interventionist, collectivist) principles rather than representing a kind of constitutional patriotism with a strong liberal program. In the best case, it is tolerating rather than promoting capitalism. Therefore, nationalist sentiments would not really help understand the processes of far-reaching economic liberalization and opening-up to the foreign capital after 1989. With some exceptions (emergence of neo-Protestant communities, a recent flirt by the Orthodox church with the idea of capitalism, etc.), the same applies to the established churches in Eastern Europe. They have deep reservations with regard to any sort of capitalism that goes beyond an interventionist version of *Soziale Marktwirtschaft*, and to global capitalism as such, and concentrate on the social costs rather than the benefits of the changes. As to the sociological carriers of the post-communist transformation, the region does not give room to new, pro-capitalist ethnic groups (except for the Chinese merchants in a few countries) that would be comparable with the Jews and the Germans in the era of early capitalism. Consequently, the bulk of spiritual capital conducive to fast and deep-going liberalization had to come from other internal sources, or external ones.

Internally, the effects of pre-communist and communist legacies may be of interest while among the external sources one cannot avoid focusing on two vast cultural packages coming from the West, globalization (Americanization) and European integration. During the past decade, I have devoted a series of essays to exploring these impacts in Eastern Europe in general, and my country, Hungary in particular[9], and come to the following tentative conclusions:

1. *The Westernizing elites.* Focusing on the ruling elites, I asked why the secular cleavage between the two dominant mentalities, 'Populism' and 'Westernization' did not cease to exist under communism, and why are they still involved in local culture wars over national isolation versus opening up to the West, discovering 'third ways' versus borrowing Western patterns of capitalism, collectivist/ethnic versus individualist/civic social philosophies,

etc. It became clear for me that while waging these wars on the rhetorical level, they tend to criss-cross the frontlines to end up with rather controversial hybrid (post-modern) programs of societal change; programs that are produced under the pressure of attaining pragmatic compromises rather than spiritual coherence.

One might think that a fair amount of spiritual capital has been accumulated in the rival camps of the political and cultural elites. Nevertheless, the populist messages have difficulties in reaching the economic elites, and do not crystallize as spiritual assets in popular economic cultures such as work and business ethics, consumption habits and the like. The liberal sources of the spirit of new capitalism are also ambiguous. Since 1989, the human rights-based and the economic as well as the conservative and the communitarian/egalitarian types of liberalism have not ceased to confront each other, damaging the spiritual capital accumulated in the anti-communist opposition, the market-socialist reforms and the shadow economy. Thereby, the harder segments of capitalism-friendly culture, which had emerged under communism in the form of quasi-market behavior and quasi-private ownership have lost much of their ideological and ethical support by now. Moreover, the idea of Westernization has also got fragmented due to the uncertainty caused by an enhanced competition between a large variety of capitalisms in the West. Borrowing spiritual capital from *the* West became a rather complicated task in the light of heated debates over globalization, the 'European Social Model', the 'Asian values', etc. As a consequence, two kinds of ambiguities confront each other: to put it simply, a populist prophet does not buy more domestic products, and a liberal entrepreneur is not less corrupt than the average citizen today.

2. *Accepting* and *resisting 'global culture'*. Turning to the external sources of spiritual renewal, I challenged, in a study of cultural globalization, the thesis of a post-communist cultural vacuum, and the related theory of sweeping globalization (Americanization, colonization). A great variety of cultural blends were described which result from a partial acceptance of *and* a partial resistance to the incoming cultural packages (which are often mixed themselves). Transfer and transformation of cultures were examined in parallel with a special emphasis upon bricolage and simulated takeover of capitalist values, norms, rules, etc. According to common wisdom, 1989 marked the beginning of cultural homogenization in the region. Since then, goes the argument, global culture has conquered, eradicated, or at least, marginalized its indigenous rivals, while the 'natives' eventually surrendered to the 'occupants' or even fell in love with the 'civilizers'. In disputing this interpretation, I focused on the ambiguities of cultural import from the

West, enumerating quite a few cases of failed globalization as well as a great number of cultural hybrids ranging from the post-communist constitutions, through welfare policies, all the way down to eating habits. These hybrids have emerged from a rivalry between the cultural exporters and from spontaneous – and predominantly passive – resistance by the importers to cultural influences from abroad. As a result, spiritual capital has been transformed while transferred. Frequently, transformation was tantamount to a kind of 'spiritual evacuation' whereby, an intrinsic moral command (e.g., paying taxes, rejecting bribes, etc.) appeared as a mere pragmatic consideration, a second best solution for avoiding punishment.

3. *America versus Europe.* In another attempt at understanding the turbulence of external impacts, I examined two major dimensions of acculturation, to put it simply, Americanization and Europeanization. Discovering a 'Little America' in Eastern Europe, I focused on the ongoing competition between the two main cultural packages coming from the West for the hearts and the minds of the people in the region. At least since the collapse of the Soviet empire, a whole series of economic, political, welfare, and other regimes wearing a US trade mark have put down roots in the region. A low share of public ownership in industry, banking, and housing, emerging forms of 'managerial capitalism', privatized pension schemes, non-progressive tax systems and decreasing tax burdens, a low rate of unionization, permissive hire and fire regulations, a high degree of social polarization, lax rules of environmental protection—could anyone disregard these systemic features of new Eastern European capitalism? Is it possible not to recognize the striking similarity between the region and the United States in terms of the style of entrepreneurship (fierce competition, informal business-making, underregulation), propensity for self-exploitation, individualism and self-reliance, suspicion toward the state, and so on? Is it fair to stigmatize that style by calling it 'Wild-Eastern' in a condescending manner?

While asking these questions, I also highlighted quite a bit of ambiguity in the reaction of the European Union to this kind of cultural change in the region. On the one hand, in demonstrating its liberal, perhaps even American, face, the EU is resolutely expanding the single market with all its freedoms toward the East. On the other, it has expropriated the old slogan of the anti-communist dissidents of the region, 'Return to Europe'. Two decades ago, the dissidents wanted their region to leave the Soviet Bloc for the West. Currently, however, the same region is strongly requested to come back from Little America to the territory of the celebrated but partly imaginary 'European Social Model'. The two competitors are incessantly spoiling each other's spiritual assets, keeping the Eastern Europeans in uncertainty, thereby limiting their chance for an emotional (transcendental) identification with capitalism as such.

4. *Spiritual capital: the local stock.* Finally, I became interested in the ways in which cultural legacies affect economic development in Eastern Europe after 1989. More exactly, I wanted to explore 'which past' matters in shaping the spirit of nascent capitalism: the precommunist or the communist one. This question was provoked by a master narrative of the current economic history of the region, according to which Eastern Europe consists of two – so-called historical – subregions, Central (more exactly, East-Central) Europe as well as Southern and Eastern Europe (whatever they should mean), to which the following syllogism applies: the former had been more Western/capitalist/modern than the latter prior to Soviet occupation, *therefore* it resisted communism more vehemently, and *therefore* it became more Western/capitalist/modern after communism. The emphasis is on a direct link between pre-communism and post-communism.

In contrast to this kind of interpretation, I suggested that communism *did* and *does* matter, it also represented a major cultural turn, and had at least forty years to remix the cultural cards, thus substantially influencing the record of the individual countries of the region in capitalist development during the past two decades. It destroyed the spirit of a certain kind of capitalism but, ironically, also contributed to the emergence of the spirit of another kind of capitalism. The rankings of the countries in an imaginary hierarchy of 'more' or 'less' capitalism have changed over the past century substantially, showing little correlation with the distant past (e.g., Slovenia preceding Czechoslovakia in the communist period, or Estonia preceding Hungary today). Moreover, the conventional cultural explanations for the success of post-communist transformation do not work well if applied to the whole region and for a longer period. For instance, geo-cultural proximity to the West loses its importance in the era of globalization. Protestantism, Catholicism, Orthodoxy: there is no such hierarchy in terms of capitalist success stories. Today, the 'Catholic' Slovenes are still better off than the 'Protestant' Estonians, and the 'Catholic' Poles may be worse off than the 'Orthodox' Romanians tomorrow. What remain as significant explanatory variables for post-1989 capitalist development are the cultural exit status of the given communist regime and the change of that status due to external effects.

As regards the exit status, one cannot capture it relying on the old, totalitarian-style concept of *Homo Sovieticus*. Actually, this cultural stereotype had been Janus-faced already under communism, and its legacy became even more complex in the period of the transformation. State paternalism and informal markets, public ownership and private redistribution, central commands and decentralised bargaining, over-regulation and free-riding, collectivist economic institutions and individual (or family-based) coping strategies, apparatchik and technocratic mentality, learned helplessness and forced creativity, etc. – one could go on listing the controversial features of economic culture in Eastern Europe prior to 1989. To a varying degree country by country, it combined the command economy with elements of a rather diluted *Soziale Marktwirtschaft*, and all this with pre-capitalist traditions and a dynamism/aggressiveness reminiscent of early capitalism. (In a sense, it was not double- but quadruple-faced.)

It sounds paradoxical but it is true: even if in a distorted manner, communism was not only a modernizer but also a school of capitalism. Industrialization, urbanization, mass education, public health, etc. are well-known achievements of 'quantitative' modernization (or simply, detraditionalization) under Soviet rule. In the course of this kind of modernization, calculative behavior, risk taking, competitive attitudes, etc. were also obligatory subjects to learn – to be sure, by default, not by design (e.g., filling the supply gaps in the economy of shortage). Communism conserved/reproduced a sort of capitalist ethos (rooted in trust rather than formal rules, personal rather than institutional transactions, small rather than large organizations, human rather physical capital etc.), part of which eroded in the West in the meantime. Ironically enough, this *Gründerzeit* ethos may grant a comparative advantage to the Eastern Europeans today.

To avoid misunderstandings, this ethos does not reproduce the old Weberian prototype of the Protestant entrepreneur, and does not have much in common with such neo-capitalist success stories as Confucianism and Evangelical Protestantism. As a crucial part of the spiritual capital of present-day Eastern Europe, this ethos has no religious foundations, contains weaker feelings of responsibility for the family or the community, it is less self-denying, less savings-oriented, etc. While in 1989, most observers expected that it is the legacy of the social market that would possibly create an organic connection between the economic cultures of Eastern and Western Europe in an enlarged EU, the past two decades have proven that another kind of cultural link is also possible. The virtues of *Gründerzeit* capitalism could qualify the countries, in *both* the Central and the Southern/Eastern subregions of Eastern Europe, for taking their fair share in globalization. Moreover, given that contemporary global/American capitalism relies, to a growing extent, on networks, informality, flexibility, decentralized knowledge production, etc., the economic cultures represented by the European Union might become a brake rather than an accelerator of a capitalist take-off in the region.

What do the above conclusions tell us about the spirit of new capitalism in Eastern Europe after 1989? They suggest, no doubt about it, that there is a considerable amount of spiritual capital accumulated in the region but this capital

- lost two important sources of past transitions to capitalism, ethnic nationalism and religion;
- stems from a peculiar mix of pre-capitalist legacies, proto-capitalist virtues emerging under communism and a large quantity of imported cultural goods that come from different 'Wests';
- therefore, the current capitalist revolution in Eastern Europe is rather turbulent (even chaotic), tends to produce hybrid cultures, and is 'dryer', much more worldly or profane than its predecessors.

Hybridity and dryness – but how do these features of spiritual capital come into being? How exactly is spiritual capital being produced? How do the imported goods combine with local assets? I cannot imagine a research field that could reveal the secrets of the formation of the capitalist spirit in today's Eastern Europe better than the transnational cultural encounters in the economy.

Transnational Cultural Encounters

This paper originates in a large comparative research project named *Dioscuri* that studied the cohabitation of 'Eastern' and 'Western' economic cultures in eight countries of Eastern Europe over the past five years[10]. In order to illuminate the basic *problématique* of the project, let me present a stylized talk between the eternal *Wessi* and the eternal *Ossi*, typical figures in German popular discourse. This is how we imagined our research terrain at the very outset.

The *Wessi* and the *Ossi*

What the *Wessi* calls Eastern Enlargement of the EU (and of the West in general) not only covers all civilizational benefits that the West generously and light-mindedly offers to the East but also refers to the Westward expansion, a sort of Western Enlargement' of the dangers originating in the former Soviet Empire. The *Wessi* is anxious about what will happen to his job, family, savings, etc., after 'those over there' (the renowned Polish plumber and Hungarian truck driver) are allowed to enter the West, either as employers or employees, for more than brief visits. Will you pay taxes properly? he asks the *Ossi* with deep distrust in his voice. Won't you accept lower wages, less safe working conditions than us? Will you protect *our* environment? How long do you want to profit from our budgets?

Won't your 'Wild-East' entrepreneurs ignore the social standards in our country? Will they observe the business contracts? Will they leave the mafia behind?

As a mirror image of how populists in Western Europe portray the Eastern 'savages' *ante portas*, one witnesses in Eastern European nationalist discourse the icon of the 'honest' and 'creative' Czech, Slovene or Romanian worker and businessman who, while matching their Western colleagues in terms of capitalist virtues, are allegedly better-educated, respect family values, religion and rural bonds. Accordingly, the West should feel honoured to receive the newcomers and be lucky to gain so much 'fresh energy and authentic culture' at such a low price.

This pride mingles with the worries of our *Ossi*. For him, the Eastern Enlargement of the West seems risky because, as a result of it, he also may lose his job. Similarly, he is also anxious about the lowering of the social standards (e.g., in child-care) in his country. Moreover, he fears the erosion of both his pre-communist traditions and the filtering of his new entrepreneurial freedoms, consumption habits, etc. in the world of more regulated capitalist regimes (cf. the *acquis communautaire*). For instance, as an employer he may have to comply with equal opportunity rules, and as a consumer he may be forced to abandon shopping around the clock. Or, to quote even more profane examples from my country, Hungary occurring in the first years after the EU accession, he is not allowed to slaughter pigs in his backyard, distil *pálinka* in the bathroom, and what is the *non plus ultra* of his fears, he must reconcile himself with the fact that the Romanians may also call their traditional drink, the *tuica*, *pálinka* (a Slovak word by the way).

Won't you use us as cheap labourers and buyers of low-quality consumer goods—a poorhouse of the West? Will you not paralyze our innovative spirit and abuse our talent? Will you accept our quest for informality or will you simply subsume it under the heading of lawlessness and corruption, and keep on stigmatizing and monitoring us? Questions such as these reflect the concerns of our *Ossi* who would prefer to see a kind of Western Enlargement that brings his old and new virtues to the West.

What, on the surface, seems to be a regular Ossi-Wessi conflict of perceptions, a two-person game, is in a closer scrutiny an interplay of at least three actors, including also a powerful challenge by global (basically American) capitalism. As the aforementioned reference to an imaginary 'Wild East' demonstrates, Eastern Europe and the United States are supposed to forge a peculiar coalition in the game, and the eternal *Wessi* finds himself in the crosshairs of similar economic cultures. For those who tend to think that this kind of *Wessi* mentality is only characteristic of the potential losers in the West (ranging from the employees in industries moving Eastward, to employers in the service sector facing Eastern competitors moving Westward), and of a few noisy trade unions, chambers and small populist parties that do their best to instrumentalise the fear from that coalition, I have bad news. That fear already sits in the minds of a whole series of influential European leaders such as the conservative French president, Nicolas Sarkozy or the former social-democratic leader in Germany, Franz Münterfering when they are heaping curses on Eastern-European tax dumping or U.S.-based *Heuschrecken-Kapitalismus* – a metaphor portraying financial investors as swarms of locusts.

'Shaken Orientalism' and the 'Temperature of the West'

The talk between the *Ossi* and *Wessi* seems to be a dialogue of the deaf, full of mutual distrust. Our research program also started off to explore East–West cultural encounters in a minefield of prejudices. The economic actors to be observed were expected to indulge in essentializing arguments about the 'Other'. We presumed to face the usual catalogue of rhetorical stereotypes that would make the understanding of the actual processes of cultural exchange extremely difficult.

As far as our Western respondents – entrepreneurs and managers working in Eastern Europe – are concerned, they did exhibit some confusion when narrating their cultural encounters with the 'natives'. On the one hand, they brought along to the region the traditional concept of *Homo Sovieticus* and characterized the local authorities, business partners and employees by means of old adjectives such as collectivist, egalitarian, unorganized, short-termist, irresponsible, passive, negativist, lazy, rule-bending, corrupt, nepotistic, paternalist, even alcoholic and thievish. Such Soviet-type people, according to the Westerners, prefer improvisation to following routine procedures, free riding to cooperative behaviour, conflict to compromise, and promise to contract, and mix up politics and business, work and private life, public and private property, etc.

On the other hand, our respondents ostensibly had great difficulties harmonizing this list with many of their new experiences, basically with the clear upswing of entrepreneurship in Eastern Europe. In any event, their traditional – Orientalist – pride *vis à vis* Eastern Europe faded. They saw less and less helpless, dependent, egalitarian-minded economic actors there while, at the same time, they witnessed the emergence of increasingly risk-taking societies with a rather creative, informal and socially not too sensitive economic culture.

This – I would call it – 'shaken Orientalism' was confronted with a sort of 'shaken Occidentalism' of our Eastern European respondents who also entered the encounters with ready-made, albeit less condescending mirror images in their mind. Accordingly, their Western partners were supposed to be socially insensitive, rigidly formalistic, overspecialized, stressed, unimaginative, etc. Of course, the attitudes varied country by country with both the Western and Eastern respondents. The Eastern interviewees, for example, developed a kind of 'thermometric language' to reveal their preferences. In quite a few in-depth interviews, especially those made in South-Eastern European ex-communist countries, the local entrepreneurs and managers often use the word 'warmness' when talking about the relationships with their business partners from Italy, Greece, or Spain, representing as a rule small and medium size firms, frequently in family ownership. They say that if they could choose, they would opt for a sort of 'Mediterranean economic culture' as they call it as opposed to a 'Nordic' one (meaning German in the first place), which they describe as megalomaniacal, rigid, and impersonal. The Americans, although they are not depicted as champions of Mediterranean mentality, also receive a couple of compliments for their easy-going, non-hierarchical, flexible, and informal business practices.

Both the traditional stereotypes and the metaphoric generalizations such as the one 'measuring' the temperature of the encounters and the ensuing cohabitation point to a multitude of key spiritual elements of Eastern European economic cultures appearing in and resulting from the cultural exchange. But how can one distill from the popular (and often populist) mind/mythology/rhetoric what actually goes on in that exchange, i.e., what elements of spiritual capital are being imported?

Going Beyond the State of the Art

Current cultural history-writing seldom offers broad empirical insights in Eastern European economic cultures. What one knows about these cultures, comes from a combination of large value surveys, a few case studies, manuals of what is called 'cross-cultural management' and anecdotal evidence[11]. Moreover, as a rule, these proofs do not refer to the very emergence of economic cultures, and do not observe their major sources simultaneously. The economic actors occur as prisoners of certain – historical or economic – arrangements rather than instinctive or conscious culture-makers. The surveys apply a few synthetic concepts such as 'power distance' or 'post-materialist values' and test them by means of standardized questionnaires, while the case studies explore specific components of economic culture (work culture, business ethics, corruption, etc.) using rather small samples but similarly impersonal techniques of data collection.

In contrast to the mainstream literature, our research focused on multiple sources of current cultural change (including spiritual one) in selected fields in many countries of the region. It put one of the major sources, the external cultural impacts under scrutiny, asking how the encounters between the economic actors in the East and the West, i.e., encounters, the number and scope of which have dramatically increased during the past two decades, influence the evolution of economic cultures in the region. By placing the transnational cultural encounters in the center of inquiry, the internal sources (communist and pre-communist legacies as well as local cultural innovation) were not neglected at all. On the contrary, they appeared as important variables explaining how the indigenous actors, that is, flesh-and-blood workers, entrepreneurs, government officials, economists, etc. in Eastern Europe, select (accept, adjust and mix) certain cultures while rejecting others, and how they exchange, accumulate and utilize spiritual capital.

Our research discussed the ways in which new capitalism is being built 'from outside'; more exactly, the ways, in which Western-made economic cultures are received by the Eastern European economies. This choice was also urged by a conspicuous gap between the scarcity of empirical knowledge concerning the reception of vast cultural packages arriving in the region from the West, on the one hand, and the abundance of high-sounding generalizations about cultural colonization, convergence, Americanization, Europeanization and the like, on the other.

In observing how the *spiritus loci* of new Eastern European capitalism is being shaped by external factors, we refrained from formulating strong hypotheses concerning the outcomes of cultural exchange with the West. The only firm assumption we made concerned the existence of the exchange itself. In other words, despite the vast power of external supply of cultures, the process of takeover was not presumed to be either smooth or uni-directional. We expected to see a blend of acceptance and rejection even mutual adjustment rather than servile imitation. In concentrating on importation, we did not exclude the possibility of finding a few cultural goods exported by Eastern Europe.

Although we presumed cultural exchange to be asymmetric, we thought that it would be a grave simplification to talk about a 'strong Western' culture that devours (civilizes) the 'weak Eastern' one, or about ongoing 'clashes of civilizations'. Instead, we expected to find a great variety of lasting cultural hybrids, some of which may even contain elements that Eastern Europe brings to rejuvenate economic cultures in the West. Thus, in an unprecedented way, Eastern Enlargement of the West was studied in conjunction with its neglected counterpart, Western Enlargement of the East, whereby the results of the latter were not *a priori* labeled as obsolete, improper or harmful. This cautious normative assumption aside, our research program took an impartial stance, and posited that Eastern and Western economic cultures come across each other in a varying mix of competition, conflict and cooperation *without* defining in advance what exactly is to be meant by these two clusters of culture. The tentative definitions were expected to rise from the actors' narratives. In taking a detached look at the cases and stories of cultural encounters, we let the actors (our interviewees) talk, and did our best to make *ex-post* rather than *ex-ante* generalizations[12].

In order to reduce the stress of deconstructing the discourse of the economic actors, we decided to study 'real' stories of cultural encounters embedded in 'real' cases and explored by loosely structured, narrative in-depth interviews. Irrespective of being close to the actual cases, both well-known methodological constraints of anthropological inquiry were considerably eased; a.) thanks to a large number of cases we studied in many countries with the help of unusually great samples of respondents, we managed to increase the level of abstraction of the final conclusions; b.) by means of covering quite a few similar (or identical) cases in different countries, we succeeded in reducing the risk of attaining incomparable research results.

The research covered *eight countries* of post-communist Eastern Europe: to follow conventional classification in symbolic geography, four of them belong to *East-Central Europe* (Czech Republic, Hungary, Poland and Slovenia), and four to *South-Eastern Europe* (Bulgaria, Croatia, Romania and Serbia). We identified *three research fields (1. entrepreneurship, 2. state governance, 3. economic knowledge)* that give room to a great many producers and mediators of economic culture[13]. In the third field, the inflow/emergence of spiritual capital could be observed in a direct manner whereas in the first two the spirit had to be 'extracted' from the incoming culture.

Our research program was not only unique in terms of the quantity of cases and depth of their studies but also in the diversity of cases. We selected small and large, old and new, public and private, etc. institutions that operate in various branches of the economy, polity and science, and embody encounters with different countries/regions in the West. With the help of 'thick description', the researchers reconstructed detailed histories of the encounters ranging from the initial expectations through various surprises/conflicts to the final compromises.

2. Importing 'Soft' in 'Hard': The Case of Banking

How do harder cultural goods carry in softer ones from the West to Eastern Europe? Why does it make sense to switch from the concept of culture to that of spirit? What kind of spiritual capital will remain in the region at the end of the day? In order to respond to such questions, I chose a spectacular case of entrepreneurship, the birth of a Western-based new transnational bank in the ex-communist countries. It was observed by means of what we called 'close comparison' of five local subsidiaries, and placed in the context of three other cases of takeover of local banks in the region.

It would be too much to say that this branch of the post-communist economies is typical in any sense. It has been one of the most dynamic and profitable area of business since 1989, though a very turbulent one in terms of institutional change. Powerful business actors from many countries of the West moved to the region, bringing along their own economic cultures, to take part in a great number of FDI operations. When they bought a bank (or a part of it) they applied similar techniques of restructuring. In granting more or (usually) less autonomy to the local partners, they dismissed a good part of the employees, got rid of the bad loans, introduced a rigorous risk management, upgraded the sales and human relations departments, integrated the back offices and reinforced the front offices, took harsh anti-corruption measures and so on, thus offering a wide terrain of research for those interested in transnational cultural encounters.

At the same time, many of the Eastern European banks we studied had gone through various acts of privatization, government-led consolidation, merger, etc. before our fieldwork began. Moreover, their Western partners had also been transformed to a large extent by major deals in the European and global capital markets, and the transformation did not stop during the period of the case studies. Hence the starting conditions for a 'normal' cultural transfer between the East and the West were favorable and unfavorable at the same time. We observed highly interesting and easily comparable cases as they evolved but occasionally it was difficult to decide if a change we wanted to comprehend had cultural causes or it was rather attributable to an accidental (even chaotic) decision contingent on some sort of rapid reorganization. Turbulence had, however, an important side effect. The radical and controversial transformations mobilized not only the intellect but also the soul of their participants who made new emotional choices, new commitments by gaining lived experiences and transcending a great many boundaries. As a consequence, they portrayed the transnational encounters according to an 'us and them' scheme, and, not infrequently, narrated the history of the encounter (as individuals or, more often, as members of a group with the same conviction) in *explicitly spiritual* terms.

A Republican Empire?[14]

During the past twenty years, a medium-sized bank (I will call it W-Bank) rooted in a small country of Western Europe has developed into a large institution by taking over a series of smaller banks all over Eastern Europe. While growing and, in the end, entering the stock exchange, it changed many of its original cultural attributes and became a multinational network from a local one, a risk-taker from a cautious player, and a cutting-edge organization from a traditional undertaking. As its leaders like to say, a group of banks turned into a banking group. Meanwhile, the mother company exerted an enormous influence on its daughters in the region by transplanting part of its original corporate culture into them, and, almost simultaneously, adjusting it to the new, global rules of the game in banking.

Below, I will not be able to decide whether or not the transplantation was successful, and will not want to discuss whether or not its results are desirable in my view. I will presume that *some kind of* cultural transfer has taken place, and only examine the spiritual content of the exported/imported cultural goods. The case studies make it clear that the W-bank acted carefully, took a gradual approach, and, instead of imposing its own culture as a whole on the new partners, offered them some opportunity of choice and co-determination. In addition, what was transferred right after the acquisition did not go fully against the indigenous cultural standards of the region. The new, Eastern European members of the bank belonged to one of the most Westernized segments of the late communist and/or post-communist economies, could continue to rely on their local roots and enjoy a rather high degree of autonomy in an unusually flat organizational structure. As one of our Polish respondents remarked, 'we are not Coca Cola where the main objective of the [local] marketing department is to translate the slogan 'we love it' into our language'.

Nevertheless, the basic institutional arrangements changed considerably by the takeover and reorganization of the local banks. No matter if it came to the market strategies or the relations with the authorities, to the internal management system or the attitudes toward the customers, there was no area of banking operations which remained untouched. The same applied to the behavior of the local managers and employees. They were confronted with a whole series of new cultural patterns ranging from an almost self-humiliating respect for the client to maintaining a distance from the political parties, from team work and information sharing to being an equal opportunity employer, from adjusting to predetermined procedures to performance – (versus position) – based authority within the company, from the appreciation of good communication skills to a strong loyalty to the bank, from cooperative behavior to strict rules, from a high level of impersonal trust to controlling personal emotions, etc.

The patterns often boiled down to seemingly banal instructions: e.g., dismantle the counters and receive the clients at desks, do not wear a mini-skirt, or answer the phone before it rings three times. To quote our respondents at random, they were asked to avoid vulgar speech, keep the door of their offices open, and not to get in an intimate relationship with the customers. They were informed about the price limit of the presents they are permitted to accept, and taught how to avoid meeting the omnipresent 'lamb brigades' (these are the agents of the companies applying for credit, who want to bribe the bank's officials dining in fancy restaurants in Serbia). Sugar-coating the critical remarks made to colleagues, not asking about each other's wages, communicating in writing, keeping the deadlines, etc. – the local employees faced many dozen similar 'suggestions' that were (or were not) included in the company's code of conduct. As a Romanian interviewee put it, in the beginning it was difficult to harmonize these norms with the national character: 'we are all Latins, we all have ideas, we all come with solutions, we all criticize, … we all step on others' toes …'

When asked/instructed to accept these patterns, the local partners had to cope not only with the usual dilemmas of the 'natives' undergoing Westernization but also with those stemming from the conviction that in a sense they were already more Westernized than some of the Westernizers. 'First-rate Easterners meet third-rate Westerners', goes the argument in one of the Hungarian interviews, complemented by a long list of self-congratulations in the other countries with regard to certain habits and skills acquired under communism. These include spontaneity, flexibility, risk-taking, informality, innovativeness and improvisation, properties that are indispensable if one has to react fast in the market, for instance, if 'there is fire in the house' as a Croatian interviewee said. When the predetermined rules fail, our fantasy and innovative drives, not to mention local knowledge, are there to help. To assess the risks, we, Easterners do not always have to apply complex mathematical models, it is enough to 'walk around the clients', boasted another respondent from Croatia. While being proud of their business instincts, an overwhelming majority of our respondents admit the poverty of their technical knowledge in banking during the first stages of cohabitation with the mother company. The message is clear: we are smart; they, the Westerners are (only) well prepared.

Ostensibly, the local employees have not always been prevented from taking instinctive, occasionally bold decisions. Hence, they have currently nothing against subscribing to the corporate identity of the bank. 'We are not a McDonald's bank', 'ours is not a totalitarian organization', etc. – our respondents reiterate these slogans rather often, and quite a few of them believe in the existence of the 'bank's spirit' that would appear in its non-hierarchical organization (subsidiarity), client-friendliness, cultural diversity, politically correct practices and the like. These features were cemented in the 'Mission, Vision, Values' statement of the company. As the author of the comparative analysis claims, a small empire is in the making. A Polish interviewee calls it a 'republic of noblemen', true, as he adds, without a *liberum veto*.

Learning Capitalism

Nonetheless, in adjusting to the empire's identity, many of the Eastern European partners realized that, despite experiencing a huge increase in their expertise about banking procedures such as product development, the introduction of new management systems or marketing techniques, there was still a great deal to learn of capitalism as such. To put it briefly, they had to interiorize both the 'philosophy' and the *modus operandi* of the new system as a whole. The employees were making efforts to understand the advantages of competition (even if it hurts them) and the disadvantages of state regulation (even if it pleases them), the constant need for innovation and the value of market information, the image of the company, etc., not to mention the complex arrangements of property rights and organizational hierarchies in a corporation heading toward the stock exchange. Perhaps more importantly, for most of them it was during the integration in the mother bank that they first 'felt on their skin' what the textbook formula of minimizing costs/risks and maximizing profits really means. This 'skin feeling' emerged in the course of the first wave of dismissals right after the takeover of a given local bank, got stronger during the recurrent HR evaluation/selection rounds, or when they were 'requested' to work overtime, or when their internet access was limited. It is astonishing how deeply they have been able to understand and accept the new rules of the game even if those seemed detrimental at the first glance (or were really such). Was this just due to sheer imposition, or an indignant approval of the *quid pro quo* principle: sacrificing leisure for high salary, private life for prestige, etc.? Or did they draw a sober conclusion: it cannot be worse than before?

The emerging mega-bank incorporates values, norms, habits, etc. that 'contaminated' the employees of its Eastern European subsidiaries in all-important fields of economic culture. Their perception of time changed radically ('from slow time to fast time', to cite the author of the Romanian study), and the space of economic action expanded enormously by becoming part of regional, European or even global competition almost overnight. Professional knowledge, openness, dynamism, accuracy, constructivism, responsibility, cooperative behavior, etc. represent values that are not only enacted in the W-Bank's official documents but also cherished in daily practice. Our interviewees report about their initial impressions/surprises in great detail. They were amazed by the value of expertise in the transforming institution, by the fact that knowledge is protected by continuous training, and that it results in promotion irrespective of one's age; by a clear definition of (meritocratic) incentives and division of responsibilities, by the fact that in this way one cannot free-ride on his/her colleagues, and that both success and failure have foreseeable consequences; by a strict divide between work and leisure as well as company and private life ('between the two families', as a Hungarian respondent remarked sarcastically), and the prohibition of nepotistic practices; by collectivist habits (team work, loyalty to the company, social gatherings during the weekends) amidst competition between the employees of the bank; by incessant specialization and standardization; by rigorous planning, evaluation and reporting (i.e., 'communist-style' activities they could finally regard as reasonable); by sustaining transparency inside the bank and guarding its secrets outside of it; by the ethos of peace (self-restraint, conflict-avoidance, tolerance) and pluralism within the institution, etc.

In other words, they were impressed by cultural patterns, many of which served to tame their learned individualism and arbitrariness as well as to keep their entrepreneurial moves within operational limits and under professional supervision. The Eastern European players were prompted to accept the fact that the game is more rewarding in the long run if its rules call for clairvoyance and cooperation (as a Polish respondent said, 'after many years I understood that ego may spoil many projects'), and are not regarded as strait-jackets that need to be loosened up by special deals from time to time.

All in all, our interview partners convey the image of a quickly expanding institution, an empire that teaches its new provinces capitalism, more exactly, a certain kind of capitalism. To a degree, this capitalism with its emphasis on the agents of entrepreneurship, local knowledge and networks, brings one back to the 19th century and/or forward to the 21st. But why are those learning so satisfied? How come that they seem to comprehend and master the new course material so rapidly? The authors of the national case studies did their best to balance the picture and deduct from the satisfaction of the respondents what might be attributed to self-justification, snobbery, fashion, newly-acquired loyalty, or fear from the employer. Even so, the sense of belonging to the bank remains extremely strong. A reason for that may be preselection, i.e., the fact that the interviewees represent one of the most capitalist-minded layers of Eastern European societies, those who had been such under communism, and who have successfully surpassed all the hurdles of adaptation within the W-Bank until now.

Another reason is gradualism and cultural proximity stemming from the initial conditions of the takeover. It was a medium-sized European institution that comes from the 'near-West' and not a large American transnational company that expanded resolutely, almost hazardously in the region while also increasing the profitability of the whole enterprise. The growth of the organization was commanded by a chief executive whose family roots stretch into Eastern Europe, and whose business moves remind the observer of a blend of ex-communist entrepreneur and American venture capitalist. With the exception of several bankers in different countries who are convinced to drive the 'flagship' of the W-Bank, the respondents cannot hide their appreciation (mixed with a bit of anxiety) toward the captain of acquisitions, who became the *de facto* leader of the whole company later. He is honored by them also because during the phase of expansion, he did not mind if they continued to stick to part of their established business routines. (They were not instructed to prepare their meals from his 'cookbook' as a Croatian interviewee said.) That phase served as a foundation enabling the Eastern European subsidiaries to become, if need be, screws in the machine of a 'Coca Cola bank' with less difficulty today. The narratives of the employees reflect anxiety over this prospect.

The potential advent of a new – more centralized (more colonial, if you please) – model of Westernization in the current history of the Bank also explains why I am so cautious about proclaiming the success of acculturation. However, precaution must not lead one to ignore the actual flood of spiritual capital to Eastern Europe under the aegis of the new transnational bank. In the course of importing (more exactly, receiving the export of) institutions such as management systems, sales procedures and work regimes the local partners got acquainted not only with the harder components of rational economic culture but also with a bunch of general market principles, elements of business knowledge, professional ethic, symbolic representation of economic power and so on. These contain a large catalogue of norms and values concerning trust, cooperation, self-discipline, mutual respect, hard work and so on. In other words, those employed by a local subsidiary of the Bank were given a chance of accumulating spiritual assets in a sort of 'on-the-job training'; assets they may capitalize on (profit from) in the future.

Rite de Passage

'The spirit of the W-Bank' may be a conventional PR item, no doubt about it, but reading the interviews and the case studies I grew more and more inclined to accept this formulation and found the term 'culture', even 'soft culture' not quite sufficient. With many of our interview partners, the process of acculturation seems to have reached a point where it transcended cognitive training and habituation, and 'went into their blood' as a Croatian respondent put it. (Expressed more pompously, it became a 'habit of the heart'.) Knowledge and creativity became lived experiences associated with a series of positive emotions, pleasant impressions and corroborated by success in general, and by improving cohabitation between foreigners and locals within the bank in particular. More than that, the new values, norms, habits and the like were offered to the Eastern Europeans as a gesture of enfranchisement or even as an act of initiation. For them, overwhelmingly young and middle-aged urban professionals, the long series of tedious job interviews, evaluations, training programs and promotion cycles they have undergone during the past one and a half decades represented stages of a long *rite de passage* that led (or may lead in the near future) to full membership in a distinguished group. Some call that group with quite a bit of exaggeration 'transnational corporate class', or with Peter Berger's irony, the 'Yuppie International'. Our respondents talk about becoming a 'Westerner', that is, about emancipating themselves, getting rid of the stigma of symbolic geography. This was a long journey, and they arrived in a safe haven. Working together with the 'real' Westerners in the bank led to the weakening of mutual stereotypes, and the common interests forged cohesion, largely increasing the social capital of the Eastern European employees. To twist Willy Brandt's solemn words, what had *not* belonged together, grew together. A Serbian manager expressed this as follows: 'I have already started to think like them, and now I do not know what is ours and what is theirs'.

Emancipation was combined with the romantic experience of being pioneers ('seeds of change', to use the Bank's language) in spreading new – allegedly superior – cultures, thereby educating the uneducated. A Serbian manager, for example, was proud of teaching his fellow-citizens the notion of a collateral or that of electronic banking while his Croatian colleague told us how they trained the employees of 'more Eastern' daughter companies in retail banking. Our respondents provide lengthy reports of their own selection process, emphasizing its professional and impartial nature, and look back on it with satisfaction and pride. (In fact, their ascendance in the hierarchy was extremely rapid due to a major restructuring of the local banks right after the acquisition.) Apparently, having been selected and promoted is one of the great formative/cathartic experiences of their lives, a real success story that has been reaffirmed by the irresistible expansion of the bank and the whole banking sector of Eastern Europe, one of the few Big Winners of the post-communist transformation[15]. Today, the local managers and employees regard themselves as lucky insiders (family members) who have common enemies and possess secrets that remain hidden for the outsiders. As a result of all these preconditions, the economic cultures borrowed by them began to crystallize into spiritual assets almost like in a religion.

To avoid misunderstandings, it is far from me to overstrain the analogy, and invoke the God of Money or talk about any mystic/transcendent imagery of banking. Nor would I attribute any importance to the fact that spirituality was exercised in the numerous training courses, sometimes perhaps in the literal sense of the word, as new age practices. Instead, I see in the bank a large array of relatively young experts from the region who had shared a basically rational concept of their profession but under the positive emotional shock (one might call it revelative experience) of finally having the chance of unfolding that profession in an institution of their dreams, this concept got filled with spiritual components. Matters of choice, that is, certain values, norms, conventions, etc. represented by the Western partner appeared as the only rational alternative, close to unquestionable (divine) truth. In the lack of a similarly strong experience to the contrary in the past, and owing to an ongoing justification of *the* alternative in the present, this 'truth' was imprinted not only in the mind but also in the soul of the Eastern European actors. (We were 'like sponges', a Romanian respondent remarked, absorbing new information.) Under such circumstances, one does not have to prove the truth any longer; involvement, enchantment, intuition or faith suffices. The external rules become internal (ethical) norms, and, for example, corruption will be avoided as a deplorable rather than only punishable way of doing business. And the converts who think they have a calling rather than a job are ready to proselytize others.

To bring this argument down to earth, let me quote some of our respondents in Serbia: 'I have noticed that the main characteristic of this [the W-Bank's] culture is some kind of strict order: it was clear what is whose responsibility, ... supervisors were respected ... but there was no fear, ... one could express his/her opinion. These experiences I had [in the West before] were confirmed in this bank. So, this was not a shock but something that gave me pleasure'. 'People who are in the bank ... from its foundation have the feeling that the bank is their own project. They feel emotionally attached to the bank'. 'We were the first bank in Serbia that introduced risk management, and that is something that people do not understand. ... The clients started to accept our way of thinking'. 'People sometimes think: now I know somebody who works in the bank and he is going to do me a favor. That is not something that our company allows. The rules of the game are strict for everyone'. 'Foreigners brought with them a Western system of functioning: they do not waste either their own or the clients' time; they brought security, ... discipline. But also they brought professionalism in communication with the clients, they brought uniformity and seriousness in doing business, and these are the things that did not exist here earlier'.

Or let us listen to employees from three other countries: (Poland) 'Having this opportunity of creating something right from scratch was a big challenge for me but also a big chance'. 'Some time ago I had the impression that these contacts [with the Westerners] revealed our inferiority complex. It has changed ... , we no longer feel inferior'. (Romania) 'People got used very quickly to new furniture, to having super-clean toilets instead of locking the toilet paper in the desk drawer. People also got used to having their training sessions in very luxurious locations'.'In the beginning, we went to training sessions because 'it was right to do so', because it was like a bonus. ... Now people think: 'what do I need?' So, all these concepts that 4–5 years ago were a bit artificially imposed, have been internalized by the people'. (Croatia) '... People have ambition which they could not realize before, and here in these multinationals they see the opportunity to quickly jump through the hierarchy and to help themselves not only financially but even more to get the awards of achievement of other kind'. 'When speaking about the real tasks in this department, first what I asked them is not 'commitment to the job' but 'loyalty to the firm'. If we do not feel like being one family, ... you cannot expect the success you dream of'. The Western colleagues were 'really open to me, eager to transfer me their knowledge. That is what I will always remember, and I feel really grateful to them'. We started our project 'not thinking only about the pure profit ... It was for us a personal challenge, we were enjoying it a lot ... because we felt we were making something new and unique'.

'Self-heroization', 'reduction of cognitive dissonance', 'childish idealism', 'systematic brainwashing', 'simulated adaptation', 'the next generation will rebel', 'look what will happen when the banking sector gets saturated', etc. – one could easily continue to challenge the narratives of the respondents. Maybe the honeymoon will end soon. As a matter of fact, our interview partners already point to those conflict areas which inhibited cultural importation in the past, and may contribute to the erosion of the spiritual capital they have accumulated thus far. The original – inherited – cultural conflicts between following the rules and bending them, professional routine and improvisation, team work and individualism, etc. have been successfully toned down to frictions until recently. Yet, they may burst out in the course of the ongoing expansion of the bank. Growth and success may have their price. The fact that the W-Bank is becoming a Big Player will enhance the need for standardization and centralization ('mcdonaldisation') while, at the same time, the global markets will possibly justify 'Eastern-style' entrepreneurship, too. I am wondering whether these two cultures can also be reconciled in the era of ever larger mergers in the banking industry hit by the current crisis. In the time of the case studies, the spirit of the bank was still defined in a contrast to the 'American way' of banking while no one among our respondents denied that many features of that spirit have a US trade mark from the very beginning. I am wondering if that trade mark is still shining despite the professional/moral imperfections revealed during the past few years.

Test Cases

The above thesis of 'spiritualization' needs, I believe, additional evidence. Besides the five new members of the W-Bank, we also studied a Bulgarian, a Czech and a Slovenian institution with different business history, size, extent and origin of foreign ownership[16]. The differences revealed quite a few new circumstances under which spiritual capital emerges (or does not emerge) in the

East–West cultural encounters but did not disprove the thesis of implicit spirituality. Rather, they pointed to the volatility of this kind of cultural capital: it is somewhat hard for it to come into being but, predictably, fairly easy to perish.

Without Catharsis

The case of the Slovenian bank, for instance, demonstrates that the fervor of spiritual identification with certain economic cultures of capitalism depends on the strength of the pro-capitalist seeds in the communist economy. Although the employees of the W-Bank in Croatia and Hungary, that is, in countries with relatively market-oriented communist regimes in the past also showed less enthusiasm for capitalist economic culture than in Romania or even Poland, the Slovenes seem to be even less 'diligent pupils'. Their institution had been one of the largest commercial banks in Eastern Europe and operated an international network before 1989; its evolution in the 1990s was more organic as it was not bought off as a whole (local ownership is still significant in the bank), kept a larger share of the former (older) employees, and the pace of institutional change in the whole country was slower. Therefore, the cultural experiences of the personnel were less formative and cathartic, they could not in fact feel themselves members of a newly enfranchised community of pioneers. They had already cherished a self-image of the 'almost-Westerner', 'the most Western Easterner' under communism (cf. 'Switzerland of the East'), hence, their adjustment to the values and norms of the new majority owner, a large transnational bank based in a small 'Far-Western' country of Europe, did not occur to be a magnificent initiation.

Early Westernization and (what was not independent from that) sluggish transformation under post-communism conserved a fair amount of old forms of behavior in the Slovenian bank. The author of the case study puts these forms under the heading of 'negative individualism'. She refers to a peculiar ambiguity of attitudes whereby one is extremely individualistic in pursuing his/her own interests but rather collectivistic in dividing responsibility for his/her individual decisions. While in the W-Bank the interviewees report (at least a wish for) fast adaptation to the Western requirements, here the Western managers still complain about the 'eight-hour mentality' of the local colleagues, the 'strange Friday afternoons' when the bank is deserted, about distrust, cronyism, and the fact that 'there is too much politics brought into the hierarchy'. 'Slovene managers are very good in networking, and maybe they even spend too much time on it', says a foreign manager mockingly. The Westerners characterize the local employees as reactive rather than proactive, who cannot plan realistically, are non-cooperative and tend to avoid risk. To quote a foreign director of the bank, 'if I am pushing them to take a decision, a risky decision, they would always turn back to me to ask, would you support this decision. Now, if I say yes, they say yes. If I say 'but it is your decision', there is no decision'.

In one of the rare self-critical passages of the local narratives, a Slovene manager comments on the attitudes of his colleagues: 'Slovenia [is] where formality is bound to status and hierarchy', rather than expertise and performance. In another one, the respondent depicts his colleagues as decision-makers who act upon feeling rather than calculation. The author of the case study cites a Western manager who speaks of a 'heroic versus engaging' style of management in Slovenia, with limited knowledge-sharing and teamwork. 'There are managers managing the manager who is managing the manager. ... For five employees you have two managers', says another foreigner.

The locals were confronted with values and norms essentially similar to those received by Poland, Hungary or Serbia (ranging from hard work, through respecting professional knowledge to banning sexual harassment). Yet, they exhibit much less desire for adaptation and much more satisfaction with their own culture that has allegedly reached the level of the West. To be sure, they admit (with some reluctance) that their Western partners are more task-oriented and productive, better-organized, open-minded and less-hierarchical but do not spare too many words on their expressly economic properties. Calculative behavior is perhaps the only exception but the single respondent who brings that up adds immediately: we could also become less intuitive if our data bases were more developed. Such self-respect borders on complacency and it would be difficult to find any traces of neophyte enthusiasm in the interviews. As a foreign manager put it, 'Slovenes are very prudent. Prudent, prudent. We did the acquisition of 100 percent of [the banks in] Poland, the Czech Republic, Hungary, Slovakia, but this here in Slovenia was the most difficult and slowest process at all. They are very prudent and think twice ...'.

The East Coming from the West

The Czech bank in our sample has also been frequently reproached by its Western partner for slowness and red tape. The mother company that came from a Mediterranean country to Prague, had started growing only in the 1990s, and began its expansion in Eastern Europe with the acquisition of a Polish and this Czech institution some years ago. The latter had had a glorious past prior to world war II, and managed to maintain part of its power and fame under communism as a quasi-Western bank specialized in foreign currency transactions. A freshly privatized organization, it did not have any friction whatsoever with its first – German – owner in terms of economic culture. As a representative of the new – Mediterranean – owner put it, 'Czechs have a German approach, which is: tell me where to go and how, and I will go there. However, what is expected is that one will begin to search for solutions'. This opinion has its counterpart on the other side: 'a [Mediterranean] manager means chaos', a 'monstrous mess'; 'strategy and vision are missing', then 'there is a fuck-up'.

The ongoing conflict between the two parties was accompanied by strong words that express old cultural/national stereotypes pertaining to order versus disorder, analysis versus intuition, rules versus emotions, rigidity versus flexibility, etc. As unusual as it may be, if compared to the previous cases, the division of roles and characteristics is reversed: it is the Western actor in the cultural encounter who laments the excessive insistence by the Easterners on professional knowledge, coherent rules and long-term planning. In the controversy, the Czechs appear as conservatives while the foreigners as 'tricky' innovators, although the former are convinced that what the latter call innovation is in fact nothing but instinctive and capricious business moves that have only proven to be successful by chance in the past couple of years. Like the Slovenes, the Czech managers and employees look upon the Western partners with some condescension, and reiterate the 'we are more Westernized' message in the interviews.

The Mediterranean managers interviewed do not bother about measuring the relative degrees of Western civilization, describe both the dichotomy and the allegedly opposing features of the two parties in a similar way but consider their own features as superior. They are proud of their sensitivity, emotional dedication and ability of reacting quickly. One of them shared his creed with us: 'When I work with ... [you], I need to know what is in your 'heart'. How can I decide if I don't know what is in the soul?'. 'I raise my voice ... not because I am angry but because of my temperament ... I am hugely surprised that [Czechs] are able to work with people who hate each other ..., that wouldn't be possible [in my country]. We need a good personal relation, ... especially if we need to perform quick changes. The Czech Republic is colder though'. Obviously, in his view, heart and soul and warmth are indispensable prerequisites of business not only to secure harmony at the workplace but also, and more importantly, to make fast responses to market challenges in the era of globalization. Thus, 'we are flexible and able to change the business model and strategy in the market', he adds. In our country, his co-patriot says, 'we close some deals only with verbal communication'. The goal is more important than the process but if one does not find good solutions the goal can be modified.

As a mirror narrative, our Czech respondents complain about a kind of cultural dictatorship, a 'suppression of the Czech way of thinking'. 'Probably it would be of help if they understood what encourages Pepik [a nickname of Czechs]', says one of them sadly. They worry about receiving inaccurate information and witnessing a frequent change of rules: 'there is always something set, and then you wait for half a year until it is revised once again'. Long lunch hours, small talk about personal matters, lengthy meetings (in bad English), accidental projects, lack of qualified people, etc. – in other words, charisma instead of reason as summarized by the authors of the case study. As regards the self-image of the locals, most of them are reinforced in their pride felt for being well-organized, analytic, systematic and careful. The scene is set for a cultural deadlock.

There is, however, a minority of the Czech managers and employees that prevent the constant conflict from developing into a 'culture war'. They, primarily young experts, discover order in the 'Mediterranean chaos', recognizing the advantages offered by the approach of the foreign partner to the market, especially in retail banking introduced after the acquisition. These experts are ready to subscribe to the idea of serving the consumer even by breaking the rules, searching desperately/aggressively for new products and sales procedures, making decisions independently, joining forces in *ad hoc* teams, while enjoying competition within the bank and being rewarded according to competence and performance, as well as attending various training courses (e.g., a Young Talents program) – and they accept all these conditions even if those are defined in a bit hectic and not too serious fashion. The foreign bank brought along not only old habits and style from its own past but also new schemes and rules that help the Czech colleagues orient in the labyrinth of present-day global markets. The most entrepreneurial-minded among the latter were not so much frustrated by the poorly coordinated changes (cleansing the back office and strengthening the front office, standardizing the products, setting up an HR department, etc.) because they understood that these innovations may open new avenues in their daily work and career development.

And they had a chance indeed. The mother company moved ahead step by step, did not apply 'carpet bombing' among the local leaders but brought only a few 'middle managers to cover a special gap' from its home country. We needed one and a half years to break through, a foreign manager says, but finally 'we have spread like a virus'. The authors of the study cannot decide whether the diffusion of Western (actually, Southern) economic cultures was due to gradual persuasion or rather imposition based on power asymmetries. In the light of the story of the W-Bank, I presume that a similar 'virus infection' would have been more effective in Romania or Serbia. In the Czech Republic, however, a great cultural distance between the two parties in the transnational encounter (combined with the reversal of the East–West roles) impeded its spread, and only a small albeit growing group of the local actors were enchanted by the incoming cultures. Yet, the Mediterranean bank did its best to spiritualize, in the literal sense of the word, the cultural goods it carried in. Economic rationality was translated into semi-intimate categories such as warm heart, personal trust or a relaxed way of togetherness, and these categories were justified by their successful use in the markets of global capitalism. The interviews demonstrate that most of the Czech respondents did not internalize that sort of translation, their adaptation was forced, and they did not even simulate adjusting to the foreign partner in spiritual sense. In fact, they were looking forward to a new merger (between the Mediterranean and a large German bank) that might bring them back to their traditional *Kulturkreis* in the near future.

Devotion through Rejuvenation

In Bulgaria the sequence of acquisitions was different: the local bank had first been taken over by a large company from the 'Near-West' (this is the subject of the case study), and the Mediterranean bank appeared as a co-owner only thereafter[17]. Until and during the first steps of privatization, the Bulgarian partner underwent a series of mergers accompanied by all possible calamities of restructuring while also suffering from the legacy of being a large state-owned company prior to 1989. 'It was a bad situation I inherited', in a foreign manager's account of the pre-acquisition story, 'sale and risk were against each other. Everybody was accusing the other one. ... It depended also on the leaders: they were fighting and the guys had to follow them, therefore they were not allowed to talk to each other which was completely crazy'. The integration in the foreign bank was expected by the insiders to bring along peace and consolidation in every respect.

Nonetheless, although the East–West cultural conflicts were not so fierce as in the Czech case, mutual adaptation took a rather bumpy road. Many locals felt disturbed by the frequent and uncoordinated changes rather than the values and norms represented by the foreign partners. They thought that the biggest and oldest Bulgarian bank deserved a smoother takeover. While being happy about their institution becoming the undisputable market leader in the country, they could not reconcile themselves with the constant coming and going of the foreign and repatriate managers and board members owing also to a simultaneous transformation of the mother company. ('Before you figure out who is who, new people are appointed'.) In contrast to the foreign partners in the previous cases, the mother company inundated its Bulgarian daughter with its own experts to supervise the 'natives', which was regarded by those as a sign of disdain and mistrust. 'He/she is already not wanted over there, in a Western capital city, this is why he/she is coming here', one of the local respondents remarked sarcastically. Instead of one clear instruction they got many from different representatives of the foreign bank: it was a 'repetition of one and the same thing. Many [Westerners] were interested in one and the same question ..., which speaks of a certain level of trust', says another Bulgarian interviewee. The locals could not see why the Bulgarian managers should have two direct superiors: one in Sofia and another in the head office abroad, both watching them: 'cross-purposes, covering, manipulations, reciprocating – basically a mist'.

Interestingly enough, the younger respondents were not troubled at all by the strong hierarchy, and recognized organization in disorganization. This was the bank, in which we found the greatest differences between the generations' attitudes to incoming cultures in the whole project. Under 35 no one expressed reservations with regard to the behavior of the foreign colleagues while over that age it was just a few who dropped a good word in for the Westerners. The case study authors are convinced that the sharpness of this divide derives from a deliberate strategy pursued by the foreign bank to base the transformation of its daughter company on young, well-trained, 'pre-Westernized' Bulgarians. Typically, the new owner fired the old (or simply let them go) and hired the young. 'We are looking for a well-educated sales-oriented staff. 37 per cent are academics in our staff here. The average age is 39 ... The Bulgarian managers are all international. The board members were all working internationally. And the Bulgarians are coming back [from the West] ..., this is a good sign', says a Western manager proudly. 'The older people are more relationship-oriented, the younger are more business-oriented', his colleague adds. 'I hope these young people will be able to forget about corruption' – to quote another Westerner. A Bulgarian manager agrees with them: 'I have personally appointed and chosen the young people simply because I think that in a competitive market one has to pick people very carefully, to train them so that targets can be met. I have picked people who were not ready – not that I would like someone ready but this would be difficult, more expensive, dependent on the corporate culture in the place he is coming from, a combination hard to get right'. A Western colleague of his illustrates the results with the following example: 'telephone manners have changed. [They say] just 'allo', no clue who or where they are. They are doing that now with the company name when they pick up the phone'.

The policy of fast rejuvenation resulted in a strong identification with the bank on the part of the privileged young employees. The 'marketization' of the bank's business strategy, ranging from the introduction of strict risk analysis and management by objectives, through a proactive sales orientation (especially in retail banking) to more demanding and motivating HR practices, were clearly and quickly justified by the dedication and loyalty of the younger generation. They were the ones who profited the most from the new matrix structure for organizing the internal life of the institution, with its horizontal linkages and opportunities for teamwork. In the eyes of their older colleagues, they became part of the Western management – a role the younger specialists accepted happily. They praise the foreigners for their openness, flexibility, politeness and informality, for their cooperative behavior (avoiding the 'this is not my job' mentality), and for the fact that they can be criticized without retaliation. The young experts enjoy being independent in a systematic organization (even though, for instance, crediting could not be decentralized properly because of the high risk of fraud), attending training courses on a permanent basis, and taking part in what one of the foreign managers calls 'market-developing – a pioneer style'. It is more than natural for them that the 'what is not allowed is forbidden' rule was turned upside down, and today 'what is not forbidden is allowed'. Expertise is appreciated and confronted with the 'no problem, we will do it (without knowing how)' approach. 'I am a Western disciple, I have learnt many things from them. ... I have always been submerged in this culture', confesses a young Bulgarian manager full of enthusiasm.

The interviews demonstrate that the young generation's devotion affects some members of the older one. The youngest among the older respondents, for example, expresses her unease in measuring by overseas standards the culture implanted by the new owner: in the English or American model the goals are clearer, the criteria are defined, so if one achieves this and that gets such and such reward or punishment. 'Your head can fly off very quickly but at least you know it is up to you'. At the same time, she admits that in this bank she developed considerably: besides enhancing her professional knowledge in banking, she learned to take risks, became more self-confident and communicative. 'I was pretty diffident and unsure of myself. I have brightened my worldview and knowledge. I learned a [new] way of communication ... argumented, short, clear. In the beginning, I was nearly silent at the meetings, ... very nervous. Now I have opinion on each single question'. An older colleague of hers goes further: 'We have started to see the business more as development rather than as a state and security. They have habituated us to this in a non-intrusive way in the course of work. ... It was useful to me'.

Unlucky Constellations

In interpreting the above three cases, I would advise against converting them into distinct types of the emergence of spiritual capital in Eastern Europe or even in its banking sector after 1989. They demonstrate, however, that what we experienced at the W-Bank's subsidiaries was a lucky constellation of preconditions for the 'spiritualization' of incoming capitalist cultures. To use economic language, a cautious and credible exporter, attractive commodities and a huge demand met in a situation in which the consumption of incoming goods presented the importers with extraordinary experiences that combined rational conviction with faith. If, however, the local actors are somehow immune, resistant or simply indifferent to the incoming culture (because they think they already master it, because they fear its adverse effects, because the foreigners offer it unconvincingly, etc.), and/or the cultural transfer does not satisfy *and* transcend certain rational considerations to result in cathartic moments (because enfranchisement is severely imposed, formative experiences are missing, etc.), then the transnational encounter will not produce a sizeable amount of spiritual capital, or it will but only for a small group.

The low level of spirituality witnessed in the Slovene case points to the lack of chances for the local actors to play a pioneering role in cultural diffusion and live through the cathartic moments of initiation. The Czech bank shows how a deep cleavage between the parties in the cultural encounter impedes acculturation, in particular, the unfolding of its spiritual processes. Finally, the case of the Bulgarian institution suggests that the foreigners may find rather skeptical partners on the spot but can create the preconditions for a successful reception of their cultural/spiritual messages. True, the Western partner has powerful incentives and means of imposition at its disposal to guide the sequence of the encounter. Nevertheless, in order to cement the new capitalist cultures, it has to go beyond the mind of the locals to reach their soul as well. If acculturation stops at a smart but dry acceptance of a certain logic of capitalism, or even at the rational perception of personal interests, then even a small crisis in the functioning of the given institution or the whole sector, or a reasonable counter-argument to that logic may jeopardize cultural reception or turn it into a second-best pragmatic/cynical/simulated transaction.

Arguably, the first-best solutions cannot be lasting without a strong commitment bordering on faith and creating ethical norms. But can they be lasting?

A Fragile Capital

In the *Dioscuri* project we were also interested in the sustainability of the outcomes of the cultural encounters. Banking has proven to be one of the rare exceptions – a case in which the incoming cultures did not have to make essential concessions and produce a large number of hybrid forms with the indigenous cultures. In neither the other fields of entrepreneurship nor state governance did we find cases of such a smooth reception with so durable outcomes. Even in the third research field, economic knowledge it was only neoclassical (mainstream) economics that spread rather rapidly. However, even there it was only certain scientific ideas that did not meet strong resistance whereas the sociological components of scientific evolution (e.g., quality of teaching, norms of recruitment and evaluation of experts, publication habits, etc.) got widely mixed with the communist legacies of scholarship. Normally, the incoming cultures did not succeed in striking deep roots in the minds of the local actors, therefore they did not have much chance for being elevated onto a spiritual level. (Of course, the 'spiritualization' of the hybrid types may also be an option.) We witnessed the most stubborn resistance in public administration where the imported cultures of governance, for instance, in the management of large-scale EU development programs tend to evaporate once the foreign partner leaves and the cultural encounter ends. The incentives of acculturation weaken when cohabitation is over while in banking the continuous coexistence of the partners and their long-term common interests serve as favorable preconditions for spiritualization. At the same time, the case of mainstream economics, more exactly, the almost religious respect it often enjoys among Eastern European economists, demonstrates that it is probably more easy to convert certain cultural goods (e.g., ideas, scientific concepts, etc.) into spiritual capital, especially if their force of rational persuasion is strong enough, and there is an (epistemic) community whose members have waited for a long time to represent these goods as a minority of pioneers against the majority of the profession. Of course, like in banking and some other types of entrepreneurship, the pressure of global competition accelerates the process of acculturation, and the success in the competition helps spiritualize the incoming cultures.

To be sure, the above description of the transnational cultural encounters in banking is not entirely devoid of hybrid outcomes. The Western banks did make concessions to their partners in the region in various areas of business, ranging from tolerating their bureaucratic stiffness or, conversely, excessive flexibility, through accepting a certain degree of corruption, all the way down to respecting the local habits of dressing. Nevertheless, this degree of hybridism did not make acculturation unstable nor prevent the crystallization of spiritual capital in most of the banks observed.

Whatever future awaits our Eastern European bank managers and employees under capitalism, they will not face it unarmed. The spiritual assets they have acquired during the past decades enable them to choose from among various coping strategies, and these strategies contain cultures that facilitate or even prescribe adaptation. No matter if they remain in banking or switch to a financial authority, become educators, or launch a new firm in any branch of the economy, their spiritual capital can be reinvested, exchanged, transformed, revalued – but also wasted. It can develop (usually slowly) but also decline (rather rapidly). Like religion, this kind of spiritual capital is volatile in the long run. The fervor of the revealing experience may fade, the 'church' may lose its credit, the commitment of the 'believers' may weaken, and their community may disperse (erasing much of the accumulated social capital). Assessing the degree of volatility is, of course, a murky task. Let me nonetheless venture to make a thought experiment at the end of this paper.

I am afraid that the new capitalist spirit of our respondents is rather fragile and short run. Enfranchisement (initiation) is a one-time event, and one cannot remain a pioneer for ages. Because the given spiritual capital has strong rational (worldly) foundations, it is sensitive to changes in the economic reality, more precisely, to the success/failure ratio of the spirit-induced strategies of the actors. Probably, an economic actor (whose 'professional aberration' is to make pragmatic calculations, check their validity, etc.) needs to reinforce his/her commitment more often than the average religious believer. Furthermore, this spirit has a rather narrow focus, therefore, if not protected by a wider world-view, it will always be exposed, like in the current crisis, to challenges by non-capitalist or expressly anti-capitalist ideologies criticizing its alleged economic, liberal, etc. narrow-mindedness, soulless pragmatism and lack of *Kultur*, that is, 'coldness' or 'dryness'. It may always be accused of being a 'habit of the stomach' rather than that of the heart. Isn't it exactly this option that annoyed Max Weber when quoting Goethe on the 'nullities' who regard themselves as the peak of human civilization?

Thus, we have arrived at the old question: would any kind of 'on-the-job training' of capitalism not promise more lasting spiritual results if it were supported by a pro-capitalist religion that is by definition less particularistic, more altruistic and warm-hearted? The success stories of Evangelical Protestantism and Confucianism in various parts of the world suggest an affirmative answer to the question. At this point, Eastern Europe witnesses the paradox of a surprising decline of liberal thought amidst a regular capitalist revolution. With a few minor exceptions, one does not see an upswing of new – capitalism-friendly – religious movements in the region, which might help loosen up the paradox. Currently, the Russian Orthodox Church seems to accept modern capitalism more than the Hungarian Calvinists. The Catholic Church in Eastern Europe prefers the concept of *Sozialstaat* to even that of the least liberal versions of *Soziale Marktwirtschaft*. Many of the new rich in the region subscribe to Buddhism rather than Protestantism. Under communism, churches lost much of their spiritual capital, above all its pro-capitalist segment. In studying the emergence of the spirit of capitalism in the banking sector of eight ex-communist countries, we did not find significant differences according to their dominant religions. If we had searched for such differences more vigorously, ... I had better stop here, asking a sociologist of religion for help. Until I get it, I insist on the concepts of implicit spirituality and surrogate religion.

Notes and References

1 This argument was put forward by the Czech writer, Milan Kundera in the debate on the concept of Central Europe during the 1980s. The prediction of decay shows an incredible continuity in the works of Zygmunt Bauman, Slavoj Zizek and others. Cf. my Westerweiterung? Zur Metamorphose des Traums von Mitteleuropa, *Transit* 21/2001, pp 3–20; Rival Temptations – Passive Resistance: Cultural Globalization in Hungary. In: Peter L. Berger and Samuel Huntington (eds), Many Globalizations. Oxford: Oxford University Press 2002, pp 146–182.

2 See, e.g., Samuel Huntington, *The Clash of Civilizations and the Remaking of World Order*, Simon and Schuster, New York, 1996; Andrew C. Janos, East-Central Europe in the Modern World, Stanford UP, 2000.

3 The discipline of Comparative Capitalism is still in its metaphoric stage in Eastern Europe. The following phrases are used to describe the allegedly neoliberal/criminal traits of the new capitalist regimes: trickster capitalism, casino capitalism, auctioneer capitalism, Chicago Boys capitalism, capitalism without compromise, uncivil capitalism, clan capitalism, mafia capitalism, gangster capitalism, parasite capitalism, predatory capitalism, etc.

4 From among the few proud reports by economists (albeit without strong cultural argumentation), see, e.g., Anders Aslund, 'Building Capitalism'. Cambridge and New York: Cambridge University Press, 2002; Leszek Balcerowicz, Socialism, Capitalism, Transformation, Budapest CEU Press, 1995; Vaclav Klaus, On the Road to Democracy, NCPA, Dallas, 2005.

5 In journalistic language Slovakia is called nowadays the 'Tiger of Tatra' while Hungary was formerly labeled as the 'Pannonian Puma'.

6 Cf. Brian Zinnbauer, Religion nd Spirituality: Unfuzzying the Fuzzy, *Journal for the Scientific Study of Religion*, 1997/36, pp 549–564; Penny Marler and Kirk Hadaway, 'Being Religious' and 'Being Spiritual' in America, *Journal for the Scientific Study of Religion*, 2002/41, pp 289–300.

7 Needless to say that this distinction is contextual to a certain extent: for example, after 1989, the myth of equality under communism proved to be a rather hard component of economic culture that influenced the 'spirit' of incomes policies of various governments from time to time. And conversely, the legal rules specifying fair business practices under the new capitalist regimes of the region could barely influence the 'spirit' of the economic elites.

8 In other words, I will not draw a sharp dividing line between cultural and social capital in this respect, and will use them in the original sense suggested by Bourdieu, Coleman, Putnam and others. For the concepts of religious capital and religious social capital, see Laurence Iannaccone, Religious Participation: A Human Capital Approach, *Journal for the Scientific Study of Religion*, 1990/29, pp 297–314; Laurence Iannaccone et al, Deregulating Religion: The Economics of Church and State, *Economic Inquiry*, 1997/35, pp 350–364; Rodney Stark and Roger Finke, *Acts of Faith. Explaining the Human Side of Religion*, Berkeley 2000.

9 Cf. my Uncertain Ghosts. Populists and Urbans in Postcommunist Hungary, in Peter L. Berger (ed), Limits of Social Cohesion, Westview Press 1998; Rival Temptations – Passive Resistance…; (ed), A zárva várt Nyugat. Kulturális globalizáció Magyarországon. (The West as a Guest. Cultural Globalization in Hungary) Budapest, 2002; Little America. Eastern European Economic Cultures in the EU', in Ivan Krastev and Alan McPherson, *The Anti-American Century*, CEU Press, Budapest 2007; Vergangenheit oder Vorvergangenheit? Kultur und Wirtschaftsentwicklung in Osteuropa nach 1989, *Berliner Debatte* 2004/5–6; Which Past Matters? Culture and Economic Development in Eastern Europe after 1989, in Lawrence E. Harrison and Peter L. Berger (eds), Developing Cultures, Routledge 2006.

10 I owe special thanks to the members of the national research teams, in particular, to Drago Cengic, Petya Kabakchieva, Irena Kasparova, Jacek Kochanowicz, Vintila Mihailescu, Matevz Tomsic, Vesna Vucinic and Violetta Zentai. The project was funded by the European Commission and run by the Center for Public Policy (CEU, Budapest) and the Institute for Human Sciences (Vienna). For more information, see

www.dioscuriproject.net, and Janos Matyas Kovacs & Violetta Zentai, *Capitalism from Outside*, CEU Press, 2010.

11 Cf. the influential works by Samuel Huntington, Ronald Inglehart and Gert Hofstede as well as the European and World Values Surveys. For the few exceptions, see, e.g., Jacek Kochanowicz and Mira Marody, Towards Understanding the Polish Economic Culture, *Polish Sociological Review*, 2003/4, pp 343–368; Hans-Hermann Höhman (Hrsg), Eine unterschätzte Dimension? – Zur Rolle wirtschaftskultureller Faktoren in der osteuropäischen Transformation, Edition Temmen Bremen 1999; (Hrsg.) Kultur als Bestimmungsfaktor der Transformation im Osten Europas. Konzeptionelle Enrwicklungen – Empirische Befunde, Edition Temmen, Bremen 2001; Alina Mungiu-Pippidi and Denisa Mindruta, Was Huntington Right?, *International Politics*, 2002/2, pp 193–213; Piotr Sztompka, Civilizational Incompetence. The Trap of Post-Communist Societies, *Zeitschrift für Soziologie*, 1993/2 pp 85–95.

12 We were prepared for the fact that our respondents would apply a rather broad concept of economic culture encompassing both softer and harder items, even policies and institutional arrangements in which these items are incorporated. In any event, we wanted to use the term 'culture' in plural to express the prevailing diversity of cultural types in both the East and the West. At the same time, our interest in transnational encounters did not rest on an identification of nations with cultures, thereby ignoring cultural exchange *within* the countries under scrutiny. Moreover, it was assumed that intra-national cultural differences between generations, genders, regions, etc., though often caused by international differences, may overshadow the latter. Finally, our project was not intended to become a comprehensive survey of all possible functional subcategories of economic culture (such as work culture, consumption culture, financial culture, etc.).

13 The group of businesspeople studied in Field 1. included, besides the owners of the firms, also top managers and their chief consultants. The civil servants in Field 2. were leading officials working on both central and local levels. As regards Field 3., the group of economists primarily included academic experts, i.e., scientific researchers and university professors. Nonetheless, advocacy specialists, cultural brokers, economic journalists, etc. were also observed. The case studies that relied, besides the in-depth interviews, on participant observation, focus group meetings, etc., were subjected to comparative analysis across the country lines. On the average, *ninety interviews, nine case studies*, two media reviews and one literature review were made in each country. They served as raw material for *ten comparative analyses* covering the whole region.

14 This section rests on still unpublished national case studies written by Liviu Chelcea and Diana Mihaloiu (Romania), Drago Cengic (Croatia), Mikolaj Lewicki (Poland), Jelena Pesic (Serbia), Violetta Zentai (Hungary), and on their comparative analysis 'The Rise of a Banking Empire in Central and Eastern Europe' by Violetta Zentai. I owe special thanks to them, as to the other authors in the project who will be cited below. (See Note 16.).

15 See, e.g., Stephan Barisitz, Banking in Central and Eastern Europe 1980–2006. From Communism to Capitalism, London, Routledge 2007.

16 Here I rely on the case studies by Tanya Chavdarova and Georgi Ganev (Bulgaria), Mateja Rek (Slovenia) and Lenka Stepanova, Irena Kasparova and Marek Kaspar (Czech Republic).

17 The Mediterranean bank is the same as in the Czech case but the Near-Western institution is different from the one in the Croatian-Hungarian-Polish-Romanian-Serbian case.

Chapter 8

ORTHODOX SPIRITUAL CAPITAL AND RUSSIAN REFORM

Christopher Marsh

In an interview conducted with members of the editorial board of *Time* magazine in relation to their naming Vladimir Putin the 2007 'Person of the Year', Putin quoted scripture when asked about his attacks against corruption, responding that 'thou shalt not steal'. When asked further about his faith, Putin confessed to being a religious person, saying that he read the Bible and kept a copy of it on his plane. Putin further elaborated by stating that society needs a moral foundation, and that in his opinion the church can provide this[1]. Indeed, in a de-secularising Russia, recovering from seven decades of forced secularization under Communist rule, many are turning to the nation's spiritual heritage both for a sense of identity and answers to how to live in post-Communist society. With more than a thousand years of history in Russia, many have a deep cultural attachment to the Eastern Orthodox faith. As they attempt to integrate this faith into their daily lives, Orthodoxy may provide significant spiritual capital that may facilitate Russia's transition from Communism to democracy and the free market.

Before one jumps to the conclusion that Orthodox spiritual capital is the answer to Russia's prayers, however, one must also consider the fact that this very same faith tradition is being drawn upon in ways that clearly could derail Russia's reform efforts. From groups that refuse to be issued tax identification numbers out of fear of being labelled with the 'mark of the beast' to radical 'Orthodox' and skinheads who turn to violence against ethnic and religious minorities, the spiritual capital that is produced through a combination of Orthodox faith and Russian nationalism may indeed prove to be one of Russia's greatest obstacles to reform and modernization, much more difficult to overcome than the legacy of central planning or over-investment in the country's military-industrial complex.

Both Western and Russian media often feed off headlines that emphasize the negative dimensions of contemporary Russian society, leading to sharply critical and pessimistic assessments of the resources for development that Orthodox Christianity offers. Stories that offer a much more positive and encouraging picture only find their way onto the back pages of Russia's media, if they receive mention at all, and almost never make it into the Western press. From women who retire from positions of power and influence in industry to rebuild Russian church life, to those who work full-time while also volunteering many hours per week for charity work, many Russian Orthodox Christians are motivated by a sense of religious calling that leads them to engage in a variety of acts of charity and compassion[2]. The story of Orthodox spiritual capital in contemporary Russia, therefore, has its bright side as well as its dark side, and as with all religious traditions, the answer to what resources are available for political, social, and economic development rests not simply in texts or complex theological formulations, but in 'lived' religious traditions and their construction in the daily lives of citizens.

Russian society faces some of the most daunting challenges of development of any society in the world today. Its social and moral fabric has faced one of history's most insidious onslaughts, further complicating the challenges of democratization, economic transformation, and the development of a healthy society. This chapter begins with a brief discussion of the concepts of spiritual capital and social capital first in general and then in the Russian context, and how these resources may be used to promote reform along the political, social, and economic fronts. It then continues with empirical analysis of some of the negative and positive dimensions of spiritual capital in Russia today. The first focuses on the negative example offered by those who draw upon the Orthodox Christian tradition – often in a perverted form that runs staunchly counter to the Russian Orthodox Church's own position – in their fight against globalization and liberalization (understood as Westernization), often resulting in xenophobic, racist, and fascist reactions. The second section offers a brighter picture, one in which people show compassion for their fellow citizens and exhibit commitments to civic, democratic, and free-market values. Finally, the chapter concludes with a brief conclusion that examines how the Russian case relates to and informs the broader discussion of spiritual capital in other cultural and national contexts.

Religious Beliefs and Values among the Russian Orthodox

In order to explore the civic, political, and social values of Russian Orthodox Christians, one must first establish a picture of the general religious beliefs and practices of Russians in order to determine just who can be considered a practicing Orthodox Christian[3]. While it is clear that Orthodox Christianity is the majority religion of Russia, estimates of the number of adherents ranges from 55 to 80 percent, depending on how one calculates the figure. The degree to which Russians are actually connected to the church, however, is a matter of great debate. What is clear is that levels of church attendance in Russia are among the lowest in all of Europe, with as few as two percent of Russians attending church services regularly, although Naletova has successfully argued that Orthodox spirituality certainly exists 'beyond the church walls'[4]. How then does one conceptualize Russian Orthodox religiosity? In the two most thorough analyses of Orthodox religious life in Russia, Chesnokova has shown that religiosity and churchliness are complex processes that cannot be gauged by any single indicator[5]. Her analysis explored the Orthodox religiosity of Russians using a complex array of indicators, including belief in God, regular church attendance, the taking of communion, the offering of confession, fasting at prescribed times, praying at home with the use of church prayer books (*molitoslov*), and knowledge of Old Church Slavonic sufficient to understand the liturgy. Understood this way, it was clear that only a very small number of self-identified Orthodox Christians were 'fully churched', while the majority of respondents exhibited extremely low levels of churchliness. These findings, although perhaps more nuanced, are quite in line with the conclusions reached by several other Russian scholars who have argued that the number of 'real', 'traditional' or 'churchly' Orthodox in Russia is no larger than 5–7 percent of the population, with other Orthodox believers being only 'nominal' Orthodox, or as Varzanova has phrased it, Orthodox only in a 'cultural sense'[6].

In order to examine the critically important issue of how differing *types* and *levels* of Orthodox religiosity may be related to individuals' value orientations toward civic life, religion and politics, and the transition from Communism, I rely upon data from the World Values Survey[7]. The first set of questions I explore here relates to the role religion plays in the lives of Orthodox believers, in terms of their beliefs in God and sin, frequency of prayer, and church attendance (see Table 8.1). While it is not very surprising that less than 30 percent of those who did not identify themselves as members of any particular religious tradition said that they believed in God, only 97 percent of Orthodox Christians felt the same way, meaning that 3 percent of Orthodox believers polled did not profess belief in God, despite identifying themselves as Orthodox Christians. While perhaps a less significant deviation from church teachings than not believing in God, only 85 percent of Orthodox said that they believed in sin, while less than 60 percent stated that they believed in life after death (54 percent) or heaven (58 percent). For the non-religious, these numbers were also quite low, 13.6 and 10.7 percent, respectively, although belief in sin was the highest of all beliefs held by this group, at almost 40 percent.

Table 8.1. **Orthodox Christians and their Religious Beliefs**

	Orthodox Christians (percent)	Non-Religious (percent)
Believe in God	97	29.6
Believe in sin	85	39.3
Believe in life after death	54	13.6
Believe in heaven	58	10.7

Table 8.2. **Orthodox Christians and their Religious Feelings and Behaviour**

	Orthodox Christians (percent)	Non-Religious (percent)
Receive comfort and strength from religion	86	20.4
How important is God in your life[a]	60.4	12.4
Moments of prayer or meditation	56	10.8
Pray outside of religious services (at least once per day)	27.9	3.8
Church attendance: once per week (once per month)	5.4 (11.0)	0.3 (1.3)

Note: [a] 7–10 on 10-point scale.

When looking at religious behaviour as opposed to only beliefs, there seems to be a sharp disparity (see Table 8.2). While 86 percent of Orthodox Christians take comfort and find strength in their religion, only slightly more than 5 percent attend religious services weekly, although 11 percent do so at least once per month. This is a similar phenomenon to that of 'believing without belonging', which Grace Davie identified as a trend in England after World War II[8], and further corroborates Naletova's finding that Orthodox religiosity cannot be gauged by church attendance alone[9]. The low levels of church attendance should not be taken to imply that the religious experience of such believers is vacuous, however, as more than one quarter pray at least once per day, while more than half (56 percent) regularly take moments of prayer or meditation. Nevertheless, there does appear to be a spiritual disconnect for many, as only 60 percent responded that God played an important part in their lives.

These levels of religiosity are much higher on every indicator for Orthodox Christians than for the non-religious. The data also indicate, however, that there are great divisions among those who identify themselves as Orthodox. The finding that only a small percentage of self-identifying Orthodox Christians attend church regularly, while some even state that they do not believe in God, leads one to wonder how individuals construe their responses in their own minds. This also suggests, however, that it is necessary to break the group of Orthodox believers down into two distinct categories. The first is that of the devout Orthodox, a category that includes only those who identified themselves as Orthodox Christians, who also stated that they believe in God, and who also attend church services at least once per month, a lower standard than that used in Protestant societies, but one which still exhibits a healthy degree of connection to the church. The remaining self-identifying Orthodox, some of whom do not even believe in God and none of whom attend church services more than a few times per year, can be labeled as the 'cultural Orthodox', following Varzanova[10]. This dataset and categorization will be used in the analyses that follow, as I attempt to identify ways in which Orthodox spiritual capital may affect Russia's transition to civil society, democracy, and the free market, whether for good or for ill[11].

Russian Orthodoxy and Anti-Semitism, Intolerance, and Xenophobia

In June 2007, a young Russian student at an Orthodox icon-painting school was arrested on 37 counts of homicide[12]. It turns out that Artur Ryno had spent more than a year targeting and killing members of minority ethnic groups in Moscow, mostly from the traditionally-Muslim regions of Central Asia and the Caucasus. For people such as Ryno – including members of some quasi-fascist groups associated with Russia's 'skinheads' – the combination of Russian nationalism and a perverted form of Orthodox Christianity is lethal.

The case of Artur Ryno is not an isolated one, although it is certainly one of the most horrific and extreme. Lesser forms of religiously-based violence include such instances as the vandalising of the Sakharov Museum in January 2003, when several Orthodox 'hooligans' smashed and destroyed an art exhibit entitled 'Danger – Religion'. The exhibit which incited such an extreme reaction as this included a Coca Cola advertisement with the words 'This is my blood' strewn across a scene from the Last Supper. Another was an icon without a face, inviting visitors to insert their head into the opening and snap a picture[13]. Not only were the charges against the culprits of the vandalism dismissed by the court, the museum curator was actually himself brought up on charges of inciting religious and ethnic hatred, further attesting to the state of religiously-based intolerance in Russia. Other artists have been the victims of lesser attacks, including pop-singer Madonna, whose concert in Moscow in the fall of 2006 was the cause for protests among Orthodox believers who considered her an 'an advocate of the Kabbalah' and vowed to prevent her from performing[14].

Who are these people whose racial and religious hatred rests upon a volatile mix of (non-canonical) Orthodox Christianity and Russian nationalism? They can be labelled with several different terms, including political Orthodox, radical Orthodox, or, perhaps the best description, the 'Orthodox nationalists'.

Of course, not everyone who holds such radical views turns to violence. Some simply turn to hatred, xenophobia, and anti-Semitism. One of the most interesting approaches to this has been that put forth by Klimchuk in his article 'On the National Origins of Jesus Christ'[15]. Klimchuk argues that this issue is quite relevant, given that 'the question of Christ's racial and national identity turns into the question of chosenness by God of this or that nation'[16]. He argues that Jesus visited India, Nepal, the Himalayas, Persia, and Egypt, and then puts forth the argument that Jesus was a Slav, substantiating his argument with the proposition that Slavs governed Palestine during the 'Babylonian captivity'. He even argues that Nefertiti's Slavic appearance is further proof of the prominence of the Slavs in the ancient world.

Even a cursory analysis of contemporary Russia indicates that issues of identity and belonging are among the most salient in society. The salience of difference varies with inclusion. In a society which has become culturally accepting and intermixed, ethnic and religious differences lose salience. In such societies, there are high degrees of intermarriage between ethnic and religious communities, and neighbourhoods are not only mixed, but people pay little attention to the ethnic composition or religious preferences of their neighbours. Russia has a long way to go toward this goal. While more than three-quarters of Russians polled considered a happy sexual relationship the most important element for a successful marriage, the other elements that were considered important indicate that religious and ethnic difference are quite salient in contemporary Russian society. Among devout Orthodox, not only was their response 10 percentage points lower than that of other Russians, more than half of devout Orthodox felt that their spouse's religious beliefs were important (see Table 8.3). More than a quarter (28 percent) also felt the same way about their spouse's ethnic background, compared to only 20.9 percent for other Russians. These data not only indicate significantly greater

Table 8.3. **Important Elements for a Successful Marriage**

	Devout Orthodox	Cultural Orthodox	Non-Religious Russians
Happy sexual relationship	77.4	86.4	87.6
Religious beliefs	58	42.6	35.2
Social background	34.4	35.6	31.9
Same ethnic background	28	23.2	20.9

Table 8.4. **People You Would Not Like to Have as Neighbours**

	Devout Orthodox	Cultural Orthodox	Non-Religious Russians
Homosexuals	56.3	57.8	58.2
Gypsies	40.7	48.3	45.4
Immigrants	14.8	11.3	11.2
Muslims	14.1	14.5	13.7
Jews	12.6	12.1	11.5
People of Different Race	11.1	9.3	8.2

levels of ethnic and religious salience among devout Orthodox, but troublingly high levels for all Russians.

This picture is further supported by data relating to tolerance, particularly for one's neighbours. The highest levels of intolerance are for homosexuals, with 58 percent of all Russians responding that they would not like to have homosexuals as neighbours. The picture is only slightly better for Gypsies, with 45 percent of all Russians not wishing to have them as neighbours. Interestingly, this number was significantly lower for devout Orthodox, with only 40 percent feeling the same way. In general, Russians surveyed exhibited moderate levels of intolerance toward ethnic and religious minorities, with an average of around 10–15 percent indicating that they would not wish to have immigrants, Muslims, Jews, or members of a different race as neighbours. From the perspective of Orthodox spiritual capital, what is most interesting is that the devout Orthodox exhibited significantly *higher* levels of intolerance on several variables, including anti-Semitism and negative attitudes towards immigrants, while when it came to Islamophobia and negative attitudes towards Gypsies they were edged out by the cultural Orthodox.

While the commitment to tolerance exhibited by the Orthodox respondents in the survey was less than encouraging, as an abstract concept all Russians generally agreed that children should be encouraged to be tolerant of others (see Table 8.5). Moreover, religious attachment alone explains the greater than 10 percentage point difference in response between the devout Orthodox (76.3 percent) and non-religious Russians (65.5 percent), with the cultural Orthodox falling squarely in between (69.5 percent). While Orthodox faith seems to be a significant resource when it comes to the value of tolerance, its impact is not sufficient to engender greater commitments to tolerance.

One last factor which significantly impacts the issue of xenophobia and intolerance is that of nationalism. Over the past decade, numerous studies have appeared which document the ways in which religion and nationalism have become interconnected, often with disastrous results[17]. These studies highlight

Table 8.5. **Tolerance and Nationalism**

	Devout Orthodox	Cultural Orthodox	Non-Religious Russians
Children should be encouraged to be tolerant of others	76.3	69.5	65.5
Willing to fight for your country	54.8	60.2	68.8

the connection between Orthodoxy and Russian nationalism, and identify that the 'Orthodoxy' that is related to Russian nationalism is not one based on the teachings of the church or an idea adhered to by all or even the majority of true believers; in fact, it appears that the *greater* one's commitment to nationalism the *lesser* is that person's connection to the church. This finding is corroborated here, and sheds light on the above findings. When asked whether or not they were willing to fight for their country – an indicator of patriotism – significantly fewer devout Orthodox than non-religious Russians responded that they would. In fact, barely more than half the devout Orthodox were willing to fight for Russia, indicating that although they can be intolerant of others, this intolerance may only signal a desire to live in a community of people of similar religious and ethnic background, but not with any willingness to engage in violence to achieve or perhaps even sustain it.

Across a range of indicators, those who identify strongly with Orthodoxy in contemporary Russia exhibit some troubling attitudes. A greater salience of religious and ethnic difference coupled with anti-Semitism, Islamophobia, xenophobia, and general intolerance is not a propitious environment for Russia's social, political, and economic transformation. While this does not, of course, motivate everyone to engage in anti-social or deviant behaviour, as Snyder has shown, attitudes such as these can become enflamed during transitions and can derail democratization efforts[18].

Russian Orthodoxy and Social, Economic, and Political Reform

Although the above analysis of xenophobia, intolerance, and nationalism highlights some of the obstacles that stand in the way of Russia's reform efforts, the picture is not entirely bleak, and in fact there are several positive signs visible. Over the past 15 years, Russia has stabilized a great deal. While the bloody feud over Chechnya has not fully subsided, further large-scale, territorially-based ethnic conflicts have not arisen in other parts of the country. On the economic front, the economy has stabilized, albeit following a period of inflation that saw

Moscow enter the ranks of the world's most expensive cities, putting tremendous strains on Russians attempting to survive and wishing to thrive in the post-Communist economy. And while democracy and justice were dealt several blows under the Putin presidency, many – apparently including the editors of *Time* magazine – felt that this was a fair trade-off in the process of establishing law and order, a feature so lacking under Yeltsin. Finally, while the cloudiness over the use of power between Putin and Medvedev is not part of a glorious moment in the history of Russian democracy, neither individual will represent its final story. In the end, there is at least a peaceful *division* of power.

Russian Orthodoxy has very much been a part of the story of Russia's recovery and stabilization, particularly over the past several years. Although the church has not been a leading force in this process, tending more to bless political actions *post facto* rather than getting directly involved in the political process, Orthodox Christians have been significant players in this process, from leaders such as Putin and foreign minister Igor Ivanov (who reportedly ensures that all of his staff are baptized Christians, even to the point of having them baptized on the spot at the foreign ministry) to ordinary citizens whose Orthodox spirituality impacts their perceptions of and behaviour in the public square.

Orthodox Christians in Russia are not distanced from community life and the plight of those around them (see Table 8.6). Nearly 80 percent of devout Orthodox responded that they were concerned with the sick and disabled, with more than 50 percent responding that they were even prepared to help in any way they could. Cultural Orthodox were not far behind, with nearly 70 percent and just below 50 percent feeling the same way. Finally, non-religious Russians were only a step behind the Orthodox, with nearly 60 percent and 45 percent, respectively, expressing concern and willingness to help the sick.

Table 8.6. **Orthodox Christians and their Views of Society**

	Devout Orthodox	Cultural Orthodox	Non-Religious Russians
Concerned with living conditions of sick and disabled[a]	78.7	67.6	58.5
Concerned with living conditions of fellow countrymen[a]	28.8	18.8	19.7
Concerned with living conditions of neighbours[a]	21.8	17.1	11.9
Prepared to help sick and disabled[b]	53.2	47.4	44.3
Prepared to help neighbours improve living conditions[b]	31.4	26.8	22.6

Notes: [a] very much and much.
       [b] absolutely yes and yes.

When it comes to one's neighbours, however, all groups are less concerned and prepared to help than they are for the sick and disabled. For example, only 31.4 percent of devout Orthodox were prepared to help their neighbours, while 26.8 percent of cultural Orthodox and 22.6 percent of non-religious Russians responded the same way. Quite interesting, however, is the fact that all three groups were more concerned with their fellow countrymen than their neighbours. While 28.8 percent of devout Orthodox were concerned for their fellow countrymen, only 21.8 were concerned for the living conditions of their neighbours, with similar disparities for the cultural Orthodox and non-religious respondents. One possible explanation for this may be the ethnic dimension of Russian life, since respondents may have had in mind their ethnic kin when being asked about fellow countrymen. In this regard, there is a marked tendency for all Russians, no matter what their religious behaviour, to identify more with their 'imagined' national community than their actual neighbourhood community[19]. To the extent that this is so, it raises serious and somewhat disturbing questions about the prospect of genuine democratization given the world-historical experience of the vibrancy of *national* level democracy being contingent upon the vibrancy of *local* level civic engagement[20].

Eastern Orthodoxy, and Russian Orthodox Christianity in particular, have received significant criticism as a religious and cultural tradition that may not be conducive to free market economics. Are societies in which Orthodox Christianity is the dominant religious tradition really condemned to backwardness? While Greece stands out as a counter-example, the challenges of post-Communist economic transformation are significantly more daunting than the process of economic transformation that Greece had to navigate over the past quarter century, not to mention the fact that Orthodoxy itself was attacked by the Communist Party during the Soviet era[21]. Weber himself argued that Orthodoxy was too mystically oriented and focused on other-worldly concerns to generate a sufficient drive to capitalist accumulation[22]. Has Russian Orthodoxy changed significantly since Weber's time that such a claim is no longer valid?

Whatever the degree of religiosity among Russians, and all stereotypes aside, there is apparently no disinclination away from work. When asked by the World Values Survey what values children should be encouraged to hold, almost 90 percent of Russians answered hard work. What is perhaps more telling is that among Orthodox Christians this number reached 93 percent, and even higher among those who attended church more regularly and prayed more frequently. While hard work is a value that Orthodox Christians seem to respect, much like Weber's Calvinists, for Russia's Orthodox Christians work apparently is not an end in itself. Less than 60 percent of Russians thought that work was very important in their lives, and only 55 percent of Orthodox Christians agreed.

Table 8.7. **Orthodox Christians and their Views on Economics and Work**

	Devout Orthodox	Cultural Orthodox	Non-Religious Russians
Children should be encouraged to value hard work	94.1	92.5	89.3
Work is important in your life: very important	60.0	78.9	86.2
Work is a duty toward society: strongly agree	65.2	58.1	52.8
Large income gap is necessary as incentive for individual effort	54.1	60.9	65.3
In order to be considered just, a society should eliminate large income inequalities: very important	43.7	52.7	58.2

Note: Figures are for the percentage of respondents at the positive end of each scale: work *rather* or *very important; agree* or *strongly agree* that work is duty; *7 to 10* on a scale of 10 for income gap as incentive; *important* or *very important* to eliminate inequalities.

What is most interesting are their attitudes towards private property and the market. Only 15 percent of Russians surveyed felt that private ownership within the economy should increase, while 33 percent actually thought that state ownership should be expanded (the plurality of respondents held an ambiguous position on the issue). What is even more surprising is that among Orthodox Christians this number rose to 40 percent, increased to 50 percent for those who prayed daily, and reached 55 percent for those who attended church weekly, indicating a very strong correlation between religiosity and preference for the state's hand in the economy.

When it comes to large income inequalities, Russians seem to hold a similar preference for state involvement in the economy, with almost 58 percent agreeing that to be just, it is important for the government to eliminate large income inequalities, compared to only 15 percent feeling that it is not important. A less pronounced but still readily apparent tendency existed for Orthodox Christians in particular and the more religious in general to be more supportive of state involvement in the economy; among Orthodox Christians and those who attended church weekly and prayed daily, almost 65 percent supported the idea of the state eliminating large income inequalities.

A somewhat contradictory message comes across when it comes to the issue of the necessity of differentials in income as a means of financial incentive. Not only are Russians in general accepting of this idea, they strongly support it; almost 55 percent of Russians agreed that large income differentials are necessary as an economic incentive, compared to only 16 percent who disagreed. As if this weren't surprising enough given the above findings,

Orthodox Christians once again led the pack, with 60 percent agreeing, although church attendance and frequency of prayer this time were associated with lower levels of agreement.

What can these figures tell us about Orthodoxy and market reform in Russia? For one, the views of Russian Orthodox Christians toward work, economic life, and capitalism do not appear to be incompatible with modern market economics, although a sizeable segment of the Russian population seems somewhat confused over the nature of market principles and the inequalities that inevitably develop and that are indeed necessary to spur on economic growth. Whether attributable to the country's Orthodox religious heritage or the Soviet glorification of work, respect for hard work in particular seems to be alive and well in Russia. As Nikolas Gvosdev points out, the fourth century theologian St John Chrysostom, who is part of the early Christian tradition in general but who is particularly revered in the Orthodox world, exhorted to his audience 'Let us not then despise labour; let us not despise work; for before the Kingdom of Heaven, we receive the greatest recompense from thence'[23].

We must be quick to identify, however, that labour does not equal capitalism, and many of the same people who said that they valued hard work also stated a preference for state involvement in the economy, from increased state ownership to state intervention to reduce large income inequalities. Since the question asked was relative (greater state involvement), we cannot and should not conclude that agreeing with this statement indicates a desire for complete nationalization of the economy or a return to state socialism. Evidence for this comes from the seemingly contradictory finding that a majority of Russians welcome pay differentials as a means of generating economic incentives. In some way, this may represent a reconciliation between the attraction and reality of modern markets and the Christian value – alive and well within the Orthodox tradition – of an aversion to an overabundance of wealth and excess.

Even a brief review of the economic values of the Russian Orthodox tradition makes clear that market economics and private property are in no way proscribed by such beliefs. Insofar as modern capitalism requires workers to sell their labour in a market-rational context, that is, to the highest bidder, there would seem to be some incongruity between the two. This lack of congruence, however, is probably no more than it is for other Christians or believers of other faith traditions functioning within market economies around the globe. While some religions may not be very clear on what sort of economic behaviours are allowed and which ones are proscribed, the fact that Orthodox Christianity is perhaps more clear than some on this issue by no means indicates that believers will follow the church's teachings, which is again often the case across the globe.

Where the beliefs of a devout Orthodox might come into conflict with the demands of the market is probably on the issue of an excessive amount of time devoted to labour and perhaps even the desire to accumulate wealth and material possessions that fuels Western capitalism. In fact, not only does Orthodoxy not provide any justification for the accumulation of wealth à la Calvinism, it actually warns against it. Unlike the Protestant ethic, therefore, whose theology provided a basis for prolonged labour and the pursuit of wealth, Orthodoxy may only allow free-market activity, entrepreneurship, and the accumulation of a modest living. While the Church and its teachings seem quite compatible with a tame version of market economics, therefore, it may not serve as a stimulus to wealth creation. This is not likely to be a problem, however, for good, old-fashioned desire for wealth is proving to be in quite plentiful supply in today's Russia. What is desperately needed is a set of moral and ethical principles to guide Russians as they operate within an economy that is still not very institutionalized or sufficiently regulated by the state or social custom.

Orthodox Christianity and Civil Society

Although showing varying levels of concern for their fellow citizens, Russians are much less engaged in civic and political life than people in many other societies, a factor that has been the topic of much criticism of Russian society and one that has even been identified as largely responsible for the traumas of the country's post-Communist political and economic development[24].

Ever since the collapse of the Soviet Union, scholars have regularly identified low levels of interpersonal trust in Russia as a major obstacle to political reform and social development[25]. As the data in Table 8.8 indicate, levels of trust are even lower for devout Orthodox than they are for other Russians. Less than a quarter of all Russians polled agreed that most people can be trusted, with the percent agreeing with that statement highest among the cultural Orthodox and

Table 8.8. **Orthodox Christians and Civic Engagement**

	Devout Orthodox	Cultural Orthodox	Non-Religious Russians
Most people can be trusted	19.3	23.6	23.1
Trust in churches: great deal (quite a lot)	73.3 (19.3)	32.6 (43.9)	5.7 (30)
Often discuss political matters	20.9	20.7	18.9
Belong to local political organization	0.5	0.2	0.6
Belong to a political party	0.5	1.2	1.1
Interested in politics[a]	34.7	41.4	38.7

Note: [a] very interested and somewhat interested.

the non-religious (23.6 and 23.1 percent, respectively), compared to 19.3 percent for devout Orthodox. This may be attributable to the religious outlook of devout believers. Orthodox Christians, not unlike many other Christians, believe in the fallen nature of this world and the existence of evil, perhaps leading to distrust for those in general society, as opposed to co-religionists or those with whom one has had frequent contact. Given these numbers, however, we should be careful about ascribing too much significance to this difference, though the topic certainly warrants further study. Here it is sufficient to note that the levels of trust among citizens in Russia are on par with those of other countries of the former Soviet Union, which tend to be *higher* than in the Balkans and Central and Eastern Europe[26].

Surveys also regularly find that the church is the most trusted institution in Russian society, with around 60 percent of all Russians expressing confidence in this important civil society institution. Using two distinct categories for Orthodox believers, we can see that there is in fact great variation in levels of trust in the church. Devout Orthodox have the highest levels of trust in the church, with over 92 percent saying that they have either a great deal of trust in the church (73.3 percent), or quite a lot of trust (19.3 percent). It is also significant that the devout Orthodox are the only group that has more responses in the 'great deal' category than in the 'quite a lot' category. The cultural Orthodox still have a high level of trust in the church, with a total of over 76 percent for both positive responses, but more have quite a lot of trust in the church (43.9 percent) than a great deal of trust (32.6 percent). The devout Orthodox thus are more trusting of the church numerically and by degree. Interestingly, and something that has remained overlooked by those who look at trust in institutions, is the fact that very few non-religious Russians have a great deal of trust in the church, although a modest 30 percent do respond that they have quite a lot of trust. The ability of the church to act as a bridge across the various factions of civil society would appear, therefore, to remain limited.

When it comes specifically to the political realm, there appears to be a relatively healthy level of interest in politics, although this is not accompanied by any significant level of political involvement. While approximately 40 percent of all respondents stated that they were interested in politics (41.4 percent for cultural Orthodox and 38.7 percent for non-religious), the number of devout Orthodox who agreed was the lowest of all three groupings (34.7 percent), perhaps reflecting an other-worldly orientation of devout believers. This idea is supported by the fact that devout Orthodox were also less likely than the cultural Orthodox and the non-religious to belong to political organizations. While 0.5 percent of devout Orthodox respondents stated that they were either members of a political party or a local political organization, there was a greater likelihood for cultural Orthodox and non-religious

Table 8.9. Orthodox Christians and their Political Efficacy

	Devout Orthodox	Cultural Orthodox	Non-Religious Russians
Sign a petition	10.7 (24.6)	10.6 (28.3)	11.5 (31.9)
Attend lawful demonstration	22.5 (23.0)	23.9 (30.5)	23.1 (32.8)
Join a boycott	1.6 (13.4)	2.4 (18.2)	2.4 (23.4)
Join an unofficial strike	0.5 (6.4)	1.5 (12.3)	1.6 (17.4)

Note: Responses are for have done (might do).

Russians to belong to a political party (1.2 and 1.1 percent, respectively). Although still representing a very small number in absolute terms, this finding is not surprising given the current state of party development in Russia.

Although involvement in the formal political realm remains low, Russians show a healthy level of political engagement and preparedness to participate in a variety of informal political activities, such as signing petitions, joining boycotts, and taking part in demonstrations and strikes. More than a quarter of all Russians are prepared to sign a petition, while more than 10 percent have actually done so. Approximately the same number are willing to attend a lawful demonstration, while more than 20 percent actually have. Significantly fewer are prepared to join a boycott, however, an act only around 2 percent have taken part in. Not surprisingly, the numbers are even less for taking part in an unofficial strike. Nevertheless, the data suggest that there is a large segment of society – nearly half – that exhibits healthy levels of political efficacy. The data are just as clear, however, in indicating that these levels are directly related to religious belief and religiosity, with identification with the Orthodox Church and religious devotion, respectively, strongly associated with diminished levels of political efficacy, with non-religious Russians registering significantly higher responses on every indicator while devout Orthodox exhibit the lowest levels on each indicator.

Orthodox Christianity and Russian Democracy

The question of civic engagement is important. Theories of development focus increasingly on it and a growing body of empirical evidence from around the world suggests that a civil society plays a critical role in pushing for democracy and is necessary to sustain democratic governance once it is attained. In today's Russia, the latter is the central issue, as the advances made in Russian democracy in its first decade are beginning to lose ground to the growing authoritarian tendencies of Putin and several other leaders in Russia who support a strong-hand approach to governance. Aside from the issue of civic engagement, therefore, we must consider the issue of support for a democratic system in Russia, since the two are not synonymous and it is entirely feasible that civic engagement might be associated with authoritarian forces that seek to bring back vestiges of the old system[27].

Some of the evidence presented in Table 8.5 certainly seems to support such an idea. When it comes to the issue of how one assesses the Communist regime, non-religious Russians are significantly less likely to offer a positive assessment of the Soviet system. While only 36 percent of non-religious Russians offered a positive assessment of the Communist regime, 46 percent – nearly half – of cultural Orthodox did so. Quite interestingly, the devout Orthodox responded more similarly to the non-religious than their Orthodox brethren, with 40 percent offering a positive view of the Communist regime. The finding that the non-Orthodox are less likely to have a positive assessment of the Soviet regime may be attributable to the fact that many of those in the survey who are non-religious are also likely to be non-Orthodox (in terms of self-identification), and therefore highly likely to include a large number of non-Russians, who tend to have a more negative assessment of the USSR than ethnic Russians. Similarly, the finding that the devout Orthodox are less predisposed to the Communist regime can be explained by the fact that the Russian Orthodox Church was systematically attacked by the Communist state, a historical fact that is not forgotten by more devout Orthodox.

Before we draw any premature conclusions about what these findings mean, however, we must consider the actual views of Russian Orthodox Christians toward democracy. While only 8.6 percent of devout Orthodox were either very satisfied or rather satisfied with the way democracy is developing in Russia, this

Table 8.10. **Orthodox Christians and their Views of Democracy**

	Devout Orthodox	Cultural Orthodox	Non-Religious Russians
Positive assessment of the Communist regime[a]	40.1	46.3	36
Satisfied with way democracy developing in Russia[b]	1.1 (7.5)	0.3 (5.5)	0.4 (5.5)
Democracy better than other political systems[c]	10.7 (35.3)	9.1 (38.5)	8.5 (38.5)
Having a democratic political system[c]	9.1 (32.1)	6.2 (41.7)	5.0 (41.5)
Having a strong leader[c]	11.8 (27.3)	13.5 (27.8)	11.4 (27.8)

Notes: [a] 7–10 on 10 point scale.
         [b] very satisfied (rather satisfied).
         [c] strongly agree (agree).

is much higher than for the other two groups, with only 5.8 and 5.9 percent, respectively, offering a similar assessment. One must be cautious in drawing conclusions from this indicator alone, however, for given the state of democracy in Russia, greater satisfaction with the way democracy is developing could just as easily be an indication of political naïveté rather than attachment to democracy.

Devout Orthodox were also more likely to agree with the statement that democracy is better than other political systems, however, further supporting the idea that Orthodoxy might not be the obstacle to democracy that some suspect. Nearly 11 percent of devout Orthodox strongly agreed with this statement, compared to 9.1 percent for cultural Orthodox and only 8.5 percent for non-religious Russians. While devout Orthodox showed a greater tendency to agree more resolutely that democracy is a superior form of governance, all three groups are statistically very similar when both positive responses are combined, with around 47 percent being positively predisposed toward democracy. Likewise, more devout Orthodox said that they strongly valued having a democratic political system than either cultural Orthodox or non-religious Russians. While devout Orthodox once again exhibited a firmer commitment to democracy, when both positive responses are combined more cultural Orthodox agreed in general.

When it comes to alternative forms of rule, it is the cultural Orthodox as a group who are the most likely to support a strong leader (13.5 percent), while the devout Orthodox and non-religious Russians exhibited almost identical levels of agreement (11.8 and 11.4 percent, respectively). It is also important to note that when both positive responses are summed, each group was more positively predisposed toward democracy than a strong leader. Although having a strong leader is not incompatible with democracy, if Lord Acton is right, then a citizenry that values a strong leader much more than democracy is not likely to remain a democracy for long.

Notes and References

1 Adi Ignatius, 'A Tsar is Born', *Time* (December 31, 2007–January 7, 2008), 46–62.
2 Some excellent examples of such behavior are offered and discussed in Wallace L. Daniel, *The Orthodox Church and Civil Society in Russia* (College Station, TX: Texas A & M University Press, 2006). See also M. P. Mchedlov, ed., *Miloserdie* (Moscow: ROSSPEN, 1998).
3 Much of the preliminary discussion here necessarily draws heavily upon my related investigation of attitudes toward religion and politics contained in 'Russian Orthodox Christians and Their Orientation toward Church and State', *Journal of Church and State* 47, 3 (Summer 2005): 545–561.
4 Inna Naletova, 'Orthodoxy Beyond the Church Walls', dissertation presented for the degree of doctor of philosophy, Boston University, 2006.

5 V. F. Chesnokova, *Protsess Votserkovleniya Naseleniya v Sovremennoi Rossii* (Moscow: Fond 'Obshchestvennoe Mnenie', 1994 and 2000).

6 M. P. Mchedlov, 'Religioznoe vozrozhdenie v Rossii: Prichiny, Kharakter, Tendentsii', *Obnovlenie Rossii: Trudnyi Poisk Reshchenii* (Moscow: Rossiiskii Nezavisimyi Institut Sotsial'nykh i Natsional'nykh Problem, 1992), 102–12; M. P. Mchedlov, 'Novyi tip veruyushchego na poroge tret'ego tysyacheletiya', *Istoricheckii Vestnik* 9–10 (2000); M. P. Mchedlov, 'Ob osobennostyakh mirovozreniya veruyushchikh v post-Sovetskoi Rossii', *Religiya i Pravo* 1 (2002): 15–18; T. Varzanova, 'Religioznoe vozrozhdenie i molodyozh''', in V. I. Dobrinina, T. N. Kychtevich, and S. V. Tumanov, eds. *Kul'turnie miry molodykh Rossiyan: Tri zhiznennye situatsii* (Moscow: Moscow State University, 2000), 167–91; T. Varzanova, 'Religioznaya situatsiya v Rossii', *Russkaya Mysl'* 4165 (1997).

7 The data used are from the 1999–2001 wave of the WVS, which was released in 2004. I initially coded all respondents as members of one of two groups; either Orthodox Christians (1,187 self-identified Orthodox believers) or non-religious Russians (those respondents who did not identify as a member of a religious community, 1,210). The remaining non-Orthodox believers are thus excluded from the analysis.

8 Grace Davie, *Religion in Britain since 1945: Believing without Belonging* (Oxford: Blackwell, 1994).

9 Naletova, 2006.

10 Varzanova, 'Religioznaya situatsiya v Rossii'.

11 For more on this classification and its correlates in contemporary Russian society, see Christopher Marsh, 'Russian Orthodox Christians and Their Orientation toward Church and State', *The Journal of Church and State*, Vol. 46, No. 2 (Summer 2005): 545–561, and 'Orthodox Christianity, Civil Society, and Russian Democracy', *Demokratizatsiya: The Journal of Post-Soviet Democratization*, Vol. 13, No. 3 (Summer 2005): 449–462.

12 The data presented in this section draws heavily upon Christopher Marsh, 'The Social Challenge of Difference: Anti-Semitism, Intolerance, and Xenophobia in Contemporary Russia', paper presented at the 14th annual law and religion symposium *Religion, Identity, and Stability: Legal Challenges of Religious Difference*, International Center for Law and Religion Studies, Brigham Young University, October 7–9, 2007.

13 Cf. Serge Schmemann, 'Hallowed Symbols Face Russian Realities', *International Tribune Herald* (February 20, 2004).

14 'Radical Christians against Madonna Concert in Moscow', *Mosnews.com* (http://www.mosnews.com/images/g/s150.shtml); accessed 05.09.2006.

15 E.A. Klimchuk, 'O Natsional'noi prinadlezhnosti iisusa khrista', *Duel*, Vol. 3, No. 146 (1998).

16 Ibid.

17 Anastasia V. Mitrofanova, *The Politicization of Russian Orthodoxy: Actors and Ideas* (ibidem-Verlag, 2007), A. Verkhovskiy, *Radikalizm: Gosudarstvo protiv radikal'nogo natsionalisma* (Moscow: Panorama Center, 2002), L. Gudkov, *O razvitii russkogo natsionalizma* (A Report from a Symposium on the Topic of *Russkiy Vopros v Rossii* held at the Liberal Mission Foundation) (Moscow: November 4, 2002), L.Gudkov, *Dinamika etnophobii v Rossii poslednego desyatiletiya* (Report at the Conference 'National Minorities in Russian Federation), Moscow, June 2–3, 2003. See also the special issue of *Nationalities Papers* on 'Religion, Culture, and Conflict in the Orthodox World', Christopher Marsh and Daniel Payne, eds. (Vol. 35, No. 5, November 2007); see in particular Vyacheslav Karpov and Elena Lisovskaya, 'The Landscape of Interfaith Intolerance in Post-Atheist Russia', and Emil Pain, 'Xenophobia and Ethnopolitical Extremism in Post-Soviet Russia: Dynamics and Growth Factors'.

18 Jack Snyder, *From Voting to Violence: Democratization and Nationalist Conflict* (New York: W. W. Norton, 2000).

19 Benedict Anderson, *Imagined Communities: Reflections on the Origin and Spread of Nationalism* (London: Verso, 1991).

20 In the Russian case, this issue has been explored most robustly by James Warhola in 'Is the Russian Federation Becoming More Democratic: Moscow-Regional Relations and the Development of the Post-Soviet Russian State', *Democratization* 6, 2 (1999): 42–69.

21 Nikos Kokosalakis, 'Greek Orthodoxy and Modern Socio-Economic Change', in Richard Roberts, ed. *Religion and the Transformations of Capitalism: Comparative Approaches* (London: Routledge, 1995), 249–250.

22 Max Weber, *Economy and Society* (Berkeley: University of California Press, 1978), particularly 551, 561, 589, 1193. See also Andreas Buss, 'The Economic Ethics of Russian-Orthodox Christianity: Part I', *International Sociology* 4, 3 (September 1989): 235–258, which attempts to attempts to follow Weber's 'The Economic Ethics of World Religions' in form and content.

23 Gvosdev, 125.

24 Richard Rose, 'Russia as an Hourglass Society: A Constitution Without Citizens', *East European Constitutional Review* 4, 3 (Summer 1995), Robert Putnam, *Making Democracy Work: Civic Traditions in Modern Italy* (Princeton: Princeton University Press, 1993), 183–185. Cf. Christopher Marsh, 'Social Capital and Democracy in Russia', *Communist and Post-Communist Studies* 33, 2 (June 2000): 183–199.

25 Richard Rose, 'Russia as an Hourglass Society: A Constitution Without Citizens', *East European Constitutional Review* 4, 3 (Summer 1995), Robert Putnam, *Making Democracy Work: Civic Traditions in Modern Italy* (Princeton: Princeton University Press, 1993), 183–185. Cf. Christopher Marsh, 'Social Capital and Democracy in Russia', *Communist and Post–Communist Studies* 33, 2 (June 2000): 183–199, and Christopher Marsh, 'Social Capital and Grassroots Democratization in Russia's Regions: Evidence from the 1999–2001 Gubernatorial Elections', *Demokratizatsiya: The Journal of Post-Soviet Democratization* 10, 2 (Winter 2002): 19–36.

26 See Helen Albert, 'The Impact of Culture on Economic Growth: A Cross-Country Study of 20 Post-Communist Societies'. Unpublished master's thesis, Baylor University, 2004, 50.

27 Such a pattern was indeed evident among Communist Party supporters in the late Yeltsin years. See Christopher Marsh, *Making Russian Democracy Work: Social Capital, Economic Development, and Democratization* (New York: Mellen Press, 2000), and Christopher Marsh, 'Social Capital and Democracy in Russia'.

Chapter 9

ISLAM AND SPIRITUAL CAPITAL: AN INDONESIAN CASE STUDY

Robert W. Hefner

One of the great coincidences of late last century was the emergence of a 'third wave' of democratization at the same time that much of the world was undergoing a powerful religious revival. Although religious organizations played a supporting role in democratic transitions in Spain, Poland, the Philippines, and Indonesia, many political analysts seemed to feel that democratization and religious revival had little to do with each other. Indeed, if they took notice of the revival at all, most analysts viewed it with concern. They worried that religion might stir up sentiments incompatible with democracy, opening the way to the scenario outlined in Samuel Huntington's 'clash of civilizations' (Huntington 1996).

Another indication of the ships-passing-in-the night approach to these two events was that one of the more potent theoretical concepts developed in the 1990s for understanding democratization, i.e., the concept of social capital, was at first rarely applied to religious organizations. In the literature on politics and democracy, social capital has been the subject of myriad definitions, not all of them compatible (see below). In the 1990s, however, Robert Putnam's seminal works on civic traditions in modern Italy (Putnam 1993) and the putative decline of social capital in the United States (Putnam 1995, 2000) catapulted the concept to the centre of political discussion.

Putnam defined social capital as 'features of social life – networks, norms, and trust – that enable participants to act together more effectively to pursue shared objectives' (1995, 664–5). As a democracy theorist in the tradition of Alexis de Tocqueville, Putnam was particularly interested in those features of social life that enable people to act more effectively in the pursuit of democratic governance. Interestingly, in his book on Italy, Putnam concluded that coming together in the pursuit of *religious* ends did not do much to enhance democracy's vigor. In fact, he found that Catholic religiosity in Italy tended to correlate negatively with civic engagement (Putnam 1993, 107). When, a few years later, Putnam turned his research gaze toward the United States, however, his findings pointed to a different conclusion. 'Faith communities in which people worship together', he wrote, 'are arguably the single most important repository of social capital in America' (Putnam 2000,6). Echoing the views of other analysts of religion and democracy in America (Verba, Schlozman, and Brady 1995; Wuthnow 1996, 1999), Putnam also argued that faith-based social capital contributes vitally to American democracy's well-being. Putnam's change of perspective was indicative of a growing interest among political analysts in religion's contribution to democratization.

In this chapter I want to explore this same issue of spiritual capital and democratic life. My discussion aims to go beyond the above-mentioned analyses, however, in two ways. First, I am interested in the organization and consequences of spiritual capital, not in Christian America, but in the world's largest Muslim-majority society, Indonesia. The question of democracy and spiritual capital in Islam is a thorny one, of course, because the Islamic resurgence has often been seen as, not strengthening, but undermining democracy by fueling fundamentalism and extremism. The reverential tone Western commentators sometimes adopt when discussing churches and American democracy has no counterpart in discussions of Islamic resurgence. On the contrary, analysts are quick to equate the latter with fundamentalism and anti-democratic violence.

It is for this reason that the Indonesian case is so interesting. It is not that Indonesia is a country of gentle civic peace and kind-hearted tolerance. In fact, Indonesia experienced one of the world's first-ever Islamist rebellions against the modern nation state – the 1948 Dar ul-Islam conflict (van Dijk 1981) – and more recently has witnessed outbreaks of terrorism and ethnoreligious violence (Aragon 2001; Barton 2004; Hefner 2005; ICG 2002a, 2002b; Klinken 2001). But this gritty reality only makes recent developments in Indonesia more interesting. During the 1990s the country experienced an Islamic resurgence at the same time that it gave birth to the largest pro-democracy movement in the Muslim world (Hefner 2000). Muslim organizations contributed directly to the movement that finally toppled the authoritarian government of President Soeharto in May 1998. Since that time the country has suffered terrorist attacks and ethnoreligious violence (Bertrand 2004). Nonetheless, Indonesia has also managed to hold two national elections, in 1999 and 2004, both of which were notable for the moderation of their outcome. The electorate's sound-headedness is all the more impressive inasmuch as during these same years Indonesia continued to suffer the destabilizing effects of the Asian economic crisis (1997–2003). For these and other reasons, the Indonesian case offers fascinating lessons on the relationship between democratization and Islamic spiritual capital.

My second aim in this case study of Islamic revitalization and democracy is to examine some of the issues surrounding the concepts of social capital, religious social capital, and spiritual capital. Although a media-friendly variant of the concept of spiritual capital has been popularized by management gurus like Danah Zohar and Ian Marshall (Zohar and Marshall 2004), scholarly treatment of spiritual capital and the related concept of religious social capital is still in its infancy (but cf. Smidt 2003). Social theorists' agreement on these terms has been difficult for several reasons. One of the more vexing is the fact that the idea of social capital from which both concepts are derived was popularized in the contemporary social sciences by Pierre Bourdieu (1973 and 1986) and James Coleman (1988, 1990), and these authors' treatment of social capital diverged on critical points. Bourdieu and Coleman's usages differ in turn from that of Putnam. The inconsistencies surrounding the concept of social capital have carried over into discussions of religious and spiritual capital, clouding issues of policy as well as analytic priority. Before turning to the Indonesian case, then, it will be helpful to clarify these terms.

Defining Spiritual Capital

In this chapter, I will treat spiritual capital and religious social capital as synonyms. More important, I will also suggest that spiritual capital comes in a variety of forms, and the varieties have quite different implications for democracy and civic peace. To understand just why this is so requires that we clarify just what it is that makes social and spiritual capital politically important.

When dealing with spiritual capital, the Islam case suggests, it is not enough to highlight networks, cooperation, and trust, as if these generic qualities are what really matter, and their effect on politics is everywhere the same. Rather, we have to pay equal attention to the cultural and ideological content that flows through these networks (cf. Stolle and Rochon 2001, 144; Smidt 2003, 11). In other words, with social and spiritual capital, culture matters, and matters deeply. Spiritual capital is as much an effect of culture and ideas as it is networks and trust.

As Putnam (2000,22) has observed, social capital 'can be directed toward malevolent, antisocial purposes, just like any other form of capital'. But we need to make clearer just why this is so. Neither social nor spiritual capital is woven of a single cloth. Both are emergent effects of participation in all manner of associations, institutions, and relationships. In the course of their genesis, social and spiritual capital take on the moral tenor and cultural rationale of those associations, including their equality or inequality, civic conviviality or anti-democratic exclusivity, ideological fervor or quietist ease. As Robert Wuthnow (2003, 192) has lamented, analysts often mistakenly assume that social capital is of one type, civic in nature and originating among 'gregarious people who happen to be well-connected to friends and neighbors through membership in middle–class clubs'. However, as Wuthnow goes on to observe, social capital is actually created in all manner of social milieus, including formal organizations and institutions as well as casual clubs. It is a feature of hate-groups and terrorist networks as much as it is bowling leagues (cf. Hefner 2001). 'Social networks and institutions may limit members' connections with the wider community; they may include some and exclude others; they may serve selfish and/or antisocial as well as 'civic' ends... and they may battle one another furiously over the nature of the 'public good" (Foley, Edwards, and Diani 2001, 272). To understand the varieties and political effects of spiritual capital in Indonesia or elsewhere, then, we need to go beyond one-size-fits all discussions of social and spiritual capital, and look not just at associations and trust but 'the ideas that 'fill' or are associated with those social structures' (Smidt 2003, 11).

For the purposes of this chapter, then, I define spiritual capital as features of faith-based organizations, including networks, norms, knowledge, and socialization, that make 'possible the achievement of certain ends that would not be attainable in its [social capital's] absence' (Coleman 1990, 302). With this definition of spiritual capital in hand, it quickly becomes clear that modern Islam produces great volumes of the stuff. Since the 1970s, in particular, there has been a vast resurgence in Muslim piety, schooling, and associational life across the Muslim world (Eickelman and Piscatori 1996; Hefner 2005). Just what this means for democracy and civic peace is, of course, another question. The mass production of spiritual capital has been accompanied by intra-Muslim contests as to the political ends to which that spiritual capital should be put. The Indonesian case suggests that whether the spiritual capital created by the resurgence helps to 'make democracy work' will depend in part on the outcome of these contests, and Muslims' decisions as to where they should invest their spiritual capital.

The remainder of this chapter illustrates these issues by way of a brief discussion of two varieties of Islamic spiritual capital that emerged in Indonesia after the fall of the President Soeharto in May 1998. The two varieties are, first, that created by the country's radical Islamist paramilitaries, which became a major force in Indonesian politics after 1998, and, second, that created by Indonesia's vast network of private and public Islamic schools, which in recent years have sought to open those schools to both general education and prodemocracy programs of civic education. The contrast between the two varieties of Islamic spiritual capital underscores that, like its counterparts in other religious traditions, spiritual capital in Islam assumes varied forms and has diverse political effects. The discussion will also shed light on some Islam-specific challenges to democracy-friendly variants of spiritual capital.

The Plural Economy of Islamic Spiritual Capital

In the months following the collapse of the Soeharto regime in May 1998, Indonesia was swept by a wave of radical Islamist mobilization the scale of which seemed to put the country's transition to democracy in question. Muslim paramilitaries (*laskar*) became active in dozens of cities and towns across much of the country, and in a few places some fell into pitched street-battles with Christians, democracy activists, and even the local police. Some of the paramilitaries had ties to local Islamic boarding schools (*pesantren*) or day schools (*madrasa*) and exploited these ties for the purposes of recruitment and propaganda. Although the results of the June 1999 elections demonstrated that the Indonesian public had little appetite for Islamist radicalism, this mattered little to the Islamist militias, who seemed determined to achieve an influence disproportionate to their numbers in society (Barton 2004; Hefner 2005).

Although many of the *laskar* were little more than neighborhood youth gangs mixing religious recreation with youthful bravado, the larger paramilitaries boasted thousands of followers under the command of charismatic preachers. The large militias were also organized into quasi-military formations, complete with commanders, officers, and named battalions. One of the best known of the big militias was the Islamic Defenders Front or FPI (*Front Pembela Islam*). Its history illustrates the ways in which it generated spiritual capital, and the distinctive ends to which it was put.

The Islamic Defenders Front was founded in the capital city of Jakarta on August 17, 1998 by Habib Muhammad Rizieq ibn Hussein Shihab, popularly known as Habib Rizieq (Jamhari and Jahroni 2004). Rizieq is a young Arab-Indonesian scholar with ties to a small network of ultraconservative Islamic boarding schools in Jakarta and the neighboring provinces of West Java and Banten. Indonesia has some 10,000 Islamic boarding schools, and most of them are notable for their moderation (Azra et al. 2007; Dhofier 1999; Prabowo and Guillot 1997). However, in the late 1990s Rizieq had woven together a small network of radical preachers and school directors into a militant front. Its leaders cited several concerns as the rationale for their organization, including the illegal distribution of pornography, the widespread sale of illegal drugs, and the growing influence of leftists and Marxists in the democracy movement. (Rizieq is vehemently anti-communist, and paints a broad stroke when identifying who is and who is not communist). In the two years following its establishment in 1998, Rizieq turned the FPI into the most potent paramilitary force in the capital, commanding upwards of 50,000 fighters.

As one might expect from a group whose sworn ambition is the armed defence of Islam, Rizieq's network was not particularly concerned with making democracy work. But the group's stated ambitions were interestingly varied. The FPI first came to national attention in late 1998, when the group joined forces with the then commander of the armed forces, General Wiranto, to form a government-backed paramilitary known as the 'Voluntary Security Guards' (*Pasukan Pengaman Swakarsa*). The Security Guards were a militia force of 125,000 civilians intended to back up the 160,000 police and soldiers deployed to protect the November 1998 meeting of the Special Session of the People's Representative Assembly (SI-MPR), an assembly convened to lay the ground-rules for the first elections to be held after Soeharto's abrupt resignation. The main groups against which the SI-MPR was to be 'protected' were prodemocracy activists and nationalists, including some retired armed forces commanders, opposed to Soeharto's hand-picked successor, B.J. Habibie. When the SI-MPR assembly finally met, more than a dozen people died in clashes between the security guards, democracy students, and residents of poor Jakartan neighbourhoods (van Dijk 2001, 340–44).

The Front's collaboration with a faction in the security forces did not end with the Special Session of the National Assembly. In June 2000, Front activists ransacked the headquarters of the National Commission on Human Rights when the latter body implicated members of the army command in the 1999 violence in East Timor. In March and April 2001, the Front joined with conservative members of the military and former ruling party, Golkar, in a campaign against an allegedly resurgent communism. The campaign targeted leftist students, union organizers, and bookstores selling Marxist literature (Hefner 2005, 284-6). In the run-up to the U.S. intervention in Afghanistan, the Front organized the largest of Jakarta's anti-American demonstrations. Finally, as Christian-Muslim violence flared in the provinces of Maluku and North Maluku in 2000 and 2001, the Front dispatched hundreds of fighters to the troubled province.

Notwithstanding these high-profile actions, the most common target for Front operations was the bars and brothels for which metropolitan Jakarta has long been famous, and which Rizieq decried as centres of vice (*tempat maksiat*). These establishments had grown in number during the late Soeharto period, and many were owned by well-connected business people. Some of the businesses were also involved in the sale of drugs. These illicit activities were of great concern to non-Muslim as well as Muslim Indonesians. Many citizens agreed with the Front leadership, then, that the government had let the situation get out of hand.

There was also a more interesting religious rationale to the FPI's programs. Rizieq explained his actions to his followers and to the Muslim public by citing the well-known Islamic ethical principle that it is the duty of pious believers to 'command right and forbid wrong' (Arabic: *al-amr bi'l-ma'rûf wa'-nahy `an al munkr*). Rooted in Qur'anic tradition, this principle implies 'that an executive power of the law of God is vested in each and every Muslim', and that, as a result, "the individual believer as such has not only the right, but also the duty, to issue orders pursuant to God's law, and to do what he can to see that they are obeyed' (Cook 2000, 9). No principle captures the distinctive spirit of Islamic public ethics, at least as expressed in jurisprudence, better than this one. None also better illustrates just why efforts to market liberal-privatist notions of religion and ethics to normative-minded Muslim often encounter serious cultural resistance.

Though easy to invoke, the principle of commanding right and forbidding wrong is not easy to implement. For centuries, Muslim jurists and theologians have grappled with the question, recognizing that 'the virtuous performance of the duty can degenerate into vice' (Cook 2009, 12). After all, who is to say just who has the right to command right and forbid wrong? Efforts to maintain public morality can degenerate into anarchic unilateralism unless the principle is tethered to some notion of social authority.

The majority of Muslim scholars and public intellectuals in post-Soeharto Indonesia had exactly these concerns about Rizieq's invocation of the principle to justify his unilateral attacks on bars, brothels, and leftist activists. However, Rizieq understood that, although many Muslim authorities might disagree with his aims and tactics, few could challenge the religious principle he invoked to justify them, commanding right and forbidding wrong. The principle recognizes a higher authority than the state, and opens the way for non-state actors to usurp some of the state's putative monopoly over legal violence.

The way in which Rizieq recruited activists to the Islamic Defender's Front also illustrates the type of spiritual capital he was intent on creating. Although most of his senior and middle-level lieutenants were teachers from his network of conservative religious schools, Rizieq recruited many of his infantry fighters from the ranks of retired urban gangsters, a group known in Indonesia as *preman* (see Ryter 2001). Now these *preman* gangsters also happen to be the ones who provide most of the muscle for Indonesia's illicit sex and drugs trade. Although some of Rizieq's ex-gang members are reported to have continued their criminal and racketeering careers under Front guise, my interviews and other research indicate that the majority were sincere in their newfound commitment to Islam (Jamhari and Jahroni 2004). Indeed, some ex-gangsters described their participation in the anti-vice raids as an effort to cleanse themselves of their earlier sins. For his part, Rizieq welcomed the former gang members with open arms, and boasted publicly that he was especially grateful for the street-fighting skills they brought to the Defenders Front cause.

In the aftermath of the Bali bombings of October 2002, the United States, Australia and other foreign powers pressed the Indonesian authorities to ban both the Islamic Defenders Front and several other Islamist paramilitaries, including, especially, a group known as the Laskar Jihad. The latter was another large militia that rose to fame in 2000 leading a campaign to battle Christian gangs in the troubled region of Maluku in eastern Indonesia. The Laskar Jihad's leadership did indeed dissolve the organization, and the action proved permanent.

A few days after the Bali bombings, the Islamic Defenders Front also announced that it was suspending operations. But the Front's suspension proved only temporary. In late 2003, the Front renewed its assaults on bars and restaurants in Jakarta. In 2004, the organization mobilized its membership to pressure provincial legislators to pass legislation allowing the implementation of Islamic law. Mid-year in 2005, the FPI joined with other militant groupings to mount a campaign against Indonesia's 300,000 strong Ahmadiyah community, a sect regarded by most of the world's Muslims as deviationist. The militia began by ransacking the sprawling national headquarters of the Ahmadiyah in West Java on July 8, 2005. The Front soon extended its efforts to other towns, closing or destroying Ahmadiyah mosques and schools, burning members' homes, and threatening to kill those unwilling to renounce their faith. Even by the standards of post-Soeharto Indonesia, the campaign was remarkable for its brazenness.

What does all this say about the Islamic Defenders Front and spiritual capital? As its well-coordinated battalions indicate, the Front produced a rich reserve of spiritual capital, mobilizing ex-gang members, Islamic school students, and poor urban workers to create an effective paramilitary organization. Clearly, however, not all spiritual capital is woven of a common cloth, and that generated by the Front was anything but civil. But this was spiritual capital nonetheless, one that showed the qualities of self-organization and a concern for the public good rightly associated with spiritual capital. Rizieq used this 'cultural frame' (Snow and Benford 1988; Wiktorowicz 2004, 16) to provide a diagnosis of Indonesia's social ills. In the process, his movement was able to exercise an influence greatly disproportionate to its actual numbers in society.

Recent events in other parts of the Muslim world remind us, of course, that the Indonesian case is not all that unusual. Where state officials are unwilling or unable to uphold the rule of law and achieve a monopoly over legitimate violence, small movements of dedicated militants may create a spiritual capital at variance with ideas of the public good endorsed by most of the citizenry.

Spiritual Capital for Democracy and Citizenship

The presence of Muslim teachers and students in Indonesia's Islamist militias showed that some school networks were being used for thoroughly undemocratic ends. A greater shock yet, however, was the October 2002 terrorist bombings in Bali, in which more than 200 people at a beachfront pub died, and for which students from an Islamic boarding school in East Java were eventually convicted. The Bali killings led some observers to wonder whether Indonesia's Islamic schools weren't being turned into training centers for *jihadi* militants. In 2002, the influential International Crisis Group issued a report that confirmed that there was a network of radical Islamist boarding schools linked by school ties, kinship, and ideology (ICG 2002a). A few Western academics began to warn that Indonesia was becoming a 'second front' for al-Qa'ida (Abuza 2003).

A closer examination of the culture and politics of Islamic education in Indonesia reveals that the situation is not nearly so dire as the second front thesis implied. Indonesia has some 10,000 Islamic boarding schools (*pesantrens*) and another 36,000 Islamic day-schools (*madrasas*). A full 15% of the country's grade-school population receive their primary education in Muslim day schools. Of these 46,000 these schools, it is estimated that fewer than 1%, about 300–400 schools, espouse some type of radical Islamist program. Of these, only a few dozen are thought to support violent *jihadism*[1]. In fact, notwithstanding this radical fringe, the mainstream among Indonesia's Muslim schools are among the most forward-looking and liberal-minded in the world.

In the remainder of this chapter I focus on the upper echelons of the Islamic educational system, and its efforts to broaden school curricula and launch programs in support of Indonesia's democratic transition. These efforts show that Indonesia's Muslim colleges are working to create a spiritual capital entirely different in ethos and aims from that of the Muslim militias. However, as we shall see, the colleges and Islamic education in general still face crucial challenges, not least of all as regards the question of how to resolve the tension between aspects of Islamic law (*shari`a*) and democracy.

There is a broader historical background to the Muslim colleges' new initiatives. Creating a system of Islamic higher education has been a dream of Indonesian Muslim leaders since the late colonial period. Interestingly, those who first promoted the idea were not conservative Islamists who rejected Western systems of knowledge, but Western-educated reformers, comfortable with modern forms of knowledge, and convinced that their methods were not merely consistent with, but vital for a modern practice of the faith. One of the most prominent promoters of Islamic higher education was Indonesia's first vice president, Mohammad Hatta. Hatta was an observant Muslim, a socialist democrat, and an ardent educational reformist. He called for the establishment of an Islamic university that, rather than just teaching traditional Islamic sciences, would open itself to Western philosophy, history, sociology, and science. Hatta also insisted that if religious law was to be made meaningful it had to be understood in a contextual and 'empirical' manner (Jabali and Jamhari 2002, 6–8; cf. Rose 1987). Hatta's views show that the ideas of educational broad-mindedness emphasized in Indonesia's state Islamic university system today build on solid historical precedents.

Notwithstanding the dreams of many Muslim leaders, government support to Islamic higher education during the first years of the republic was minimal. It was only after 1960 that the government authorized the establishment of a State Islamic Institute system (IAIN), which was created by linking two pre-existing faculties in Jakarta and Yogyakarta. Over the next ten years, local Muslim leaders and government officials in cities and towns across Indonesia established dozens of institutes. By 1973, there were some 112 IAIN campuses. Most, however, were underfinanced and poorly staffed.

Under the leadership of the Minister of Religion, Mukti Ali (minister 1971–1978), beginning in 1975 the Ministry of Religion undertook an ambitious modernization of the State Islamic colleges. The Department reduced the number of schools from 113 to 13. It also initiated what was, as far as conservative Islamists were concerned, a controversial program of faculty enhancement that sent senior professors and administrators from the state Islamic colleges, not to the Middle East, but to Canada, the United States, and Western Europe. A program of faculty upgrading soon followed. The program was built around an exchange program between Indonesia's Department of Religion and the program in Islamic studies at McGill University in Canada, where Minister Ali had been a graduate student. By 2001, 99 IAIN instructors had studied at McGill; twelve had received their Ph.D. Upon returning to Indonesia, these scholars were appointed to key administrative positions in the Department of Religion and the state Islamic colleges, in a careful effort to accelerate the reform of the state-supported educational system.

At the centre of these reforms was the desire to take Islamic education beyond the traditional canon and to encourage the adoption of historical and contextualizing methodologies like those used in modern departments of religious studies in the West. Today, every student admitted to the state Islamic university system is required to fulfill divisional studies requirements that begin with courses on Islamic history and general hermeneutic and contextualizing methodologies for the study of Islam. Since the early 2000s, in addition, seven of the state Islamic Universities have begun a far-reaching restructuring that includes building new faculties in non-religious fields like medicine, psychology, social science, and business (Yatim and Nasuhi 2002). Since 2003, finally, all students entering the IAIN system have been required to take a civics course on democracy, civil society, and human rights. The curriculum for this program was developed during 2001–2002 in collaboration with a U.S.A.I.D.-financed program run by the Jakarta office of the Asia Foundation.

Through these and other initiatives, then, the State Islamic system has transformed itself into a cultural broker for new models of Islamic education and democratic politics to the country's forty-six thousand Islamic schools. This change has occurred at the same time that the state Islamic system has become the preferred venue of higher education for graduates of the country's *madrasas* and Islamic boarding schools. Today, rather than going to the Middle East for higher education, most educators go into the state Islamic system. There they are exposed to courses in contextual hermeneutics and democratic theory for which there is, quite literally, no counterpart in the Muslim Middle East (Azyumardi, Afrianty and Hefner 2007; cf. Kusuma and Munadi 2002).

Is this shift in higher education really likely to strengthen democratic currents in Indonesia's Muslim schools? The editors of a 2002 report on the 'IAIN and the modernization of Islam in Indonesia' reached a hopeful conclusion on this point (Jabali and Jamhari 2002, 114).

'The large number of IAIN alumni who go on to become *kyai* [directors] or religious teachers [ustadz] in pesantren certainly gives rise to the hope that they will bring with them a new Islamic culture that is modern, contextual, liberal, and rational, like that which is being developed in the IAIN.... With the model of understanding developed at the IAIN, Muslim Indonesians, who of course represent the majority of Indonesians, will be educated so as to be able to understand the important meaning of modernity, progress (*the idea of progress*), societal pluralism, and tolerance toward people who profess other religions'.

Notwithstanding the report's optimism, the precise impact of IAIN programs on the broader Islamic school system, however, remains uncertain. It is not that there is a broad-based opposition to the educational reforms. Indeed, interviews I conducted with one hundred faculty and administrators at four campuses during July and December 2006 indicated that the overwhelming majority (92%) support the civic education program, and a comparable majority agree with efforts to turn the state Islamic colleges into general universities with an Islamic studies subprogram[2]. But the long-term impact of these programs is going to depend on an even more ambitious transformation of the culture and teaching of Muslim public ethics.

Public Ethical Ambivalences

As has many commentators have noted, there is a cultural tension in modern Islamic jurisprudence between democratic ideals, with their emphasis on popular sovereignty and democratic legislation, and conservative and even many mainstream interpretations of the historical *shari`a*. Many among the latter scholars insist God alone is sovereign, and His sovereignty is such that the role of human political actors cannot extend to crafting legislation, but must be limited to interpreting and implementing God's laws.

The question of the shari`a and democracy is a complicated one, to which major works have been dedicated by democratic-minded Muslim reformers (An-Na`im 1990; El Fadl 2004; Zubaida 2003). It is not my purpose in this chapter to review this debate. Rather, I want to explore Indonesian Muslim educators' views on this thorny issue. In an effort to gauge those views, in January 2006 I worked with staff at the Center for the Study of Islam and Society (PPIM) at the Hidayatullah National Islamic University in Jakarta to carry out a survey of 940 Muslim educators in 100 madrasas and Islamic boarding schools in eight provinces in Indonesia. The purpose of the survey was, among other things, to talk with educators in the front lines of Muslim education, and explore their views on shari`a, democracy, gender and public ethics.

The survey was coordinated in the field by eight staff members from the PPIM, and administered by senior college students hired and trained by the PPIM in each of the eight provinces. The survey had 184 questions, the aggregate results of which are too complex to present here. The tables presented below summarize the data that dealt with Muslim educators attitudes toward democracy, Islamism, and pluralism.

Indonesian Pesantren and Madrasa Teachers' Views on Democracy, Islamism and Pluralism

A. Support for Democracy

1. Democracy, compared to other forms of governance, is the best form of government for a country like ours	85.9%
2. Democracy is a source of political disorder	8.1%
3. Every citizen is equal before the law regardless of his or her political views	94.2%
4. Every citizen must be allowed to join any political organization	82.5%
5. Mass media must by protected by law to protect them from arbitrary actions of government	92.8%
6. Our economy will be better if the government gives more freedom to each citizen to do as he or she wishes	73.4%

7. Free and fair contestation between political parties improves
the performance of government of this country   80%

B. Support for Islamism

1. Islamic governance, i.e. governance based on the Qur'an
and Sunna and under the leadership of Islamic authorities
like ulama is the best for this nation.   72.2%
2. The state should enforce the obligation to implement
Islamic law (shari'a) for all Muslims.   82.8%
3. The amputation of the hand of a thief as prescribed in
the Qur'an should be enforced by the government.   59.1%
4. General elections should be limited to candidates who
understand and agree to fight for the implementation
of Islamic teachings in the polity.   63.9%
5. Only Islamic parties should be allowed to participate
in general elections   24.3%
6. The Muslims who do not perform their religious duties should
not be allowed to serve as members in the National Assembly   74.3%
7. The ideals and practices of Islamist organizations, like the
Darul Islam, Negara Islam Indonesia, Front Pembela Islam,
Laskar Jihad, etc., to implement Islamic law (shari'a) in the
society and polity should be supported   64.4%
8. The practice of polygamy should be legal and allowed in
Indonesia.   75.7%
9. Females should not be allowed to take distant trips without the
accompaniment of a close family member or relative   79.6%
10. The government (police) should engage in surveillance
(mengawasi) so as to insure that Muslims perform
the Ramadan fasting   49.9%
11. The government (police) should close the restaurants
during day of the month Ramadan   82.9%
12. The government (police) should engage in surveillance
(mengawasi) if the two persons (male and female) in the
street are married couple or together with his or her relative 66.6%

C. Muslim and non-Muslim [Christian]: Approval of...

1. Non-Muslims should be allowed to become President of this country 6.5%
2. Non-Muslim should not be allowed to be a teacher in public school 19.9%
3. Non-Muslim should be allowed to perform their religious
rites in this area   20.1%

4. Non-Muslims should be allowed to build the place for
   worship [church] in this area   39.8%
5. Islam is the best *umma* (religious community)   92.5%
6. We are not supposed to cooperate with non-Muslims in
   anything   10.5%
7. We are not allowed to say greetings like 'asslamu'alaikum'
   or 'Merry Christmas' to non-Muslims [Christians]   73.5%
8. Islam is the only true religion and therefore non-Muslim
   should convert to Islam   58.7%

D. Gender Issues

1. Generally speaking, males are superior over females   61.3%
2. Like males, females have the right to run for membership
   in the legislature   81.6%
3. It is best that women not be allowed to run for president   55.8%
4. Women are too weak to serve as judges in court   51.3%
5. In a family there are two children, son and daughter, while
   the family socio-economic condition is only able to support
   one child. In this situation, the son, rather than the daughter,
   should go to school.   57.2%

As one might expect, the most interesting feature of the data concerns educators' views on democracy and the *shari`a*. On one hand, an impressive 85.9% of Muslim educators agree that democracy is the best form of government for Indonesia. Equally striking, the educators' support is neither formalistic nor based on a crudely majoritarian understanding of democracy. Rather the educators' views extend to subtle matters of civil rights, including support for the equality of all citizens before the law, no matter what their political persuasion (94.2%); citizen freedom to join political organizations (82.5%); legal protections for the media from arbitrary government action (92.8%); and even the notion that open party competition helps to improve the performance of government (80%). These figures are as high or higher than survey data on similar issues from Western Europe and the United States (Norris and Inglehart 2004).

If this was all there was to educators' attitudes on Islam and democracy, it would be smooth sailing. However, educators' political views do not stand alone, but co-exist with the educators' understanding of God's law. For example, notwithstanding the strength of their commitment to democracy, 72.2% of the educators believe the state should be based on the Qur'an and Sunna and guided by religious experts. A full 82.8% of these educators think the state should work to implement the *shari`a*, although their support for the *shari`a* gets shaky at a few points. For example, it drops to 59.1%, when the regulation in question concerns

the amputation of thieves' hands, or government efforts to require performance
of the Ramadan fast (49.9% agree). On these matters, at least, a substantial
number of educators seem to have second thoughts about a too-literalist
implementation of the law. Nonetheless, when asked whether inobservant
Muslims should be allowed to serve in the National Assembly, 74.3% of
educators feel they should not. A full 64.4% agree with Muslim militants'
campaigns to implement Islamic law.

It is on matters of women and non-Muslim religious minorities, however, that
the tension between educators' enthusiasm for democracy and their
understanding of the *shari`a* veers in a direction many outsiders might feel is
contradictory. Some 93.5% of the educators believe that a non-Muslim should
not be allowed to serve as president. A full 55.8% feel that women should not
be allowed to run for the office. 51.3% feel that women do not have the
intellectual or emotional capacity to serve as judges. About twenty percent
would bar non-Muslims from teaching in public schools; a similar percentage
would ban non-Muslims from performing religious services in the area
surrounding the school at which the educator-respondent works. Twice that
percentage would bar non-Muslims from erecting houses of worship in the
same area. In short, on matters of gender and non-Muslims, the educators'
commitment to democracy seems hedged, to say the least.

We see in this small sample of Indonesian Muslim public opinion the tip
of a bigger public ethical problem. Educators' stated commitments to
democracy, rights of political association, and press freedoms are as strong as
any where in the democratic world. However, where a democratic principle
runs up against an issue on which the *shari`a* and its interpreters have
something to say, the majority of educators feel that piety requires that they
defer to conventional understandings of the *shari`a*. This deference results in
judgments that many observers, including most Muslim democrats, would
regard as inconsistent with democracy.

What are we to make of this tension? The example draws us back to the
above discussion of the Islamic Defenders' Front. However much state officials
and other Muslim scholars disagreed with it, the Front was able to undercut the
state's monopoly over legal violence by appealing to what many Muslims regard
as an incontestable religious principle: that there is an authority higher than that
of government, the authority of God's law. Rizieq and his followers invoked
this principle to legitimate their sometimes violent actions against vice and
'opponents of Islam'. To judge by the evidence of the above survey of
educators, the majority of Indonesia's `ulama* disagree with the Front's actions.
But most could not take exception to the principle of *shari`a* and public ethics
with which Rizieq justified his actions. These examples point to a distinctly
Islamic form of spiritual capital, one based on the cultural conviction that the
shari`a must serve as the ground for politics and public ethics. This ideal makes

it difficult for moderate and democratic Muslim educators to endorse a public revision of Muslim attitudes on women, minorities, and other matters where those attitudes are thought to be based in the *shari`a*.

In an essay on Islam and the challenge of democracy a few years ago, Khaled Abou El Fadl (2004) argued that the prospects for a *sustainable* accommodation of Islam and democracy will remain remote until sound religious arguments in support of democracy are formulated by leading Islamic jurists and then accepted by many in the scholarly community and the Muslim public. Throughout his essay, El Fadl also suggests that at present no such systematic reintegration of Islam and democracy has been formulated. This latter view may be too dire. Indonesia's Islamic colleges have made great progress drawing up and disseminating Muslim rationales for democracy and civic freedoms. Nonetheless El Fadl's broader point seems right. Sustainable democracy in the Muslim world depends upon, not just broad changes in state and society, but a change in a specialized but broadly influential subculture, that of Muslim jurists and `ulama. More particularly, sustainable democratization depends on influential scholars' making further progress into still unsettled fields, including questions of religious freedom (especially apostasy), religious minorities, and the position of women.

Muslim political culture in Indonesia is, of course, still a work in process. Indonesia's democratic transition and the state Islamic universities' programs for civic education are just a few years old. However, as El Fadl, Abdullahi Ahmed An-Na'im and other Muslim democrats have suggested, until there is a more systematic and widely accepted reformation of scholars' understandings of the law, their and the public's commitment to democracy may continue to suffer an unsteady ambivalence.

Conclusion

By way of conclusion, one might ask: What does Muslim education have to do with spiritual capital? After all, isn't spiritual capital a sub-species of social capital, and are not both varieties generated in the informal associations of bowling leagues and bridge clubs, not formal settings like Islamic schools?

In answering this question and justifying the comparisons that I have made in this chapter, I am reminded of Robert Wuthnow's essay in a collection entitled, *Religion as Social Capital: Producing the Common Good* (Smidt 2003). The volume is a well-written and sensible one. This fact makes it all the more interesting that Wuthnow, who has written volumes on religion and American democracy, can barely hide his frustration with what he regards as the anti-institutional bias in studies of social and religious capital. The bias is one that privileges 'interpersonal relations and the behavior and beliefs of individuals, especially in small, local, or informal and voluntary settings' (Wuthnow 2003, 191) but somehow ignores the fact that social capital is also created in institutions, including government, schools, and legal systems that support the fair application of the law. Wuthnow comments that concentrating on bowling leagues and buddy networks runs 'the risk of being a step backward in social theorizing, not a step forward' (p. 192). It is not that these little groups cannot contribute to a democratic culture, he implies, but that they are only part of the story. Wuthnow takes particular exception to the tendency to ignore 'the public and private system of elementary, secondary, and higher education – virtually none of which was present when Tocqueville visited – that currently shapes the values and lifestyles of nearly all Americans' (ibid.).

My observations on spiritual capital formation here in Indonesia are informed by a conviction similar to Wuthnow's. Islamic spiritual capital is created in formal institutions as well as informal relationships. Its ethos and values are also not of a single stripe. By organizing and socializing armed militants, the Islamic Defenders Front has been able to create a disciplined spiritual capital committed to an undemocratic understanding of the public good. By contrast, Indonesia's state Islamic colleges are trying to create a spiritual capital that will flow with rather than against democratic currents.

The survey data discussed in this chapter also indicate, however, that the college programs have not yet resolved the tension between democracy and *shari`a* on matters related to women, non-Muslims, and the place of *shari`a* in the state itself. Reforming religious understandings of these issues is going to take time, and, if it is to succeed at all, the effort will require a sustained interaction among all levels of Muslim social and intellectual life.

Let me be clearer about just what this might entail. The problem of democratization in the Muslim world is at once cultural, jurisprudential, and political. It has to do with the creation and control of religious authority and public ethics in societies where modern religious leadership has become fractiously differentiated, so much so that freelance adventurers like the Islamic Defenders Front's Rizieq feel emboldened to launch unilateral moral strikes. In his little essay on *The Place of Tolerance in Islam*, Khaled Abou El Fadl observed that 'The essential lesson taught by Islamic history is that extremist groups are ejected from the mainstream of Islam' (2002, 6). Unfortunately, however, much of the earlier edifice for constraining freelance extremists today lies in ruins. The *massification* of religion facilitated by print technology, mass education, and religion's fractious pluralization have all weakened Islam's extremism-damping institutions. Where these events are accompanied by weakened state legitimacy and capacity, the consequence can be a plague of commanders of the good. As Khaled Abou El Fadel, Muhammad Qasim Zaman (2002), and others have shown, the Islamic jurisprudence offers abundant resources for religiously humanist toleration as well. But these resources have to be recovered and amplified by respected and influential scholars, and then backed up by powerful public institutions, to create an Islamic spiritual capital capable of strengthening democracy and preventing pre-emptive moral strikes.

This effort to create a democratic spiritual capital has one important support. It is the realization that to follow the path of freelance adventurists like Bin Laden and Rizieq is to take Islamic piety itself down the path to ruin. 'The modern world has also undermined a right that has always been a source of evil and corruption', writes Abdolkarim Soroush (2000: 64), 'that is, the right to act as a God-like potentate with unlimited powers'. Yet it is just this God-like authority to which Bin Laden and Rizieq lay claim. The struggle to circumscribe their claims of preemptive authority will not be easy. However, as Soroush, El Fadl, An-Na`im, and others have made clear, the recognition that such an absolutist understanding of God's law threatens Islam itself is a *religious* source from which a new tradition of Muslim politics and civility is emerging.

Notes

1 This estimate is based on my two-year collaborative project on Islamic education conducted with the Institute for the Study of Islam and Society at the Hidayatullah National Islamic University.
2 Interviews with faculty at the National Islamic University Kalijaga, Yogyakarta, January 12, 2005, July 12 and 17, 2003

References

Abdillah, Masykuri. 1997. *Responses of Indonesian Muslim Intellectuals to the Concept of Democracy (1966–1993)*. Hamburg: Abera Verlag Meyer & Co.

Abuza, Zachary. 2003. *Militant Islam in Southeast Asia: Crucible of Terror*. Boulder: Lynne Rienner.

An-Na`im, Abdullahi Ahmed, *Toward an Islamic Reformation: Civil Liberties, Human Rights, and International Law*. Syracuse: Syracuse University Press, 1990.

Aragon, Lorraine. 2001. 'Communal Violence in Poso, Central Sulawesi: Where People Eat Fish and Fish Eat People'. *Indonesia* 72 (October): 45–79.

Azra, Azyumardi, Dina Afrianty, and Robert W. Hefner. 2007. 'Pesantren and Madrasa: Muslim Schools and National Ideals in Indonesia'. In Robert W. Hefner and Muhammad Qasim Zaman, eds., *Schooling Islam: The Culture and Politics of Modern Muslim Education*, pp. 172–98. Princeton: Princeton University Press.

Barton, Greg. 2004. *Indonesia's Struggle: Jemaah Islamiyah and the Soul of Islam*. Sydney: University of New South Wales Press.

Bertrand, Jacques. 2004. *Nationalism and Ethnic Conflict in Indonesia*. Cambridge: Cambridge University Press.

Bourdieu, Pierre. 1977. *Outline of a Theory of Practice*. Cambridge: Cambridge University Press.
———. 1986. 'The forms of social capital'. In John Richardson, ed., *Handbook of Theory and Research for the Sociology of Education*, pp. 241–58. New York: Greenwood.

Coleman, James. S. 1988. 'Social capital in the creation of human capital'. *American Journal of Sociology* (supplement) 94: s95–s120.

———. 1990. *Foundations of Social Theory.* Cambridge, MA: Harvard University Press.

Coleman, John A. 2003. 'Religious Social Capital: Its Nature, Social Location, and Limits'. In Corwin Smidt, ed., pp. 33–47.

Cook, Michael. 2000. *Commanding Right and Forbidding Wrong in Islamic Thought.* Cambridge: Cambridge University Press.

Dhofier, Zamakhsyari. 1999. *The Pesantren Tradition: The Role of the Kyai in the Maintenance of Traditional Islam in Java.* Tempe: Monograph Series, Program for Southeast Asian Studies, Arizona State University.

Dijk, C. van. 1981. *Rebellion Under the Banner of Islam: The Darul Islam in Indonesia.* Verhandelingen van Het KITLV No. 94. The Hague: Martinus Nijhoff.

———. 2001. *A Country in Despair: Indonesia between 1997 and 2000.* Leiden: KITLV Press.

Eickelman, Dale F. and James Piscatori. 1996. *Muslim Politics.* Princeton: Princeton University Press.

El Fadl, Khaled Abou El Fadl. 2002. *The Place of Tolerance in Islam.* Boston: Beacon Press.

El Fadl, Khaled Abou. 2004. *Islam and the Challenge of Democracy.* Princeton: Princeton University Press.

Fattah, Moataz A. 2006. *Democratic Values in the Muslim World.* Boulder: Lynne Reinner.

Foley, Michael W., Bob Edwards, and Mario Diani. 2001. 'Social Capital Reconsidered'. In Bob Edwards, Michael W. Foley, and Mario Diani, *Beyond Tocqueville: Civil Society and the Social Capital Debate in Comparative Perspective*, pp. 266–80. Waco: Baylor University Press.

Hefner, Robert W. 2000. *Civil Islam: Muslims and Democratization in Indonesia.* Princeton: Princeton University Press.

———. 2001. 'Multiculturalism and Citizenship in Malaysia, Singapore, and Indonesia'. In Robert W. Hefner, ed., *The Politics of Multiculturalism: Pluralism and Citizenship in Malaysia, Singapore, and Indonesia'*, pp. 1–47.

———. 2003. 'Civic Pluralism Denied? The New Media and *Jihadi* Violence in Indonesia'. In Dale F. Eickelman and Jon W. Anderson, eds., *New Media in the Muslim World: The Emerging Public Sphere*, 2nd Edition. Bloomington: Indiana University Press.

———. 2005. 'Muslim Democrats and Islamist Violence in Post-Soeharto Indonesia'. In Robert W. Hefner, ed., *Remaking Muslim Politics: Pluralism, Contestation, Democratization*, pp. 273–301. Princeton: Princeton University Press.

Huntington, Samuel P. 1996. *The Clash of Civilizations and the Remaking of the World Order.* New York: Simon & Schuster.

ICG Asia. 2001. 'Communal Violence in Indonesia: Lessons from Kalimantan'. Jakarta and Brussels: Asia Report No. 19, International Crisis Group.

———. 2002a. 'Al-Qaeda in Southeast Asia: The Case of the 'Ngruki Network' in Indonesia'. Jakarta and Brussels: Asia Briefing, International Crisis Group.

———. 2002b. 'Indonesia Backgrounder: How the *Jemaah Islamiyah* Terrorist Network Operates'. Jakarta and Brussels: Asia Report No. 43, International Crisis Group.

Jabali, Fuad and Jamhari. 2002. *IAIN dan Modernisasi Islam di Indonesia* [State Islamic institutes and the modernization of Islam in Indonesia]. Jakarta: UIN Jakarta Press.

Jamhari and Jajang Jahroni, eds. 2004. *Gerakan Salafi Radikal di Indonesia* [Radical Salafiyyah movements in Indonesia]. Jakarta: Raja Grafindo Persada.

Klinken, Gerry van. 2001. 'The Maluku Wars: Bringing Society Back In'. *Indonesia*: 71 (April): pp. 1–26.

Kusmana & Yudhi Munadi. 2002. *Proses Perubahan IAIN Menjadi UIN Syarif Hidayatullah Jakarta: Rekaman Media Massa* [The process of changing the IAIN into a National Islamic University]. Jakarta: UIN Jakarta Press.

Mujani, Saiful. 2003. Religious Democrats: Democratic Culture and Muslim Political Paarticipation in Post-Soeharto Indonesia. Ph.D. Dissertation. Columbus, Ohio: Department of Political Science, Ohio State University.

Norris, Pipp and Ronald Inglehart. 2004. *Sacred and Secular: Religion and Politics Worldwide*. Cambridge: Cambridge University Press.

Prabowo, Taufiq and Claude Guillot. 1997. 'Les pesantrèn ou centre d'enseignement de l'Islam à Java'. In Nicole Grandin and Marc Gaborieau, eds., *Madrasa: La transmission du savaoir dans le monde Musulman*, pp. 181–94. Paris: Éditions Arguments.

Putnam, Robert D. 1993. *Making Democracy Work: Civic Traditions in Modern Italy*. Princeton: Princeton University Press.

———. 1995. 'Bowling Alone: America's Declining Social Capital'. *Journal of Democracy* 6 (January): 65–78.

———. 2000. *Bowling along: The collapse and Revival of American community.* New York: Simon and Schuster.

Rose, Mavin. 1987. *Indonesia Free: A Political Biography of Mohammad Hatta*. Ithaca: Cornell Modern Indonesia Project, Monograph 67, Southeast Asia Program.

Ryter, Loren. 1998. 'Pemuda Pancasila: The Last Loyalist Free Men of Suharto's New Order'. *Indonesia* 66 (October): 45–73.

Smidt, Corwin, ed. 2003. *Religion as Social Capital: Producing the Common Good*. Waco: Baylor University Press.

Snow, David A., and Robert D. Benford. 1988. 'Ideology, Frame Resonance, and Participant Mobilization'. In B.Klandermans, H. Kriesi, and Sidney Tarrow, *From Structure to Action: Comparing Movement Participation Across Cultures*, pp. 197–218. Greenwich, Conn.: JAI Press.

Soroush, Abdolkarim. 2000. *Reason, Freedom, and Democracy in Islam*. Oxford: Oxford University Press.

Stolle, Dietlind and Thomas R. Rochon. 2001. 'Are All Associations Alike? Member Diversity, Associational Type, and the Creation of Social Capital. In Bob Edwards, Michael W. Foley, and Mario Diani, eds. *Beyond Tocqueville: Civil Society and the Social Capital Debate in Comparative* Perspective, pp. 143–56. Hanover: University Press of New England.

Verba, S., K.L. Schlozman, and H.E. Brady. 1995. *Voice and equality: Civic voluntariam in American politics*. Cambridge, MA: Harvard University Press.

Wiktorowicz, Quintan. 2004. 'Introduction: Islamic Activism and Social Movement Theory'. In Quintan Wiktorowicz, ed., *Islamic Activism: A Social Movement Approach*, pp. 1–33. Bloomington: Indiana University Press.

Wuthnow, Robert.; 1996. *Christianity and civil society: The contemporary debate*. Valley Forge, PA: Trinity International Press.

———. 1999. 'Mobilizing civic engagement: the changing impact of Religious involvement'. In T. Skocpol and M.P. Fiorina, eds., *Civic engagement in American Democracy*, pp. 331–63. Washington DC: Brookings Institution Press.

———. 2001. 'Can Religion Revitalize Civil Society? An Institutional Perspective'. In Corwin Smidt, ed., pp. 191–209.

Yatim, Badri & Hamid Nasuhi. 2002. *Membangun Pusat Keunggulan Studi Islam: Sejarah dan Profil Pimpinan IAIN Syarif Hidayatullah Jakarta 1957–2002* [To build a center of excellent for Islamic studies: a history and profile of Jakarta's IAIN Syarif Hidayatullah, 1957–2002]. Jakarta: IAIN Jakarta Press.

Zaman, Muhammad Qasim Zaman. 2002. *The Ulama in Contemporary Islam: Custodians of Change*. Princeton: Princeton University Press.

Zohar, Danah and Ian Marshall. 2004. *Spiritual Capital: Wealth We Can Live By*. San Francisco: Berrett-Koehler.

Zubaida, Sami. 2003. *Law and Power in the Islamic World*. London: I.B. Tauris.

Chapter 10

SEPARATING RELIGIOUS CONTENT FROM RELIGIOUS PRACTICE: LOOSE AND TIGHT INSTITUTIONS AND THEIR RELEVANCE IN ECONOMIC EVOLUTION*

Gordon Redding

Recent studies have revived an ancient debate and pointed to some form of correlation between the religious base of a society's culture and the state of its progress towards wealth. Some accounts have been highly controversial, and in particular those in the 'clash of civilizations' debate led by Huntington[1]. Others have been more literally 'measured', as for instance the work of the World Values Survey led by Inglehart, studies of 'social axioms' by Bond and Leung and the earlier chapter in this book by Harrison on the roots of progress[2]. Others such as Sen have argued forcefully against the stereotyping that hides inside it an unstated assumption that religion *per se* is a direct cause of a society's main features[3]. All accounts remain in the shadow of the sophisticated and extensive treatment of the question by Weber, often represented too simply by later scholars[4].

In this concluding paper I wish to explore an aspect of the issue that seems rarely addressed in discussions of economic progress, and that is the way in which societies vary in the degree of religious penetration of the societal fabric. My intent is to shift the focus of attention away from the *content* of religion, and to place it instead on the *amount of societal 'space'* a religion occupies. My working assumption is that if a society contains free space in which individuals are required to, and are at liberty to, invent order themselves if they want conduct

* I wish to acknowledge with gratitude the contribution of Leslie Young to a number of the ideas in this chapter.

regularized, then *along with other factors*, that context is conducive to the emergence of an institutional fabric appropriate to economic progress. In other words – given a free hand people are likely to invent forms of order that foster their capacity to trade and to accumulate wealth. Thus, in such cases, the content of the religion is largely irrelevant to the question of 'progress'. Instead the key lies in the nature and extent of the institutional fabric. Such an approach is supported by new work in cross-cultural psychology on the comparison of cultural tightness-looseness across societies[5]. In this the objects of comparison are (i) the clarity and pervasiveness of a society's social norms, and (ii) the strength of sanctioning used to enforce them, some societies being 'tighter' than others.

I do not say that the religion has no influence on the shaping of the institutional fabric. It does. It shapes a great deal of the meaning in the culture's underlying categories of sense-making. It also interacts significantly with the society's working out of its patterns of horizontal order (the question of identity) and of vertical order (the question of authority). But it does not penetrate the institutional fabric to the same degree in different societies. Some religions are all-embracing and penetrate deeply. Others – bearing essentially the same messages about human conduct – do not. My interest is in the medium, not the message.

It is also a crucial part of the argument that the religion might well contribute to economic action by the transfer from it of frameworks for organizing. An obvious case is the double-entry bookkeeping developed to account for indulgences in late mediaeval Christianity. In the Chinese case, Weller has noted that the popular traditions of local worship, with their management committees, contractual relations with deities, paper spirit money, and Kharmic accounting system, have offered much to modern economic behaviour.

I will consider first the newer perspectives on societal evolution now emerging from the 'complexity economics' school. Here the core idea is that of complex adaptive systems inside which adaptation and experimentation are keys to the survival and growth in wealth of both the social organisms and their societal envelope. I shall then turn to the features that, in general terms, are conducive to economic growth, and then to how they show themselves in real life in societies, usually as 'institutions'. The role of religion is then examined in terms of the way it interacts with the processes of shaping the institutions, placing emphasis on the capacity of religion to amplify or suppress economic variety and experimentation. In this latter set of thoughts religions are seen more in terms of their mode of application than their content. Two simple starting assumptions are (a) that most religions serve the universal need for a 'sacred canopy' inside which people may establish a connection with the cosmos and (b) that religions answer to the need of *homo sapiens,* as a species, to act cooperatively to survive. These twin needs cause them to share a great deal in their approaches to guiding human beings.

The Complexity of Societal Evolution

The evolution of societies, and of the economies within them, is a matter of immense complexity. Religion plays a significant part in the process but it would be no more than an act of faith to assume that it is a dominant cause of economic outcomes. There are too many variables in the equation. In consequence it is better to proceed by acknowledging the complexity, and by seeing how it may be brought to some minimally comprehensible account. Two related disciplines are drawn on for that purpose – those of societal business systems analysis, and of complexity economics. Uniting the two is the notion of the complex adaptive system as the unit of analysis. For the purposes of this paper the system in question will be taken to be the economic component of a particular society, usually – but not always – a nation state.

That economic component is seen as a system of coordination, i.e. a stable pattern of conduct for cooperation and exchange. What that means is that for an economy to produce wealth in large quantities, it needs to solve two core problems. The first of these is the extent of economic exchange within a society. At a simple level of analysis one might pose this as the question of how to do business with strangers. The more this is possible the greater the amount of exchange that can take place. When a society can evolve in such a way that virtually anybody can do business with virtually anybody else inside that society, then the chances of wealth creation are higher than in a society where exchange is restricted to particular relationships. It is in essence a simple mechanical fact, and within it is a multiplier effect that is logarithmic as exchange becomes both denser and more extensive. The second problem is somewhat more subtle and less simply mechanical. It is whether the system of exchange between economic actors is conducted at high levels of efficiency in the use of resources. Is there, in other words, waste or slack in the system? To take an example it was recently noted that about 400,000 people per day go in and out of Beijing to do business dealings, mostly by train, and this massive investment of administrative effort is due to the need in China for dealings to be settled interpersonally. It cannot be efficient unless its costs are counterbalanced by big savings in other transaction costs. In any society the usual feature relied upon to drive out waste is the discipline of competing in an openly understood market. The analogy of surviving as a species in the natural world is telling, but it requires a definition of the unit that does the surviving in the economic world.

New thinking in complexity economics takes its inspiration from complex adaptive systems thinking in the bio-sciences[6]. Here one of the core questions is what unit does the living and dying? Such a unit is the 'interactor' that mediates the relationship between an environment and the sets of living components, i.e. people working to exchange and accumulate resources. The interactor is the business, seen as the person, or the organized group of people, who transform matter, energy, and information from one state to another with the goal of making a profit. This usually but not always overlaps with 'the firm', but the latter category is too loose for this theory, as a firm may contain more than one business and those businesses may have different capacities to survive and grow. In the technical language of this field a firm can display different 'fitness functions', but a 'business' will have just one. A single viable living business will have put together a combination of routines and competencies, and these are tuned to its surroundings so as to give it a chance to survive and grow.

Economic behaviour in such businesses is co-ordinated in three ways, all interconnected. They may be termed *ownership*, *networks* and *management*. The first occurs when organizations emerge, usually in the form of firms under a particular structure of ownership. So an American multinational enterprise has a different ownership and control structure from a Chinese family business, or a Japanese *keiretsu*. These units are then connected (or not, as the case may be) across the economy, in ways studied as 'networks', dense in Japan, more or less illegal in the US. So too does coordination take place within the management process inside the firms as people, technology, and capital are brought together and connected. The pattern of such combinations is not random. There is a clear sorting out (or evolution) of types of 'business system' when the three features are seen together and their internal complementarities understood. They form distinct systems of capitalism, and because of the powerful role of institutions in their being shaped, the clearest determinant of their currently evolved patterns, is the nation-state. These are societal artefacts from a long process of complex adaptation as the 'varieties of capitalism' literature now makes clear. Religion is part of the set of institutions and cultural features in which they are embedded. But it is one of many determinants.[7] It also stretches across national boundaries, although its national interpretation may give it local flavour, as with the Church of England, Russian Orthodoxy, or the Indonesian version of Islam.

Seen historically the survival rate of companies (carrying one or more businesses) is low. A study by Wiggins and Ruefli cited by Beinhocker found that, of 6772 companies seen over 23 years, only 5 percent were able to sustain superior performance over ten years, less than 0.5 percent over twenty years, and (going beyond their period) only 0.04 percent over fifty years.[8] What is termed the Red Queen phenomenon leaves companies running faster and faster to stay in the same place. It is beyond the scope of this book to investigate that particular phenomenon, but it does presage a focus on the question: What characteristics of organization are associated with economic growth in conditions of such competition? How does natural selection work in an economy? By extension I will later take the same enquiry further by asking how a society supports the presence of such features. I aim to define them in terms abstract enough to transcend national boundaries, but to return to the societal effect later, at a different level of analysis.

The Organizational Origins of Wealth

Recent analysis of stock-market performance concludes that if there is a universal 'magic formula' for firm survival and growth it is 'differentiate, select, amplify, and repeat'[9]. This argues for constant experimentation and the accumulation of options, just as with animals that survive or become extinct on the grounds of their adaptability.

In organization theory an extension of this logic is worked through into the common conclusion that organizational growth comes from exhibiting three features: (a) efficient and well-coordinated use of resources, i.e. good, tight, management, (b) a capacity to learn about what is relevant, and/or is changing in the environment and absorb it into the organization's collective thinking, and (c) a capacity to adapt and change the organization itself.

Switching to the societal context, it is possible to lay out a series of requirements for support, visible in the institutional fabric of a society, that would enhance an organization's ability to meet the survival and growth needs of efficiency, learning and adaptiveness. Again, these supporting features are seen here in the abstract so that they might be thought about across different societies, but they will lead later to more specific considerations of practical implementation, and of effects on them stemming from religion.

Favourable Institutions

In a detailed study of seventy-two rich and poor countries, Easterly and Levine explored the question of what leads to wealth. Their data showed that endowments stemming from location, climate and resources had little impact on the accumulation of wealth. Nor did macro-economic policies. What made the difference was the set of institutions the society was able to construct. When effective, these stabilize order and exchange. Key among them are the rule of law, property rights, economic transparency, a banking and finance system, and established professions or their equivalent[10]. Their conclusion (p. 33) was that 'institutional quality seems to be a sufficient statistic for accounting for economic development'. Their institutions index aggregated 300 indicators, the principle underlying components of which were:

1. Voice and accountability
2. Political stability and absence of violence
3. Government effectiveness
4. Light regulatory burden
5. Rule of law
6. Freedom from graft

If we accept that institutions are the key to growth, three questions follow. What kinds of institutions work to enhance the growth process? What is the role of culture in their emergence? What is the role of religion in the interplay of culture and institutions? These questions will lead us to a concluding analysis of the architecture of the institutional framework and the freedom or otherwise within its structure for individuals to add their own institutions.

The 'Functioning' of the Institutional Framework

I use the word 'functioning' in inverted commas, as I am not a functionalist. But until more people become accustomed to the vocabulary of emergence, co-evolution, and complex adaptive systems, it is perhaps enough to qualify its use by saying that institutions are seen here as evolving jointly with a societal culture, and jointly also with a business system, the three levels being in constant reciprocal interaction. In simple terms, the base layer of culture is the realm of meaning, the middle layer of institutions is the realm of order, and the top layer of the business system is the realm of coordination of economic action.

As the realm of order, institutions become what North sees as the 'rules of the game'[11]. Their function is largely to reduce complexity to manageable limits by categorizing behaviour, and proper conduct, into identifiable, i.e. learnable components. These can then be codified, diffused, and compliance with the rules monitored. You can play football once you know what an offside decision is about, what constitutes a foul, what a goalkeeper is permitted to do, and it is easy to explain to millions of people. Once you know the rules of the stock exchange you can raise capital, and account for it under the scrutiny of specialists.

In an economy, and especially when it rises in effectiveness and complexity, a set of institutions evolves to deal with three major challenges for economic actors: (1) How to gain access to capital? (2) How to gain access to human labour, skill, and technical knowledge? (3) How to trust in the reliability of exchange relations and of information, so that uncertainty can be managed?

Many societal bodies become involved in the processes of dealing with those questions: government, unions, banks, educational institutions, agents of the law, professions etc. But the challenges are always the same. They will be termed here the institutional fabric of Capital, Human Capital and Social Capital. The question within this book is about the possible influence of Spiritual Capital (lying in the culture domain within the realm of meaning) on the other three. To examine that, we need to see what the other three do, and how (obviously in the broadest of terms). In doing so, I propose to use anecdotes to illustrate the main argument rather than to present data, as very few data exist for most of the questions at issue.

Capital

A society's institutions of capital are usually designed to foster two responses. First is the sourcing of capital, and the development need is for all the available capital in the society to be put to the maximum use – within the usual constraints of risk and of cost effectiveness in transactions. In layman terms it is a matter of getting the money out from under the mattress. It is also often a matter of bringing it to life when it is lying moribund for lack of institutional help, as de Soto has revealed for the case of the unused value of property in many third world countries[12]. Underlying many handicaps to such capital being accessed is the poverty of the institutional fabric, and the sense among many victims of such systems that there is nothing they can do about it. At the same time, the work of the Grameen Bank has demonstrated that, given a chance, people disadvantaged in this way are fully capable of using to a high level of efficiency any capital available to them.

The second response that a developed system fosters is allocative efficiency. This appears when capital is put to work to yield good returns, visible in productivity data. The private sector in China is now achieving higher productivity than either the state or local corporate sectors, and suggests a chain of connections going back into the psychology of ownership, and of capital sourcing. Elsewhere the yields of return on capital are higher in the US capital market than in European markets, and this begs the question of how the incentive structures emerge from the surrounding institutional fabric, and where in turn that fabric came from.

An important institution, with an arguably major impact on the allocation of wealth, is inheritance law. In societies with traditions of partible inheritance, the accumulated wealth of a nuclear family is broken up and divided at each generation. In Islam this feature is deeply rooted, and specified in the Koran. To some observers this non-negotiable transfer of wealth inhibits the building of business dynasties, and thus large organizations, stable through time[13]. It stands in stark contrast to the Japanese and many Western traditions of primogeniture, under which many organizations last centuries. In the Islamic and Confucian traditions the religious roots of partible inheritance are clear. The Western roots of the business enterprise, in European mediaeval corporate structures, are clearly pragmatic responses not to religious dogma, but to the need to preserve the revenues of the church (from the sale of indulgences) against the instabilities arising when the abbot of the monastery died. The modern corporation that eventually emerged from that origin is designed to be a legal entity able to transcend the limited human lifespan.

Human Capital

The second of the three fundamental requirements for economic progress is Human Capital. As with capital itself, the question is what is there to work with? The answer suggests two main features, each present in different degrees. One is the *quantity* of skill and knowledge available as inputs to the economic process. The other is the *quality* of that human input seen as a combination of (a) willingness to contribute to the process of productivity gain, and (b) conditions of availability such as occur under union regulations, mobility, security of employment etc.

The society's institutions shaping such features are essentially the system of education, and the organization of labour markets. In each there is great variety between societies. For organizations to meet the needs noted above for learning and adaptiveness, the need is obvious for a 'thinking' workforce, and preferably one with high skills, but a warning is necessary that this applies most in contexts where technology is central to the firm's growth, and it can be handled in the developing context with more reliance on managerial skills. China has successfully become 'the workshop of the world' without a great deal of employee participation in the creative process. Labour market flexibility is obviously crucial to a firm's adaptiveness, and where labour is not normally moving in and out of companies, but is instead retained in conditions of long tenure or 'lifetime employment' its contribution to that adaptiveness is likely to be in creativity within the production process.

As with capital there is also here a less visible additional influence with much power, and that is the degree to which the institutional fabric supports worker 'empowerment'. Two anecdotes will illustrate this for the case of Islam.

In most Islamic societies, authority is centralized, and this is reflected in traditions of management. Communication is mainly top-down and workforce empowerment is underdeveloped compared to equivalents in Japan and many Western economies. A case is reported by d'Iribarne of a subsidiary of a Western multinational manufacturing company, located in Morocco, in which techniques of total quality management (TQM) were introduced by a French executive[14]. Built into this highly structured and codified system was a mode of operating that could only work effectively under conditions of empowerment. It depended heavily on open upwards communication, worker creativity and inventiveness, and the taking of initiative. The Moroccan workers, accustomed to a highly ordered social context – but not to empowerment – took to this new set of regulations with instinctive appreciation for clear rules, and within a year were using the system to its full to express their thinking. This enhanced the organization's efficiency and the factory was soon being compared favourably with the group's Asian factories for the spectacular nature of its improvement. It would seem that, by accident, a potential for empowerment rarely exercised in the authoritarian societal context, had been suddenly realized. But it also says much about the limited degrees of freedom in some contexts, where such 'liberating' catalysts do not arrive.

The second anecdote, also from the world of Islam in interaction with the West, comes from Stockholm and the suburb of Rinkeby, populated largely by an immigrant community mainly North African in origin. It concerns a school that in the early 1990's had descended to such a state of disrepair, poor performance, and low morale, that the local authority had decided to close it. At the last minute a final experiment began, under a new headmaster, to change the situation. He called a public meeting, told the parents he would give them the kind of school they wanted, in exchange for their taking responsibility for its physical condition and maintenance. Establishing a governing council including parents, teachers, and pupils he began, and maintained, an extensive process of consultation and involvement. What they wanted was language training, with a view to entering the labour markets of Europe, and in exchange for their collectively repairing the school's buildings and equipment, he provided a large new language laboratory, open to anyone in the community day and night the whole year. School scholastic performance rose rapidly, and within five years it was among the best performing schools in Sweden, with entry to it actively sought by families across the city. It took national sports trophies, and the average number of languages in which its students were competent upon leaving rose to five. Not only was the school a great success, but the community also stabilized, is now free of graffiti, and has full employment.

The issue here is not so much the liberating effects of empowerment, which are obvious, but the sources of such a change. They appear in each case to lie in the finding of new social space, outside a culture's traditional structures, in which new forms of expression, and new patterns of behaviour, can be fostered. In each case the catalyst was an outside influence. Two questions then arise: Do societies that already have enough internal spaces for such experimentation have an advantage? And what is the role of religion in filling the societal space and so inhibiting the experimentation? As an illustration of this opening up of free space, let us examine the description by Berger of the historical diverging of Catholic and Protestant societies[15].

The Catholic is seen as having the sacred mediated to him through a variety of channels – the church sacraments, the intercession of saints, supernatural forces in miracles – 'a vast continuity of being between the seen and the unseen'. The sky is crowded with angels and saints. Protestantism removed most of these intermediaries. 'It broke the continuity, cut the umbilical cord between heaven and earth, and thereby threw man back upon himself in a historically unprecedented manner'. Man's connection to the sacred was reduced down to one 'exceedingly narrow channel' – the Bible as the conveyor of God's word. As long as this conception was plausible, the forces of secularization could be held back, but such a defence could not be maintained. It was 'amenable to the systematic, rational penetration, both in thought and in activity, which we associate with modern science and technology....Protestantism served as a historically decisive prelude to secularization.' Hence the 'distinct and peculiar rationalism in Western societies' that lies at the heart of Weber's quest to explain the Protestant ethic and the spirit of capitalism.

Social Capital

The third field of institutional structuring is that of social capital, in other words trust. It occurs in two main forms: personal trust and 'system' trust. It is this that largely determines the extent and the density of economic exchange in a society.

Interpersonal trust, illustrated most clearly in the very heavy reliance on *guanxi* (connections) in China, comes into play especially in conditions where uncertainty is high, information is in short supply and unreliable, there is volatility in the business environment, and opportunism is common. Such trust works well to facilitate efficient exchange when members of trading networks share values, and such values are often grounded in religion. The Maghribi traders described by Greif as operating successfully throughout the eastern Mediterranean in the mediaeval period were Jewish, as were also later banking networks in Northern Europe[16]. Traders of Indian, Arab, Chinese, Italian extraction operated in networks, each with membership kept within the culturally defined group, or sub-group.

The effects of such religio-cultural identity are two-fold: firstly it makes it easier for members to understand the other person, and so to predict behaviour, and this reduces risk: secondly there is protection from improper conduct because membership in the group has high value, and peoples' conduct will be monitored for reliability. Cheating may well lead to exclusion and that has a high cost.

The other form of trust –system trust – is that fostered by the availability of institutions to underwrite or reduce risk. Primary among these is law, but also regulated conduct of the kind seen in professions. Crucial too is the availability of reliable information.

The impact of social capital on economic exchange is suggested in Inglehart's international studies of societal values, using the very large data resources of the World Values Surveys[17]. Clear correlations exist between trust and per capita societal wealth, and the highest results on both appear in the Protestant regions plus Japan. So too does self-expression appear to play a part in generating prosperity as societies learn to be 'looser' without losing their order. Other regions display varying degrees of relative poverty per capita, with Islam at the lowest level, and Catholicism and Orthodoxy in low to middle positions. A similar pattern, supported by analysing ten indices across 117 countries is reported by Harrison in chapter 2. Other accounts of a more narrative kind such as those of Braudel, Landes, and North, provide ample evidence to illustrate the influences at work[18]. North in particular, after decades of dedication to the study of institutions and their effects, has recently acknowledged the significance of the cultural dimension. Let us examine how looseness and tightness help to explain the growth or otherwise of human initiative in the economy.

Looseness and Tightness

A 'tight' society is one where the social norms are powerful, codified clearly and in detail, and applied to all within the defined membership, with sanctions to ensure compliance. A loose society is the opposite. Its norms may be powerful but they are laid loosely on the social fabric and much social space is free of them. When a society is seeking economic growth, whether via the concerted interventions of individuals at the base, or by the organized evolution of development policy by government, or both combined, a key to the success or failure of those interventions is whether they are designed to foster economic efficiency. Do they make it easier for organizations to display efficiency, learning and adaptiveness? Do they make it easier to do business with strangers? Do they foster the acquisition of scale in operations, and so better returns to capital invested? Do they stabilize and regularize the ownership of wealth? Do they provide incentives to strive that are legitimate within the society's value system?

Whether they do so or not is largely a result of how such initiatives come about, specifically what kind of people start them, and how do they engage others in their being institutionalized. Briefly, if they are started by people with knowledge of business, and an interest in its progress, they are likely to be technically appropriate. If too they serve a wider constituency with benefits, they are likely to be seen as legitimate. Thus the 'invention' of insurance methods, the joint-stock company, the instruments of banking, professions, and the conventional instruments of trade and transport, were all by people doing such things, and all brought wider benefits than to just their proponents.

If the creation of new institutions is to proceed along such lines, it needs to be conducted in circumstances where there is free societal space in which such thinking can proceed. This means that religious rules of conduct do not penetrate to stifle innovation. To illustrate that, consider the role of fatalistic beliefs in Buddhism, and the impact they have in preventing the 'activism' that might otherwise come from a belief in the possibility of mastering nature and events. Consider the emphasis on the religious socializing of children in the Catholic family, and its production of quite programmed minds. Consider the strictures of Islam as regards the use of capital, the rights of inheritance, the roles of women, or the rituals of prayer.

To analyse this interface between religion and the shaping of societal spaces, I propose to conclude with the identifying of four features to be seen comparatively. Each of these is a condition of the relationship between a religion and a society, and I would argue that together they shape the structures and attitudes of economic exchange by determining whether there is enough space for economic actors to create an evolving set of institutions appropriate to wealth creation. The features are interconnected in many ways. They are

1. The extent to which religion exists as a discrete domain within a society, and does not take over large areas of daily life by prescribing rules of conduct. This includes the possibility of its being co-opted for purposes of power holding.
2. The extent to which a religion leaves room for individual interpretation of its principles.
3. The degree to which the religion permits alternative mental frameworks to be used.
4. The degree to which a religion permits the incorporation of calculative rationality in the conduct of economic life.

Religion as a Discrete Domain

Attention was given above to the restricted nature of Protestantism, and the narrow focussing of its attention on the individual soul and its redemption. It is noteworthy how much discretion is transferred to the individual in this context. Rules of conduct are restrained except for the encouragement for people to seek in the Bible for their own guidelines. The priesthood is not constructed as a powerful hierarchy, nor as a monopoly conduit of religious knowledge. The congregation is not treated as a subordinate body. Instead the priest is a catalyst, a guide, and an available point of contact, and is not a source of authority except in re-stating the understood ideals shared.

So too in most Chinese religions, the priesthood is a small, local, discreet mediating force, and not a dominant source of instruction. Nor is there a large coordinated hierarchical structure with heavy weight in the society. As Weller in chapter 4 has observed of the workings of spiritual capital in contemporary Chinese society it is mainly a matter of local temples, house shrines, and ancestor veneration, and it makes little contribution to the creation of civil society. It can and does however influence individualism, the work ethic, education, civility, trust, and it can limit the power of leaders. The crucial element of individualism is here a matter of individual achievement within the broader social values rather than the Western version with its separated self-actualizing achiever.

As Weller notes, the social organization of religion in Chinese society remains strictly local. Every village and urban neighbourhood will have its own temple, but there are typically no resident priests that would tie these bodies into broader clerical hierarchies. The temples are symbols of local solidarity. And it is the low level of organization, the absence of powerful sacred texts, the loosely connected nature of surrounding schools, groups of priests, and religious bodies, that gives the religion its resilience and its capacity to re-interpret its context.

The two religions most clearly associated with high levels of societal trust are Confucianism and Protestantism. In Confucianism there are two responses – those of the Chinese and the Japanese, the latter being much more strongly associated with high wealth. I would argue that two historical features especially have contributed to the growth of extensive institutional trust in Japan: the highly stable and professional administration of the Tokugawa era, and its legacy of strongly supported societal order; and the Japanese tradition of primogeniture that saw the long survival of commercial organizations. Thus Japan has the advantage of using both personal and institutional trust in the workings of its economy. As with China its religious institutions are localized and do not constitute a large power block in the society. As with China also, the religion does not intrusively invade the space in which business is conducted and organized, and strongly secular institutions have grown in consequence.

The opposite (i.e. low trust) examples of Catholicism and Islam are noteworthy for two principal features: the aligning of the religion with the state hierarchy, and the use of religion by that hierarchy to claim authority; and the attempt in both cases to saturate the society with the religious ideals, and to control conduct in detail. The examples of *shari'a* banking, or of required welfare contributions, serve to illustrate the point for Islam. The extent of Catholic-based education and family-based communion rituals in many countries illustrates the Catholic case. There is, of course a historical momentum here. Many societies have gone through revolution to change this domination. Turkey, France, Indonesia, England, the Lutheran states, all adopted either secularism or their own religious institutional structures in order to create new space in which to express new ideas.

One of the visible effects of a loss of monopoly influence by religion in a society is that it loses power overall as the new variants of it that emerge do not command the same legitimacy as the original body did. This is now visible in Indonesia as reported by Hefner in chapter 9, with Islam diffracting and being weakened by freelance adventurers. It would appear that this trial has to be gone through before a society can evolve historically to display high trust. High trust is connected with high individual discretion. So the good society as designed by the early religions transits to the good society as designed by its members. Is the difference that between the contexts of these alternative good societies? Is the overtly religious society an essentially pre-modern one? Is the modern one necessarily more secular? Are the good society and the good economy mutually exclusive or are they inextricably linked?

Whether the religion is kept compartmentalized, and away from direct involvement in political and economic life, is a key determinant of the amount of discretion left to economic actors to follow their instincts and to build the order they need. But there are other features of the process to consider in addition, and I now turn to the question of the self as focus.

The Individual as Interpreter

All religions serve individuals in their search for 'the meaning of life'. They offer an explanation of how the individual fits into the universe. But they vary in the extent to which they foster interpretation of their message by members. As societies become more secular, the clarity and consistency of the religious message across society breaks down, and is often replaced by various religious 'fashions' or sects. It may occur that the state and the family remain rooted in the society's base religion, but history shows that economic life creates what Berger (1967: 129) sees as a 'liberated territory' in which capitalistic and industrial processes may be pursued. From this beach-head the secular impulse moves out to occupy other spaces in the society and to secularize them also. Religious pluralism often follows, as does also a decline in the power of the original religious structure. After a century of secular life France now has more fortune-tellers than priests. American spiritual life is vibrating with competitive denominationalism as its purity fades.

In this process two forces come into play to emphasize the individual as interpreter. The splitting of a core religion into compartments, clearly visible in Protestantism, introduces individual choice and private religiosity, and often restricts religious practice to the private sphere, most obviously that of family. The connections of people into such frameworks are generally made individually in conditions of wide choice. The public or business sphere is rarely invaded by this spiritual influence and is lived in as if it were a separate compartment. In that sphere the otherwise religious individual conducts an essentially non-religious rational life.

A second force is the simple abandoning of religious practice, as the rationale of the business sphere takes over, and as new ideals (rationalism, career, consumerism, atheism etc.) spread. Under the pressure of either or both of these forces, individual choice, and the taking of individual initiative, lead to an increase in the likelihood of new societal structures and an enhancing of the economy's capacity to display efficiency, organizational learning, and adaptiveness. The recent secularization of China (if we take the fading Communist ideal as a proto religion) illustrates the power of this response. The inflexibility of most Islamic economies illustrates the costs of restraining individual initiative.

Openness

A *cause celebre* recently before the courts in Malaysia concerned the plea of a female citizen to change the religious denomination in her passport from Muslim to something else. The highest civil court decided it had no jurisdiction in the matter and that it could only be determined by a *shari'a* court. This latter felt constrained by the dogma that apostasy is punishable by death. The lady was locked in. In Malaysia the religious writ over-rides the civil. For the majority Muslim citizenry, the rules of Islam are inescapable. And yet its economy remains dominated by the minority group – the ethnic Chinese, as also occurs throughout Southeast Asia. In Malaysia, the ethnic Chinese account for about 35 percent of the population but about 60 percent of the economy, following quite open legal discrimination to favour Muslim ownership of industry. In Indonesia – a quite specifically secular state since its foundation – the ethnic Chinese hold about 60 percent of the industrial and commercial assets, with about 4 percent of the population. In the Philippines, with a population about 90 percent Catholic, but with extensive animism in the mixture for many, the ethnic Chinese control also about 60 percent of the economy, with a population proportion of less than 2 percent.

For both Islam and Catholicism rules of membership are tight, and penetration of religious perspectives in thinking runs deep into everyday life. Christian networks run through the elite ranks of Philippines society. Its turbulent politics is partly accounted for by them. The fall of Marcos was engineered by a set of religiously defined committees. The originally Spanish oligopoly of landowners remains united by their Catholicism. Religious ideals, especially surrounding family conduct and education, are visible in daily behaviour. In Indonesia the conduct of business life is constantly interrupted by prayer breaks, and an air of quiet piety among many people is clearly noticeable in comparison with some other cultures.

For the Chinese, by contrast, religion is a loosely worn cloak. It is common in Chinese society and in their overseas locales, to find people who worship at a Buddhist temple, follow a Taoist view of aspects of life, believe in the folk wisdom of *feng shui*, and live in a Confucian family. They venerate ancestors at shrines, and they believe in fortune telling. In some cases this crowded universe might include a Christian component. But, although their religious smorgasbord might well influence behaviour, it does so in a way that is non-exclusionist. It contains a mixture of cosmologies within an overarching naturalist perspective of the person in harmony with nature. The religious institutions are local rather than national and they impose far less restraint on conduct than do their equivalents in Islam and Catholicism. It is the comparison of looseness and tightness that is most striking here, rather than the comparison of dogmas. Again, the fundamentals of family, help to others, and cooperativeness, remain universal themes in them all.

Rationality

The distinct and peculiar rationalism noted by Weber – in his consideration of Europe's bursting out from its relatively tiny space – was the rationalism of calculation. Its essence lay in mathematics, and then later in science, and in the technical commercialization of that science in industrialization. These are deeply secular processes. And although many major Western scientists and mathematicians held religious beliefs personally, they did not usually work to bridge their inventions to their religion, and their thinking appears not to have been constrained with a religious cosmology. In fact it was the very opposite in crucial cases such as that of Galileo. They may be collectively represented by Laplace, who, when asked by Napoleon to explain why God had no place in his theory of the universe, replied 'I have no need of that hypothesis'.

The museums of Toledo, Venice, Genoa, and other trading and cultural centres, attest to the flourishing of mathematics in Islamic societies hundreds of years ago coinciding as it did with higher levels of tolerance of religious diversity, and greater openness and exchange. One might then ask of Islam whether the decline of its reputation for science is attributable to its teachings *per se* or the tendency to exclusionism that it acquired in later centuries. If the latter, then it may well have resulted not from the religion, but from the way the game of power was played in certain societies, and the religion used to legitimate its seizure and retention.

Room to Manoeuvre

It is a theme of this chapter that the content of religions does not vary enough to explain economic success and failure, but that the use of religion within a society does vary substantially, and crucially for the determining of patterns of economic coordination and exchange. If individuals find societal 'spaces' in which they are free to work out new forms of order, many of them will choose to do so in ways that maximize their ability to accumulate wealth. This will lead to societal prosperity, although the trajectories of such progress do not follow one formula, except for the broad components of capitalistic competition and markets.

If the crucial variable is the institutional fabric, then it is still naïve to see that without its cultural underpinnings, and it is at this level that the impact of religion comes into play. It does so by shaping meaning. This operates in three modes. One is the defining of purposes. To what end are we working? And by what means should we pursue that end-state? The second and third are the fundamental understandings of identity and authority or horizontal and vertical order. American individualism is not fully understood without taking account of its Protestant roots in the person's own relation with the almighty. Chinese familism cannot be seen without its Confucian rationale.

The religion helps to shape the 'spaces' of societies, leaving some societies full of vacuums, where order needs still to be created. When the people sitting on a bench in Venice eight hundred years ago were saying 'We need some standard ways of moving money around, so let us design them' – a process began that finished up as the banking (from the bench) we know today. They had room to manoeuvre and used it to good effect. They may well have been acting as good Christians, or devout Jews, but they had the opportunity, and the need, to act outside the other rules that governed their lives. It is this freedom, above all else, that made them rich. The mechanisms that explain the connections are those of successful evolution in the natural world. Unless there is experimentation, internal variety, and a habit of learning, organisms cannot flourish. In economies it is the same.

Notes and References

1 Huntington, Samuel P (1996) *The Clash of Civilizations and the Remaking of World Order*, New York, Simon and Schuster.
2 Inglehart, Ronald (1997) *Modernization and Postmodernization*. Princeton N.J., Princeton University Press. Bond, Michael H. and K. Leung (2004) 'Culture-level dimensions of social axioms and their correlates across 41 countries', *Journal of Cross-Cultural Psychology*, 35, 5, 548–570.
3 Sen, Amartya (2006) *Identity and Violence: the Illusion of Destiny*, New York, Norton.
4 Weber, Max (1930) *The Protestant Ethic and the Spirit of Capitalism*, London, Unwin. Weber, Max (1978) *Economy and Society*, Berkeley CA., University of California Press.

5 Gelfand, Michele J., L.H. Nishi and J.L. Raver (2007) 'On the nature and importance of cultural tightness-looseness', Cornell Center for Advanced Human Resource Studies Working Paper 07–05.

6 Beinhocker, Eric D. (2005) *The Origin of Wealth*, London, Random House.

7 Redding, Gordon (2005) 'The thick description and comparison of societal systems of capitalism' *Journal of International Business Studies*, 36, 123–155.

8 Wiggins R.R. and T.W. Ruefli (2002) 'Sustained competitive advantage', *Organization Science*, 13,1, 81–105.

9 Beinhocker, *opus cit*, p 403.

10 Easterly, William and R. Levine (2002) 'Tropics, germs and crops: how endowments influence economic development', Working Paper 9106, National Bureau of Economic Research, Washington DC.

11 North, Douglass C. (1991) *Institutions, Institutional Change, and Economic Performance*, Cambridge, Cambridge University Press.

12 De Soto, Hernando (2000) *The Mystery of Capital*, New York, Basic Books.

13 Jacobs, Norman (1958) *The Origin of Modern Capitalism and Eastern Asia*, Hong Kong, Hong Kong University Press. Kuran, Timur (2003) 'The Islamic commercial crisis: institutional roots of economic underdevelopment in the Middle East' *Journal of Economic History*, 63,2, 414–446.

14 D'Iribarne, Philippe (2007) 'Islam et management: le role d'un univers de sens' *Revue Francaise de Gestion*, 171, 141–156.

15 Berger, Peter L. (1967) *The Sacred Canopy*, New York, Anchor Books.

16 Greif, Avner (2006) *Institutions and the Path to the Modern Economy*, Cambridge, Cambridge University Press.

17 Inglehart, Ronald and C Welzel (2005) *Modernization, Cultural Change, and Democracy*, Cambridge, Cambridge University Press.

18 Braudel, Fernand (1982) *The Wheels of Commerce*, London, Collins. Landes, David (1998) *The Wealth and Poverty of Nations*, New York, Norton. North, Douglass C. (2005) *Understanding the Process of Economic Change*, Princeton, Princeton University Press.

www.ingramcontent.com/pod-product-compliance
Lightning Source LLC
Chambersburg PA
CBHW022354280326
41935CB00007B/183